The Man of Letters
in New England
and the South

✐ The Man of Letters in New England and the South Essays on the History of the Literary Vocation in America

LEWIS P. SIMPSON

Louisiana State University Press

BATON ROUGE

ISBN 0–8071–0216–4
Library of Congress Catalog Card Number 72–94151
Copyright © 1973 by Louisiana State University Press
Manufactured in the United States of America
Printed by Heritage Printers, Inc., Charlotte, North Carolina
Designed by Dwight Agner

FOR MIMI AND DAVID

⊷§ Contents

ᴥᶳ Preface

I USE THE comprehensive term *man of letters* in the title of this collection of essays not only to suggest that I am concerned with a variety of literary figures but also to indicate that I am interested in the significance of the use of letters in American culture. I am not simply writing about literary persons of one kind or another but about their possession of letters—in some cases about their being possessed by letters. I am concerned with the vocation of letters in America. If my concern is largely historical, it also bears upon the present moment. Although I have given my essays a semblance of unity, they are discrete studies—undertaken at different times, mostly in the past five years, and under the pressures of several expediencies. Revisions here and there have not been intended to alter their separate origins.

The organization of the essays in two sections asserts the extent to which I believe that the regional, or sectional, emphasis in American culture has influenced the man of letters. As I remark in the last essay in the volume, however, I think that we must recognize Poe and Mark Twain as special cases of the Southern writer. The reader, incidentally, will discover specific comparisons between the South and New England only in the essays in the second section. Implied comparisons are of course general. The studies of Joseph Stevens Buckminster,

Preface

William and Frederic Tudor, Emerson, Howells, Poe, and the Southern Agrarians present episodes in the history of the literary vocation in America. Those on Mark Twain, Faulkner, George Marion O'Donnell, and Southern nationalism deal in one way or another with the American man of letters as bard and prophet. I should perhaps add that altogether my studies represent an approach to a larger study of the literary vocation in America.

I acknowledge the many professional and personal obligations I have incurred in the pursuit of my work. Most of these must go unmentioned since they are too numerous. I will take advantage of the limited space to express deep appreciation to two administrative heads of Louisiana State University at Baton Rouge: Max Goodrich, dean of the Graduate School; and Thomas A. Kirby, head of the Department of English. I must also express my hearty thanks to three members of the staff of the Louisiana State University Press: Charles E. East, director; Leslie E. Phillabaum, associate director; and Martha L. Hall, the editor of this book. Finally, I wish to acknowledge the assistance several years ago of the John Simon Guggenheim Memorial Association. This has been of great continuing value to me, as have three grants from the Louisiana State University Council on Research.

L. P. S.

Baton Rouge
November, 1972

⋙ Acknowledgments

PRIOR PUBLICATION of the essays in this volume has occurred as follows:

"Joseph Stevens Buckminster: The Rise of the New England Clerisy" appeared as "Joseph Stevens Buckminster and the New England Clerisy" in *Essays in Honor of Esmond L. Marilla*, ed. Thomas A. Kirby and W. J. Olive (Baton Rouge: Louisiana State University Press, 1970).

"The Tudor Brothers: Boston Ice and Boston Letters" appeared as "Boston Ice and Letters in the Age of Jefferson" in *Midcontinent American Studies Journal*, IX (Spring, 1968).

"Emerson's Early Thought: Institutionalism and Alienation" appeared as "The Crisis of Alienation in Emerson's Early Thought" in *American Transcendental Quarterly*, Pt. I (Winter, 1971); reprinted in *Emerson's Relevance Today*, ed. Eric W. Carlson and J. Lasley Dameron (Hartford: Transcendental Books, 1971).

"Poe's Vision of His Ideal Magazine" appeared as " 'Touching the *Stylus*': Poe's Vision of Literary Order" in *Studies in American Literature*, ed. Waldo McNeir and Leo B. Levy (Baton Rouge: Louisiana State University Press, 1960). This essay has been considerably revised.

"Mark Twain: The Pathos of Regeneration" appeared as "Mark Twain and the Pathos of Regeneration: A Second

Acknowledgments

Look at Geismar's *Mark Twain*" in *Southern Literary Journal*, IV (Spring, 1972).

"William Faulkner and the Fall of New World Man" appeared as "Isaac McCaslin and Temple Drake: The Fall of New World Man" in *Nine Studies in Modern Literature*, ed. Donald E. Stanford (Baton Rouge: Louisiana State University Press, 1965).

"O'Donnell's Wall" appeared in the *Southern Review*, n.s., VI (October, 1970).

"The Southern Novelist and Southern Literary Nationalism" appeared as "Southern Spiritual Nationalism: Notes on the Background of Modern Southern Fiction" in *The Cry of Home: Cultural Nationalism and the Modern Writer*, ed. H. Ernest Lewald, and is reprinted by permission of the University of Tennessee Press. Copyright © 1972 by The University of Tennessee Press.

"The Southern Writer and the Great Literary Secession" appeared in the *Georgia Review*, XXIV (Winter, 1970).

I
THE NEW ENGLAND IDEAL

I arrived in Boston . . . when all talents had more or less a literary coloring, and when the greatest talents were literary. These expressed with ripened fulness a civilization conceived in faith and brought forth in good works; but that moment of maturity was the beginning of a decadence which could only show itself much later. New England has ceased to be a nation in itself, and it will perhaps never again have anything like a national literature; but that was something like a national literature; and it will probably be centuries yet before the life of the whole country, the American life as distinguished from the New England life, shall have anything so like a national literature. It will be long before our larger life interprets itself in such imagination as Hawthorne's, such wisdom as Emerson's, such poetry as Longfellow's, such prophecy as Whittier's, such wit and grace as Holmes's, such humor and humanity as Lowell's.

William Dean Howells (1895)

Joseph Stevens Buckminster: The Rise of the New England Clerisy

NOT LONG after he first came to live in Boston in the later 1860s, William Dean Howells heard an "eminent" Unitarian minister deal severely with Hawthorne "for what he considered his libel of the New England Puritan clergy in venturing to imagine the Reverend Arthur Dimmesdale and his dark history possible to any man of his cloth." [1] We easily assume the irony of this stricture on Hawthorne: a Unitarian pulpit, although strictly disapproving of Dimmesdale's irregular affection for one of his parishioners, might well have sympathized with his dark fate in a society dominated by the Calvinist God declared by William Ellery Channing to be immoral. On the other hand, considering *The Scarlet Letter* in the context of the history of the ministry in New England, we may wonder why Dimmesdale's blighted career was not more vehemently questioned in New England's pulpits, particularly in Boston's. If it could be taken as a depreciation of the Puritan clergy, it could be construed as a libel of the continuing office of the New England ministry. For two and a half centuries, in spite of all divisions in the faith, New Englanders had venerated this office. They revered the pulpit as the chief voice of their

---

1 William Dean Howells, "The Personality of Hawthorne," *North American Review*, CLXXVII (December, 1903), 882.

3

society. Although they gave no credence to the doctrine of apostolic descent, they yet looked upon the occupants of the pulpit as a spiritual succession. The ministry was a discipline and a government, in effect an order resembling a priesthood.

But at the same time, the New Englander's conception of a providential instead of an apostolic succession to the sacred desk encouraged a strong individuality in New England ministers and tended to inspire the people to identify piety for the ministerial office with intense devotion to specific ministers. Consequently, there was always an inclination in New England to elevate attachment for the individual minister above piety for the whole office of the ministry, creating a degree of dissociation between the institutional sense of religion and the ministry. The tendency to dissociation was the most pronounced in Boston—or, it is more accurate to say, in the Boston-Cambridge community, a spiritual and intellectual homogeneity. From the days of Thomas Shepard in the seventeenth century to those of Channing in the nineteenth, the clergyman chosen by Providence for a Boston pulpit enjoyed a partiality of treatment envied by his colleagues in the hinterland.[2] The regard for the person of the minister became more pronounced in Boston in the generation following the American Revolution, when the rise of Unitarianism (the "liberal religion") began to undercut the feeling for the old Congregational order. Eventually the religious liberals in eastern Massachusetts came into conflict with their orthodox brethren. By the time this became open and flagrant, much of the older life had changed. The "city set on a hill" had, by Puritan standards, become a secular city; and religion had yielded its

---

2 See Lewis P. Simpson, "The Intercommunity of the Learned: Boston and Cambridge in 1800," *New England Quarterly,* XXIII (December, 1950), 491–503.

centrality to money and politics. In the face of these developments the corporate authority of the pulpit in Boston declined markedly. In 1812 William Ellery Channing, the young minister of the Federal Street Church, said: "People here . . . are attached to religious institutions, not so much by a sense of the value of religion as by their love to their minister; and I fear that their zeal will grow cold, when their ministers are removed. I wish that there were more attachment to the truth, and less to the man who delivers it."[3]

Implied in the situation Channing describes—that of a Unitarian and secular world which responded more to affection for the person in the pulpit than to concern for the truth of the other world his office represented—is a crisis in the concept of the clerical vocation in Boston. The historical prelude to this well-known crisis, which was made public when Ralph Waldo Emerson quit the ministry a generation later, is a crisis occurring quietly in early nineteenth-century Boston. It is defined in the careers of William Emerson (Emerson's father), Samuel Cooper Thacher, or, notably, William Ellery Channing himself. The key figure in it is Channing's contemporary and fellow liberal Joseph Stevens Buckminster, who was pastor of Boston's Brattle Street Church from 1804 to 1812. In his brief and brilliant career, cut short by his early death in 1812, we discover an appealing and dramatic episode in the inner history of the ministry in Boston.

Its bearing on the important relationship between clerical and literary vocation in the great age of Emerson, Hawthorne, and Thoreau may be elaborated first in a general thesis about the mid-century period, followed with a somewhat detailed examination of Buckminster's significance.

---

3 William Henry Channing, *The Life of William Ellery Channing* (Centenary Memorial Ed.; Boston, 1880), 124–25.

I

Occupant of a historic, fashionable, and influential pulpit when he was scarcely beyond twenty years of age; handsome and graceful, if delicate, in appearance; an eloquent orator; suffering from an insidious disease that would kill him when he was twenty-eight—Buckminster was inordinately cherished by Boston. He was the personification of the kind of minister the Bostonians had always prized and, it would seem, valued increasingly as the worth of religion depreciated: a minister such as Thomas Shepard had been in Puritan days, a "poore, weake, pale-complectioned man" who was a "gracious, sweet, heavenly minded, soul ravishing minister." Buckminster was, as a matter of fact, something like what Arthur Dimmesdale was to Boston before the awful confession on the scaffold: a young, frail, and learned minister whose "eloquence and religious fervor had given him the earnest of high eminence in his profession."[4] There is indeed a certain logic, poetic and historical, in associating the impression the fictional person of Dimmesdale makes upon Boston with that the real person of Buckminster made upon his community. Both the fiction of Dimmesdale and the reality of Buckminster relate to an age when the response to the pulpit in Boston had become more literary than religious. Both relate to a shift in New England spirituality, as Buckminster indicates in an essay in the *Monthly Anthology and Boston Review*, from a "scholastico-theological" basis to a moral, rational, and essentially literary one. This is not the same, it must be remarked, as saying a movement from a spiritual tradition to a secular outlook. The nonmaterialist ideal of living remained powerful in Boston, "a place for

4 The life of Thomas Shepard is discussed in Samuel Eliot Morison, *Builders of the Bay Colony* (Boston and New York, 1930), 105–34.

the education of spirits."[5] The shift that may be defined occurred within the spiritual tradition; and it assumed the character not of a despiritualizing of the tradition but more nearly of a consecration to secular letters. By the time of Hawthorne's maturity this transition was complete. Its fulfillment is to be seen in *The Scarlet Letter*, in which the Puritan institution of religion, especially the ministry, is worked on by a perfected literary imagination—consecrated, with an intensity like Flaubert's, to the literary art. Its fulfillment is also to be seen in more superficial ways. The satire on Calvinism in Oliver Wendell Holmes's "The Deacon's Masterpiece, or the Wonderful One-Hoss Shay" is a case in point. More to the point is Holmes's depiction of Buckminster in his *Life of Ralph Waldo Emerson*: "Joseph Stevens Buckminster was the pulpit darling of his day in Boston. The beauty of his person, the perfection of his oratory, the finish of his style, added to the sweetness of his character, made him one of those living idols which seem to be as necessary to Protestantism as images and pictures are to Romanism."[6] This literary trivialization of Boston's regard for a distinguished cleric would have been considered impious in Buckminster's own time. One generation later, the lighthearted irony is in good taste. In Holmes the spiritual life of Boston tends to become a genteel cosmopolitanism.

But this relaxation—or transformation—of piety for the ministry can hardly be summed up in any simple way. Its historical origins go straight back to the humanistic education the New England fathers brought with them on their mission into the "Desarts of America." More immediately, during the early nineteenth century it was shaped by the effort of Boston

5 Channing, *Life of W. E. Channing*, 122.
6 Oliver Wendell Holmes, *Works*, (Boston and New York, 1892), XI, 21.

7

clergymen—together with Cantabrigians and Bostonians in the teaching and legal professions—to establish in the Boston-Cambridge world a functional association between "liberal Christianity" and the humanistic ethos. The effort was crucial. At the beginning of the American national existence, it substantially provided for the reintegration in New England of the intellectual and spiritual order that descended from the Puritan priesthood. The Boston clergy became the nucleus of a New England *clerisy*—an extraordinary body of literary intellectuals and artists who created a cultural renaissance. Insofar as this development has been remarked by literary historians, it has been mostly connected with the career of Channing. But Joseph Stevens Buckminster, though Channing's immediate contemporary, performed in advance the role the longer-lived Channing played in asserting the possibilities of the literary power inherent in a Unitarian humanism. Indeed perhaps more intimately and dramatically than Channing's, Buckminster's career was directed by the generational conflict of pieties and values out of which the clerisy of the mid-century age evolved.

II

Joseph Stevens Buckminster was born to the Reverend Joseph Buckminster and Sarah Stevens Buckminster on May 26, 1784, in Portsmouth, New Hampshire, where his father spent virtually his entire career, from 1779 to 1812, as pastor of the North Church. Both parents came of sound New England clerical stock. Educated at Yale, Joseph Buckminster was never a happy youth, suffering from a disposition to melancholia that would disturb him during recurrent periods throughout his life. Evidently his depression was related to deeply felt doctrinal uncertainies; he never fully resolved his doubts con-

8

cerning the concept of innate depravity, even though he early declared for strict adherence to this doctrine and as well that of the Trinity.[7] Settled at Portsmouth, Joseph Buckminster proved to be a faithful parson and a consistent and worried foe of religious liberalism. Recognized as a representative of the best traditions of the New England ministry, he was, in the opinion of Henry Adams, "an able and estimable clergyman."[8]

Sarah Stevens Buckminster died on July 17, 1790, praying that Joseph Stevens, then eight years old, would seek his vocation in the ministry. Her supplication may have assured what was virtually predestined. A small yet handsome boy, with chestnut curls and hazel eyes dominating a beautiful countenance that in manhood became classic in proportion and expression, Joseph Stevens early showed promise of spiritual and intellectual genius. In the fall of 1795, when he was ten years of age, Buckminster was sent to Exeter Academy. Never once disciplined while he was at Exeter, he applied himself solely to his books, taking time from them only to ponder the admonitions his anxious father thrust upon him in a steady flow of letters, not only while he was at Exeter but later when he went to Harvard. The father's advice finds a summary in one grand exhortation: "Take care of your clothes, your health, your morals, and your soul!"[9]

Although by the time he was twelve young Joseph Stevens was qualified for college, his father was reluctant to enter him for another year. He remained at Exeter, carrying on in the

---

7 See Eliza Buckminster Lee, *Memoirs of Rev. Joseph Buckminster, D.D., and of His Son, Rev. Joseph Stevens Buckminster* (Boston, 1849), for biographical information about the Buckminsters.

8 Henry Adams, *History of the United States* (New York, 1890), I, 81.

9 Lee, *Memoirs*, 96.

meantime a mild argument with his father about whether he should attend conservative Yale or liberal Harvard. But the parental prejudice was not adamant, as it was never to be finally, and in 1797 Joseph Stevens was admitted to Harvard as a sophomore of the highest standing. If the elder Buckminster believed his parental influence would be sufficient to counterbalance the growing latitudinarianism at Cambridge, he was to be sharply disappointed.

Now his precocity and imperative to perfection began to shape the legend of Joseph Stevens Buckminster: his devotion to learning and his wide erudition, his frank and independent but temperate expression, his exquisite sensibility, and his moral purity. Significantly he allowed his interest in what was then called belles lettres to dominate his studies. He soon attained a decided degree of literary cosmopolitanism. His commencement oration, "The Literary Character of Different Nations" reflects the encyclopedic literary curiosity of the eighteenth-century man of letters. Buckminster even included a glance at German literature; superficial and general, it points to the time a few years later when he would be studying German biblical scholarship, and to the day not much later, when George Ticknor would become a student at Göttingen.[10]

At sixteen, and looking no more than twelve, Joseph Stevens was influenced by his father to return to Philips Exeter as an assistant—this instead of becoming an usher in the Boston Latin School. Joseph Buckminster was wary of Boston's "diversity of amusements . . . variety and character of company . . . floods of books . . . proximity to Cambridge." [11] Why the youth did not embark immediately upon further preparation

10 An excerpt from Buckminster's oration is given in James W. Alexander, *Life of Archibald Alexander, D.D.* (New York, 1854), 258.
11 Lee, *Memoirs*, 101.

for the ministry is not clear; likely his father already sensed a rebellion against orthodoxy in his son and thought that time and isolation from Boston and Cambridge might quell it. But the appeal of a new dispensation had already possessed Joseph Stevens. During the two years he served at Exeter, lamenting his fall from scholar to drill master, he dutifully read Jonathan Edwards on original sin but to the accompaniment of Joseph Priestley's *Harmony of the Gospels* and *Corruptions of Christianity*. The appeal of Priestley was more than doctrinal. A philosophe, a wide-ranging man of letters, eighteenth-century "clerk," Priestley was a model of the kind of scholar Buckminster wanted to become.

The autumn of 1802 saw Buckminster well along in an exhaustive program of studies, when in the midst of his labors Providence suddenly arrested the "son of promise and the son of hope." He suffered an unforeseen and severe epileptic attack, a violent warning that his life might be brief and dreadful. The threat of such an affliction was heightened by its association with madness. Following yet another seizure, Buckminster wrote in his private journal: "The repetition of these fits must at length reduce me to idiotcy! Can I resign myself to the loss of memory, and of that knowledge I may have vainly prided myself upon?" He could. Acceptance of "the perpetual lesson of humility with which God has visited me" was a response built into his character.[12] But he could accept no compromise with his plans. Humility was a discipline; so was ambition. He needed the resources of both in the struggle with his father that soon developed.

During his three years at Harvard, Joseph Stevens had formed a friendship—exactly when and under what circumstances is uncertain—with the minister of King's Chapel, the

12 *Ibid.*, 122, 296.

Reverend James Freeman, whom the young man found to be "one of the richest sources of improvement which Boston, so fertile in such sources, could afford."[13] Freeman, then in his late forties, had come to King's Chapel in 1782. Long the worshipping place of the officials of the British Crown, this old Boston church had become the home of a unique brand of religious liberalism, employing in its services a modification of the Book of Common Prayer and existing apart from the Episcopal communion in the United States. Urbane, versed in languages, secretary of the newly formed Massachusetts Historical Society, Freeman was called by his namesake James Freeman Clarke, "the father of liberal and rational Christianity, as we understand it, in the United States."[14] The claim is excessive, but Freeman did have an influence on a whole generation of aspirants to the pulpit, seemingly on none more than Buckminster, who found in him virtually a second father. In 1800 he wrote ecstatically to a friend that Freeman "like Socrates" shows a devotion to the young and "has often had an Alcibiades."[15] In 1803 Freeman took steps to have Joseph Stevens placed as his assistant at King's Chapel. Joseph Buckminster was overcome by both righteous and, we must suppose, jealous indignation. "I fear you have suffered your great partiality for Mr. Freeman as a man to warp your judgment and seduce your heart, respecting some of the important doctrines of our holy religion, and the foundation of our hopes as sinners," he wrote. "Could he have taken such a step, unless he had believed it would be agreeable to you?" In a more chilling question the father demanded: "Could he flatter himself that a descendant of the venerable and firm, though catholic, Stevens, and the independent and honest strain of Buckminsters,

13 *Ibid.*, 119.
14 James Freeman Clarke, "Character of James Freeman," *Western Messenger*, I (January, 1836), 480.
15 Lee, *Memoirs*, 119.

could be induced to aid in the support of sentiments that he did not believe, or that he was so pliant that, by art and industry and flattery, he could be moulded into anything?" In conclusion, Joseph Buckminster gave a peremptory command: "You must decline their proposal, and at once excuse yourself from their services." [16] The thunder from on high was too loud, and the son obeyed. But his obedience was prompted as much by his reluctance to break away from the Congregational order as by his respect for his father, for he did not give up his disposition to liberal opinions.

Joseph Buckminster pushed the advantage of a victory he thought he had gained, urging Joseph Stevens to take up his residence with an orthodox parson in a small community—with Dr. Lathrop at Springfield, or Dr. Dana at Ipswich, or Dr. Morse at Charlestown. But the Metropolis was shortly again demanding his son, this time in the most alluring way possible. The elegant, wealthy, and notably liberal Brattle Street congregation approached Joseph Stevens about filling the pulpit left vacant by the death of their minister. Faced with such an unexpected and formidable invitation, he seems to have been almost overwhelmed. Anxiously he traveled to Portsmouth to see his father personally; not to argue with him, for apparently he never did, but to attempt to find some way of justifying his liberal views to him. The visit was futile, leaving the father and son equally in despair. Out of his sense of obligation to his father, and to the historic order of the ministry, nevertheless, Joseph Stevens wrestled again, week after week, with the doctrine of the Trinity, once more studying Jonathan Edwards and "all the most orthodox works." But when Priestley died during this year (1804), he confided to his journal that "the friends of rational religion and religious liberty should bless God for granting our age such a strenuous

16 *Ibid.*, 132–33.

and learned friend, and for continuing him so long, the admiration and glory of science and of religion in its various departments." He told his father that "from what I know of my own mind I despair of ever giving my assent to the proposition that *Jesus Christ is God, equal to the Father*."[17] In the face of this complete confirmation of his son's apostasy, Joseph Buckminster exclaimed in desperation: "You had better be a porter on the wharf than a preacher with such views."[18] He advised Joseph Stevens to study either law or medicine. In the privacy of his diary, the son cried out: "O God, assist, guide, and direct me what course of life to pursue! Save me from prejudice, from indifference, from ambition, and from worldly views."[19]

Since neither law nor medicine was really a possibility for him, Joseph Stevens Buckminster had one alternative to the ministry. He had the qualifications to become a teacher. But he actually had no alternative in the crisis of vocation he faced. Teaching meant no more than being a drill master, a somewhat glorified one at Harvard if he should ever be asked to Cambridge. In the New England world at this time only the ministry offered the promise of a fruitful career combined with letters. And it was letters as much as the pulpit Buckminster could not give up.

Joseph Buckminster seems, in a way, to have understood his son's literary ambition, and this may be one reason why, after all his protestations, he suddenly gave up his overt objections to Joseph Stevens' taking the appointment of Brattle Street. At any rate—moved by various motives, including undoubtedly, a feeling for the historic succession of father and son in the New England ministry—Joseph Buckminster broke off the

17 *Ibid.*, 146. Cf. Joseph Stevens Buckminster's journal, *ibid.*, 224.
18 *Ibid.*, 147.
19 *Ibid.*, 148.

quarrel and accepted an invitation to deliver his son's ordination sermon at Brattle Street Church.

Still, Joseph Buckminster did not come down to Boston to confer an anti-climactic parental blessing on his son's decision in favor of Brattle Street liberalism. He came to warn him publicly about the dangers and duties of the ministry. Drawing the text of the ordination sermon from Titus, the elder Buckminster uses St. Paul's admonition to Titus, his son in the faith, as the basis of "a parental and apostolic charge" to Joseph Stevens (and his congregation) concerning the authority of the sacred desk and the pastoral responsibility of the clergy. The sermon emphasizes the authority of the ministry and the "recovering of sinners from the degradation of apostasy to glory, honour and immortality" in "an age of infidelity and bold speculation." Pointedly observing that he is speaking in a "region of literary polish and refinement," Joseph Buckminster dwells on the impediments to the salvational message created by an undue respect for rationalism and for "the beauties of style and the elegances of composition." "A studied neglect of scripture language," he says, "or an apparent contempt of its plainness and simplicity in performing the offices of our sacred function, so that while the Bible furnishes us with a text, Plato, Seneca, or Aristotle fills up the page, is a matter of grief to the pious, and of banter to the profane. It is to 'begin in the Spirit, and to be perfect in the flesh.' "[20]

In warning that in the minister's excessive devotion to literary learning lies the danger of apostasy to the faith, Buckminster echoes the Puritan tradition of the plain style. But the warning he felt had as much relevance for the Boston of the

20 *A Discourse Delivered at the Ordination of the Rev. Joseph S. Buckminster to the Pastoral Charge of the Church in Brattle-Street* (Boston, 1805), 14–15, 16–17.

15

nineteenth century as for the Boston of the seventeenth, possibly a great deal more. Indeed the minister who at the conclusion of the ordination service offered Joseph Stevens Buckminster the right hand of fellowship on behalf of the Boston ministers was at the very moment a primary figure in the editing and publication of the *Monthly Anthology and Boston Review,* one of the few significant magazines of the early Republic. The Reverend William Emerson asked the God who "erst hallowed the lips of the youthful Isaiah" to touch the candidate's "tongue with the fires of celestial eloquence," knowing that the God who favored the voice of Buckminster had in latter days hallowed the lips of Edmund Burke.[21] Five years later William Emerson was to be buried to the exquisite periods of Buckminster's already legendary eloquence. In the funeral sermon the Brattle Street minister spoke about William Emerson's attachment to the literary responsibility of the clergyman as one of the fundamental services he rendered to his world.[22] Buckminster knew how true this was. If he had been associated with Emerson in "pulling down the strong holds of infidelity and vice" (Emerson had discreetly used the conventional phrase in his remarks at the ordination) in Boston, he had been far more closely connected with him in propagating the faith in letters and learning. He had been his colleague in editing the *Monthly Anthology,* in founding the Boston Athenaeum, and in other good works of letters. From the elder Buckminster's implied point of view, his son and William Emerson shared not a common faith but a common infidelity—an undue love of the flesh which is literature. How

21 *Ibid.,* 35. On the *Monthly Anthology and Boston Review,* the Boston Athenaeum, etc., see Lewis P. Simpson (ed.), *The Federalist Literary Mind* (Baton Rouge, 1962).

22 "On the Death of William Emerson," in *Works of Joseph S. Buckminster with Memoirs of His Life,* ed. Henry Ware, Jr. (Boston, 1839), II, 324.

16

deeply Buckminster was involved in this apostasy may be gauged by his vision of the man of letters, a counterimage to his father's ideal image of the minister.

III

This vision, it must be said, was affected by, but not inspired by, the rather wide acquaintance Buckminster and his circle had with the European scene. To a degree Perry Miller misrepresents Buckminster's character as a man of letters when he says that Buckminster was a "domestication of European graces in ungainly New England" or that he was "the most accomplished and cosmopolitan figure of the age."[23] The records show that during his only European sojourn, in 1807, he was charmingly awkward and uncomfortable. Buckminster allowed himself the pleasure of attending the theatre in London only after he had made a calculated decision: "In a place where my example cannot be of evil influence . . . I should reproach myself if I were to leave England without having observed what constitutes so great a part of the national character." In Paris, Buckminster accepted a degree of boredom as necessary to his spiritual health. "Paris must be in some measure dull to any person who is not willing to relieve his *ennui* by rushing into scenes of guilty amusement," he explained to his sisters.[24]

What the Bostonians prized in Buckminster was not so much the cosmopolitan manner of the European cleric. It was his incarnation for a new age of the rigorous New England ascetic ideal. The nineteenth-century critic J. T. Tuckerman said that Joseph Stevens Buckminster presents a remarkable illustration of "the poetry of the New England character." In

23 Perry Miller (ed.), *The Transcendentalists: An Anthology* (Cambridge, Mass., 1950), 17.
24 On Buckminster's stay in London and Paris, see Lee, *Memoirs*, 265–67, 278–92.

a time when the "national life was so fresh as yet to be experimental," he represented not only "grace and sensibility" but also the "unchallenged purity" derived from early discipline in "self-denial, self-control and aspiration."[25] It was as one of their cherished dreams fulfilled that Buckminster stood before the audience at the Harvard Phi Beta Kappa celebration in 1809 to deliver the chief address of the day, "On the Dangers and Duties of Men of Letters." This vision of the life of letters is the most important statement about the literary vocation in New England prior to Ralph Waldo Emerson's famous Phi Beta Kappa address, *The American Scholar*, in 1837. Like Emerson's pronouncement, Buckminster's represents a quest for vocational identity which has both personal and general significance. By implication it is an effort to define Buckminster's role in society and at the same time to speak for—to anticipate—the forming of a new intellectual order in his society. Today Emerson would entitle his address "The Function of Men of Letters in Our Time," but specialization had not yet made functionalism so vital in conceiving the nature of a vocation.

Buckminster commences with the problem of the future of letters in a new nation. Far from assuming the fabled *translatio studii*, the progress of letters from East to West as predetermined American history, he foresees an American future that may be fatal to literature. He compares Athens to the "unlettered" Assyrian empire; and the "polished republick of Geneva" to the Czar's "vast dominions," and to Napoleon's "desolated continent." America "in the course of national aggrandizement" will also become an empire of unparalleled extent. Can it also be a "nation of men of letters"? Born "in an

25 J. T. Tuckerman, "Joseph Stevens Buckminster," *Southern Literary Messenger*, XXIV (January, 1857), 50.

age of tremendous revolution," marked by the wreckage of "ancient literary glory," the present generation is still under the influence of the "foul spirit of innovation and sophistry" which arose in the French Revolution. Buckminster, it is significant to say, finds the influence of this force in a literary instead of a religious decline in New England. Before the American Revolution, he says, "we find, or think we find . . . more accomplished scholars than we have since produced; men, who . . . felt more than we do the charm of classical accomplishments . . . who had not learned to be ashamed of being often found drinking at the wells of antiquity." The American Revolution, followed so closely by the far more disruptive one in France, has created a crisis marked by the introduction of "the pernicious notion of equality," a concept "which has not only tainted our sentiments, but impaired our vigour, and crippled our literary eminence." American literary aspiration has become subject to a sinister force, "the secret influence of publick opinion." This can only be overcome, and with difficulty, by a "spirit of criticism" directed toward establishing and maintaining correct models for literature. But faction, the insidious monster born of public opinion, threatens all criticism. The young man of literary promise is lured by some faction of the people—the way Milton was, Buckminster says, by the "vulgar and usurping" party of Cromwell a century before. Save for his blindness, Milton might have entirely wasted his genius in "more praises of Cromwell and more ribaldry against Salmasius."[26] On the other hand, if the youth shuns the politics of his age completely, he will destroy his

26 Joseph Stevens Buckminster, "On the Dangers and Duties of Men of Letters," *Monthly Anthology and Boston Review*, VII (September, 1809), 146–50. Buckminster's opinion of Milton—considering Buckminster's heritage it is highly ironic—was undoubtedly influenced by Samuel Johnson's.

talents in pleasant but enervating retirement. Who best illustrates the character of the man of letters in all his virtue? To the youth of Cambridge and the assembled Boston-Cambridge community (everybody came to the annual Phi Beta Kappa celebration), Buckminster holds up the great pagan Cicero. There may seem nothing fundamentally noteworthy in Buckminster's idealization of Cicero, who had been thoroughly assimilated to the Christian humanism of the Renaissance and the eighteenth century. But the implication of the devotion shown to Cicero is distinctive.

The history of letters does not at this moment suggest to me a more fortunate parallel between the effects of active and inactive learning than in the well known characters of Cicero and Atticus. Let me hold them up to your observation . . . because, like you, they were the citizens of a republick. They lived in an age of learning and of dangers, and acted upon opposite principles, when Rome was to be saved, if saved at all, by the virtuous energy of her most accomplished minds. If we look now for Atticus, we find him in the quiet of his library, surrounded with his books; while Cicero was passing through the regular course of publick honours and services, where all the treasures of his mind were at the command of his country. If we follow them, we find Atticus pleasantly wandering among the ruins of Athens, purchasing up statues and antiques; while Cicero was at home blasting the projects of Catiline, and at the head of the Senate, like the tutelary spirit of his country, as the storm was gathering, secretly watching the doubtful movements of Caesar. If we look to the period of the civil wars, we find Atticus . . . recommending himself to Caesar by his neutrality, courted by Anthony, and connected with Octavius, poorly concealing the epicureanism of his principles under the ornaments of literature and the splendour of his benefactions . . . . Turn now to Cicero, the only great man at whom Caesar always trembled, the only great man whom falling Rome did *not* fear. . . . If, my friends, you would feel what learning and genius and virtue should aspire to in a day of peril and depravity, when you are tired of the factions of the city, the battles of the Caesars, the crimes of the triumvirate, and the splendid court of Augustus, do not go and repose in the easy chair of Atticus, but refresh your virtues and your spirits with the contemplation of Cicero.[27]

Buckminster's appeal to the Ciceronian image was a way of identifying the Boston-Cambridge literati, not altogether with ancient literature, but with the literary present, the eighteenth-century dominion of letters. Cicero, Peter Gay says, was a "culture hero of the Enlightenment."[28] Adapting his writings to a variety of attitudes, philosophes and men of letters found in Cicero one attitude they all held in common: in the words of the Roman intellectual and statesman himself, "The whole glory of virtue lies in activity." To the eighteenth-century literary mind this meant primarily literary activity—the disciplined use of words in writing and speaking to provide moral guidance to society. The man of letters functions in the world in which he lives; and if he becomes isolated in scholarship or in mere literary dilettantism, he becomes useless.

Late in his address, almost as an afterthought it would seem, Buckminster gets around to the relationship between letters and Christianity, that is, Protestant Christianity. The passage is curious. It reads in part:

Protestant Christianity has in former times given learning such support, as learning never can repay. The history of Christendom bears witness to this. The names of Erasmus, of Grotius, of Bacon and a host of luminaries of science [that is, of letters and learning], who rise up like a wall of fire around the cause of Christianity will bear witness to this. They cry out in the language of Tully: *O vitae dux! o virtutis indagatrix, expultrixque vitiorum! quid non modo nos, sed omnino vita hominum sine te esse potuisset.* Without this for the guide and terminus of your studies, you may "but go down to hell, with a great deal of wisdom." My friends, infidelity has had

27 *Ibid.,* VII, 150–51.
28 Peter Gay, *The Enlightenment: An Interpretation: The Rise of Modern Paganism* (Vintage Paperback Ed.; New York, 1968), 189.

one triumph in our days; and we have seen learning, as well as virtue, trampled under the hoofs of its infuriated steeds, let loose by the hand of impiety. Fanaticism, too, has had more than one day of desolation; and its consequences have been such, as ought always to put learning on its guard.[29]

Such an eclectic weaving of Protestantism, "liberal" Roman Catholicism, and Classicism in an implied pattern of opposition both to infidelity and religious fanaticism documents a subtle change in the Boston-Cambridge mind. Allegiance to religious doctrine is transferred to a humanistic moralism. To put it another way, Buckminster's comment indicates that in the secularization of the Boston mind, there had occurred a spiritualization of secular letters; that is, to a greater degree than at any time before in the history of the mind in New England. Many years later remembering the appearance of Buckminster before the Phi Beta Kappa audience, George Ticknor caught a moment in this kind of spiritualization almost perfectly: "His bright and beautiful features, transfigured with enthusiasm as he uttered these glowing words, and his eager manner, as he leaned forward with the earnestness of his emotions, are still present to us. The very tones of his voice stir us still as with the sound of a trumpet. They sank deep into many hearts; and more than one young spirit, we have reason to think, was on that day and in that hour, saved from the enthralment and degradation of party politics and party passions, and consecrated to letters." [30]

The phenomenon of the divinization of humane letters in New England during the period of the early Republic has been too little regarded in the historical study of American literature. In it lies an important reason for the unusual coherence and community (existing in dissension as well as in agree-

29 "On the Dangers and Duties of Men of Letters," 156–57.
30 George Ticknor, review of Lee, *Memoirs*, in *Christian Examiner*, XLVII (September, 1849), 169–95.

ment) which mark the literary life in Boston until the latter part of the nineteenth century. In the early nineteenth century the image in the New England mind of the old theocratic polity begins to become the image of a literary polity. (This is not only analogous to but a part of a process we see taking place in Western civilization from the Renaissance onward into the twentieth century, the climax occurring in the eighteenth century.) The *Respublica Christiana* in New England becomes the *Respublica litterarum*. The Boston intellectuals seek quite consciously to fulfill in New England and the new nation the eighteenth-century representation of literary order. This aspiration is writ large in Buckminster's constant sensitivity to the problem of literary and intellectual discipline in the infant republic, and is dramatically fixed in one essay in "The Remarker" series in the *Monthly Anthology*. The essay deals with the lack of a critical tribunal in the United States and declares the right to establish one which will represent the universal commonwealth of literature.

The commonwealth of learning is the only permanent example of pure and original democracy. In this state, under the protection of truth and reason, whose authority alone is acknowledged, wars may be carried on with the utmost innocence, though not always with impunity; for here every man is sovereign, and every man also under the jurisdiction of every other. The laws of *civil society* have in no degree abridged the independence of the state of nature as to errour and ignorance. No man can be excluded by the social compact from his inalienable right to be a fool; and, on the other side, every man retains the right of the sword, and may exercise it without a commission.

On the basis of this concept of literary government, Buckminster postulates a highly legalistic, authoritarian theory of criticism that is a *reductio ad absurdum* of the neo-classic doctrine of literary standards. "Every candidate for fame," he goes so far as to assert, "has it in his power to consult innumerable precedents, statutes and declarations of criticism, by which the verdict of the publick and the sentence of the reviewer may be previously and probably conjectured."[31] But the significance of Buckminster's attitude does not lie in his absurd literary zealousness. It is to be found in his attempt to express his feeling for the existence and perpetuation of the literary realm —in his sensibility of literary order. The man of letters belongs to the literary realm. Independent of the realm of politics, it is as well, Buckminster implies, independent of the realm of religion, or of any union of the civil and ecclesiastical realms. This is not to say that Buckminster is willing to abrogate the responsibility of the man of letters to either the State or the Church. He suggests that the responsibility to letters and learning is a responsibility in its own right. His function is to be a citizen of the Republic of Letters, enlisted in the "cause of truth and learning," which is the cause of "God . . . and will not be deserted."[32] Word and deed, thought and action interact. The man of letters is a constant actor in a drama of existence in which the struggle is to maintain civilization against barbarism. He serves "the Word" in the sense that Pope means "the Word" in the *Dunciad*.[33] In the interrelated life of the three realms of existence—Church, State, and Letters—the duty of the man of letters is to represent the realm of letters.

While he discussed the theory of the man of letters in speeches and essays, Buckminster never failed to represent the literary republic in tangible ways. Always pressing upon the limits of his frail health, he was constantly engaged in the writing, scholarship, and editing demanded by the *Monthly*

---

31 Joseph Stevens Buckminster, "The Remarker, No. 5," *Monthly Anthology*, III (January, 1806), 20, 22.

32 "On the Dangers and Duties of Men of Letters," 158.

33 See Aubrey L. Williams, *The Dunciad: A Study of Its Meaning* (Baton Rouge, 1955), especially Chaps. 5 and 6.

Anthology and in attending to the routine affairs of the Anthology Society and the magazine. He was occupied too in buying books for the Boston Athenaeum (which began as the
Anthology Society Reading Room in 1805) and for his unusually fine personal library. Then, too, he was busy pursuing
his pioneering literary and philological studies of the Bible.

Never properly recognized is the significance of Buckminster's agency in purchasing books for the infant Athenaeum
while he was abroad. This task required judgment and hard
work, and the patience to put up with the overly enthusiastic
requests of the dedicated first librarian of the Athenaeum, his
friend and fellow Anthologist William Smith Shaw. The almost pathetic eagerness of Shaw and Buckminster to supply
the "want of books" in their world, and otherwise to make
themselves useful in a literary way, was directly related to a
spiritual emergency they at times felt was more precisely economic than political. If the vacuum left by the decline of the
old religious community was in danger of being filled by demo-
crats and atheists, it was in just as much danger of being taken
over by Philistines. While he was in Paris, Buckminster spent
much of the time he had free from his Athenaeum obligations
purchasing books for his own library. On this collection he
lavished all of a substantial bequest left to him by his maternal
grandfather. "Although I may, by the Providence of God, be
cut off from the enjoyment of these luxuries of the mind, they
will be a treasure to those who may succeed me, like the hoards
of a miser scattered after his death," he wrote privately. "I feel
that, by every book which I send out, I do something for my
dear country, which the love of money seems to be depressing
into unlettered barbarism." [34]

The "luxuries of the mind"—books thought of as necessities

---

34 Lee, *Memoirs*, 259.

of civilization, that is to say, the authority of the lettered mind conceived as the basis of civilization—this attitude, as well as the repudiation of Calvinism, was a motive in a rational religion and an inspiration in Buckminster's effort to introduce the textual methodology of German biblical scholarship into New England. In 1808 he engaged with William Wells, scholar and bookseller of Cambridge, in editing and publishing, under the patronage of Harvard, an American edition of Griesbach's New Testament, a critical text of the first importance. This New England edition of Griesbach preceded its publication in England; when the English booksellers placed orders for the American Griesbach, the Boston scholars were well pleased. But this kind of printing was expensive and the volume in no great demand. When a supplementary volume was proposed—one that would contain among other aids an English translation of Griesbach's prolegomena to his large critical edition—an insufficient number of subscriptions caused the cancellation of the project. For lack of financial support Buckminster was likewise forced to give up an ambitious two-volume edition, with critical paraphernalia, of the best versions of the prophetical books of the Old Testament. The literary study of the Scriptures, nevertheless, was established through Buckminster's work. In 1811 the Samuel Dexter Lectureship in Biblical Criticism was set up at Harvard, and in August of this year Buckminster was appointed to fill it.[35] He would not live to do so, but Andrews Norton, who would become the great Unitarian biblical scholar, was already a youthful disciple of Buckminster and the new criticism of the Bible. Under his direction the literary and historical criticism of the Scriptures became a part of Unitarian orthodoxy, the orthodoxy finally to

35 See Josiah Quincy, *History of Harvard University* (Cambridge, Mass., 1840), II, 310–11.

be challenged by Ralph Waldo Emerson in an address Norton would ironically call "the latest form of infidelity."

IV

Buckminster poured the remaining energies of his life, excepting the strength he carefully reserved for his pastoral duties, into the preparations for his new task. Planning to begin lecturing early in 1813, he went to work at once to become fluent in German, started a review of his past reading, and began to plan his lectures.

He toiled through the winter and into the late spring of 1812. Interrupted in May by the traditional obligations of Election Week, he filled a busy schedule, official and social, during the week. On the Sunday following he appeared to become ill while in the pulpit, stepped down, then returned to complete his sermon. A few days later he suffered a violent epileptic attack, and save for brief intervals did not regain consciousness. George Ticknor remained constantly with him during his final illness. After seven days he died, his head resting on Ticknor's arm. Far away in Reedsborough, a village in the remote western part of New York, the elder Buckminster, on a journey for his health, lay fatally ill with an infection resulting apparently from an incision made in his arm to bleed him. "My son Joseph is dead," he said to his wife. She replied that he had dreamed. "I have not slept nor dreamed; he is dead," he said. This incident became famous in New England. Two months later young Edward Everett memorialized it in his Phi Beta Kappa poem at Harvard, when in a tribute to Joseph Stevens Buckminster he said:

> Go with your sire, for Heaven in judgment kind,
> The chain of filial friendship spared to unbind.
> Or was that cord of love so finely spun

That joined the secret souls of sire and son,
That each unconscious, owned the fatal blow,
And nature felt what reason could not know! [36]

The father and son, having refused to break the bonds of family and sacred desk, were taken up into heaven together. And so the story of the Buckminsters, made to order for New Englanders who loved a drama of holy living and holy dying in the ministry, had a happy ending and became a legend. But the legend of the Buckminsters, though it expressed the historic desire of the New Englanders to make New England a unified spiritual mission to the world, had no forceful symbolic meaning. Beyond the pleasant sentiment of cultural harmony it evoked, it did not bring the Boston mind and the outlying Calvinism any closer together. The clash of attitudes between Joseph and Joseph Stevens Buckminster was too fundamental for reconciliation, save perhaps ultimately in the lonely and exquisite irony of an Emily Dickinson. What is significant for literary history in the Buckminster story is that in the crisis of vocation pressed upon him so directly by his father, the younger Buckminster set up an image of the Boston ministry as an order with a distinctive vocation to literature. Both in words and deeds he gave his age leadership in letters, and thus became the focus of an incipient community of Boston-Cambridge literary intellectuals. The focus was the most intense within the circle of his intimate friends in the Anthology Society—among them, besides Shaw and William Emerson, Arthur Maynard Walter, Samuel Cooper Thacher, William Tudor, Jr., and George Ticknor. But the circle extended outward to include a larger group—John Thornton Kirkland, John Sylvester John Gardiner, and John Quincy Adams, to mention three among a dozen or more others. Together Buckminster's

36 Lee, *Memoirs*, 472; William B. Sprague, *Annals of the American Pulpit* (New York, 1857–69), VIII, 405.

literary friends and acquaintances constituted a major segment of an evolving order of men of letters in the Boston and Harvard world that may properly be designated a clerisy. The term is usually connected with Samuel Taylor Coleridge because of the prominence he gives it in *Church and State* and elsewhere in his writings. It is interesting to see that, lacking any direct relationship to Coleridge's ideas, the New England clerisy bears a resemblance to the clerisy Coleridge wanted to see established in England. This was to be an order of the literary and learned which would be a "national church." But in an approximate or loosely analogous sense. It would be a spiritualized literary authority responsible for the intellectual and spiritual well-being of the nation. Coleridge's notion of a clerisy is an aspect of his effort to grapple with the leading problem of his age: the bearing of intellect on society when religious authority has lost its assimilating power over the primary civilizing agency in society, the use of letters.

Who makes up the clerisy? Poets, philosophers, and scholars, Coleridge says. "The sages and professors of the law and jurisprudence; of medicine and physiology; of music; of military and civil architecture; of the physical sciences; with the mathematical as the common organ of the preceding; in short, all the so-called liberal arts and sciences, the possession and application of which constitute the civilization of a country, as well as the Theological"—Coleridge's view of the composition of the clerisy is that of the Republic of Letters. This spacious view was possible before the age of specialization. To Coleridge, literature is a comprehensive activity of mind; and the clerisy is charged with securing "for the nation . . . that character of general civilization, which equally with, or rather more than, fleets, armies and revenue, forms the ground of its defensive and offensive power." [37]

37 From Samuel Taylor Coleridge, *The Friend,* as quoted in *The*

Following the same humanistic idea of the large usefulness of men of letters, Buckminster says in "The Dangers and Duties of Men of Letters":

> Learning is not a superfluity; and utility must, after all, be the object of your studies. The theologian, like Paley, who makes truth intelligible to the humblest; the preacher, like Fenelon, who imparts the divine warmth of his own soul to the souls of his readers; the moralist, like Johnson, who "gives ardour to virtue and confidence to truth;" the jurist, like Mansfield, who contributes to the perfect administration of justice; the statesman, who stems the torrent of corruption, and directs the rising virtue of an indignant people; the philosopher, who leaves in his writings the pregnant germs of future discoveries; the historian, and the poet, who not only preserve the names of the great, but, in words that burn, inflame us with the love of their excellence, are of more value to the community, than a whole cabinet of *dilettanti*, and more worthy of your imitation than Magliabechi, reposing on the ponderous tomes of his library, a mere *corpus litterarum*.[38]

Something like this vision of an active, responsible, assimilating order of letters and learning was fulfilled in New England by Buckminster's surviving contemporaries and by the remarkable and numerous generation of men of letters that announced itself in the 1830s. Richard Henry Dana, George Bancroft, William H. Prescott, Francis Parkman, John L. Motley, Theodore Parker, Longfellow, Holmes, Lowell, Emerson, Thoreau, Hawthorne—these and many others in one way or another were joined in the community of aspiration that centered in the Boston-Cambridge, explicitly the Boston-Cambridge-Concord, area during the three decades before the Civil War. Brahmins or Transcendental rebels, of the Establishment or the Movement, addicts of society or haters of it,

---

Political Thought of Samuel Taylor Coleridge, ed. R. J. White (London, 1938), 165–66. A convenient, scholarly anthology of Coleridge's scattered comments on politics.

38 "On the Dangers and Duties of Men of Letters," 155.

book lovers or book rejecters (as Emerson tried futilely to be) —these New Englanders—poets and storytellers, essayists, historians, and philosophers—were all scholars or men of letters. They were all conscious, often no doubt painfully so (who more than hard cases of isolation like Hawthorne and Thoreau?) of the dangers and duties of their common vocation for literature. They shared the sense of belonging to an order opposed to the order of "things"—the materialist order, economic and political. Inheritors of the poetry of the New England ascetic character, indeed through Buckminster and his friends of the asceticism of the old order of the Puritan ministry, they were a clerisy responsible for the spiritual education of the nation. The responsibility was hard on some of them. It wore them out and made them eccentric. It may have killed some of them—Theodore Parker, for example. But they knew a state of consecration to a saving cause. They were the last generation of New Englanders to know this kind of comfort.

31

❧ The Tudor Brothers: Boston Ice and Boston Letters

> The frost covers the windows, the wheels creak, the boys run, winter rules, and $50,000 worth of ice floats for me upon Fresh Pond.
>
> *Frederic Tudor, "Ice House Diary"*

> But in this country, avarice and ambition are more nearly identified than in any other.
>
> *William Tudor, "Discourse before Phi Beta Kappa"*

> Ice is an interesting subject for contemplation. They told me they had some in the ice-house at Fresh Pond five years old which was as good as ever. Why is it that a bucket of water soon becomes putrid, but frozen remains sweet forever? It is commonly said that this is the difference between the affections and the intellect.
>
> *Henry David Thoreau, Walden*

IN THE sixteenth chapter of *Walden*, called "The Pond in Winter," Thoreau transforms the carrying of Walden water to India by the worldwide New England ice trade from a commercial fact into a symbol of a "passage to more than India," to use Whitman's famous phrase. In the 1840s, as Thoreau observes, ice cut from the winter-frozen ponds of New England —cut regularly from major sources such as Fresh Pond at Cambridge, and irregularly, or seldom, from less favored ponds —was being consumed in quantity by "the sweltering inhabitants of Charleston and New Orleans, of Madras and Bombay and Calcutta." Invoking the Hindu scriptures ("In the morning I bathe my intellect in the stupendous and cosmogonal philosophy of the Bhagvat Geeta. . . ."), Thoreau in a transcendental vision sees "the pure Walden water" mingling "with the sacred water of the Ganges," and then in its mystical voyage being wafted beyond all reckoning, to "ports of which Alexander only heard the names." [1]

This transcendent culmination of the description of Walden Pond in winter contrasts with the dramatic depiction of the rape of the Walden ice immediately preceding. In the winter of 1846–1847, Thoreau says, an ice crew made up of "a hundred Irishmen, with Yankee overseers," arrived one day at Walden Pond on the cars of the Fitchburg Railroad. Efficiently equipped for their work of destruction, commonly called an "ice harvest," the men labored for sixteen days, returning to Boston late each afternoon in the cars and coming back promptly in them early each morning. They systematically ravaged Walden Pond's blue ice, stacked ten thousand tons in cakes on the shore, and covered the great stack with hay and boards, leaving their harvest to be transported to its far-flung destinations. It was a ruthless business operation conducted, Thoreau says he learned, by "a gentleman farmer, who was behind the scenes, wanted to double his money, which as I understood, amounted to half a million already; but in order to cover each one of his dollars with another, he took off the only coat, ay the skin itself, of Walden Pond in the midst of a hard winter." [2]

In view of the mercenary actualities of the ice trade, Thoreau's transformation of the literal voyage to Bombay and Calcutta into an ideal literary voyage may well seem to be a somewhat contrived symbolism. But his conjunction of the economic and literary history of mid-nineteenth-century New England rests in a logic that, if Thoreau was not fully aware

---

1   Walter Harding (ed.), *The Variorum Walden* (New York, 1963), 225.
2   *Ibid.*, 222–23.

of it in historical detail, was part of his integral consciousness of his cultural situation. This situation emerges when his treatment of the ice trade is seen in the light of the relationship of ice and letters in the history of Boston—that is, of the Boston community, including Cambridge and Concord—during the Federalist Age, and the years immediately following. Because Philadelphia was the intellectual capital of Jeffersonian America and, in a negative sense, because the Federalist-dominated politics of Boston has not been congenial to our cultural historians, the importance of Boston in the early nineteenth century to the history of the American literary mind has been underestimated. And yet during the first two or three decades of this century, significant preparations were made in the commercial and literary capital of New England for both her actual and her literary voyages in the great mid-century period—the time of Emerson, Thoreau, and Hawthorne and of Boston's strongest national influence on our culture.

Among the many interesting ways to estimate the significance of the Boston of Federalist times is to study the lives and adventures of two largely forgotten brothers of a once prominent Boston family. One of them, Frederic Tudor (1783–1864) was the "gentleman farmer" whose ice crew took the skin off Walden Pond while Thoreau looked out at the depredation from the window of his hut. Thoreau states that Tudor was worth half a million dollars at the time. Likely he was closer to being a millionaire. He was by this time the "Ice King," the leading entrepreneur in the New England ice industry. He had won his preeminence the hard way, for years his chief resource being mostly a desperate confidence in his dream of wealth. Frederic Tudor's older brother, William, is not mentioned by Thoreau in *Walden* (nor elsewhere, it would seem), but his presence, was felt at Walden Pond in the winter of 1846–1847—not so much because he was the one who had the idea of the ice trade in the first place as because he was an inept merchant with literary inclinations. Frederic called William "worthless," an opinion confirmed over and over again in Frederic's view by his brother's literary projects, for example, founding the *North American Review*.

I

In the Federalist Age, Boston associated its destiny not primarily with the vast American continental frontier but with the new Republic's great seafaring frontier. Freed from its long deference to British colonialism, the mercantile imagination of the port city, in spite of the Napoleonic world war and Jefferson's despised neutral trade policies, prepared the way for a golden seafaring period following the Treaty of Ghent.

As early as 1790 the *Columbia*, captained by Robert Gray, had heralded the opening of Boston's Pacific trade, when she sailed into her home harbor after a three-year voyage loaded with Chinese teas, textiles, and porcelain. Her cargo had been purchased in Canton with furs procured in Oregon in exchange for Boston copper, iron, and cloth. In 1810 Captain William Sturgis, a twenty-eight-year-old Bostonian, organized the firm of Bryant and Sturgis; for more than thirty years this firm, specializing in the Northwest fur trade, controlled over half of the Pacific trade of the United States. "Next to a beautiful woman and a lovely infant," Sturgis said, "a prime sea-otter is the finest natural object in the world." It was more a financial than an aesthetic judgment, and few took exception to it. Investors and shipmasters in successful Pacific voyages made enormous profits. For example, Captain John Suter, a shipmaster in the best Bible-reading tradition of New England seafaring, sailed for Canton with an investment in cargo and equipment representing not over $40,000. In spite of difficulties trading with the Indians, the nineteen-year-old captain accumulated enough furs and sandalwood to trade for $156,743 worth of chinaware, Souchong and Hyson tea, oriental silk, and other treasures in Canton. When he returned to Boston in 1810, the net profit from his adventure was $205,650.47. Common seamen profited in the Pacific enterprises also. Yankee lads from the lonely farms of the interior sought berths on ships engaged in the fur trade, knowing that if they survived the long voyage to Canton and back, they could make five to six hundred dollars in wages, plus an additional sum from the sale of all the Chinese articles they could pack in their sea chests. A New England farm boy might become comparatively well off on his earnings from one or two oriental voyages.[3]

The enormous profits from the China trade encouraged the speculative spirit in Boston commerce and lay behind the development of the ice trade, a more venturesome and precarious, if less spectacular, innovation in New England commerce.

The historic possibility of the ice trade was created when Frederic Tudor, in an act of rebellion left Boston Latin School at the age of thirteen to become the youngest apprentice of Ducosten and Marshall, a firm on State Street. Although he was about the right age, he refused to follow his three dutiful brothers and be a Harvard man. He scornfully denounced Harvard as a place for loafers. "To a man who is to be a gentleman in the world," William Tudor vainly told his errant

3 Captain William Sturgis is quoted in *Boston Looks Seaward: The Story of the Port, 1630–1940*, comp. Writers' Program of Works Progress Administration (Boston, 1941), 84. See also *Voyages of the Columbia, Collections of the Massachusetts Historical Society*, LXXXIX, xxv–xxvii, 145–49; Samuel Eliot Morison, *Maritime History of Massachusetts, 1730–1860* (Boston, 1921), 71; Robert A. East, "Economic Development and New England Federalism," *New England Quarterly*, X (September, 1937), 430–46.

brother, "nothing can compensate for the want of a college education."[4]

Frederic Tudor, however, had not yet found true independence; in setting himself against Harvard he may have been primarily expressing his resentment of his older brother, who was doing all of the right things. Frederic soon left State Street for the Tudor family home at Rockwood, where he hunted, read a great deal, and interested himself in agricultural experiments. He also speculated modestly in Cuban molasses and cigars; and when he was seventeen, in the company of a younger brother on a voyage for his health, he visited Cuba. Eventually Colonel Tudor set Frederic up in the commodity market in Boston. Speculator and man about town, Frederic Tudor at the age of twenty-two seemed to be on the way to becoming merely another State Street operator, when William suggested at a fashionable party that ice from the Tudors' pond in Rockwood would be a profitable commodity in Caribbean ports. The time was the summer of 1805; very likely the Bostonians at the party were enjoying iced drinks and iced confections made with ice taken from nearby ponds and preserved through the hot months in a family ice house. William, it would seem, did not make his suggestion seriously. He was more interested in helping the newly formed Anthology Society edit the *Monthly Anthology and Boston Review* (1803–1811) and establish its reading room, soon to become the

4 Henry G. Pearson, "Frederic Tudor, Ice King," *Proceedings of the Massachusetts Historical Society*, LXV (November, 1933), 172. Although he is an important figure in the history of American and world commerce, Frederic Tudor has had no adequate biography. Pearson's essay, which is strong in quotations from the basic documents, especially Tudor's diary, is the only comprehensive source of information about Tudor. Daniel J. Boorstin has studied Tudor's career briefly in *The Americans: The National Experience* (New York, 1965), 10–16. See also Stewart Holbrook, *Lost Men of American History* (New York, 1946), 114–23.

Boston Athenaeum, than he was in business. Besides, in 1805 the Tudor family fortunes had never been higher, and William, the eldest son, could afford to practice the cavalier philosophy he had set down in a letter written from Europe to his mother in 1799: "I am afraid I shall be full of plans when I return; but then you know it is not necessary to execute them; and there is a pleasure in talking."[5]

But the notion of trading ice in the West Indies caught Frederic up in a vision of instant fame and fortune. On the leather-bound cover of a journal he started at this point, which he came to call his "Ice House Diary," he boldly printed a motto: "He who gives back at the first repulse and without striking the second blow despairs of success[,] has never been, is not, and never will be a hero in war, love, or business."[6] These words proved to be a prophecy of a strenuous and hazardous but ultimately highly successful commercial career.

With an impulsiveness characteristic of his whole career, Frederic Tudor borrowed money, secured a brig—with a name of good omen, the *Favorite*—and took his first cargo of ice into the Caribbean. The citizens of his port of destination, St. Pierre, Martinique, were eager for ice, especially after Tudor showed them how it might be used, but by then much of it had melted away; and in the initial ice venture he lost $3000 to $4000 of the $10,000 put into it. Arrangements for storing Tudor's highly perishable cargo were to have been made by his advance agents, his brother William, and a cousin, another young Bostonian, James Savage. Savage was later to become the successful treasurer of the Provident Institution for Savings in Boston, but he was no more provident at this time than the cavalier William Tudor. Consequently, although both agents found the voyage in West Indian waters exotic, they did noth-

5 Pearson, "Frederic Tudor, Ice King," 173.
6 *Ibid.*, 175.

ing to prepare for Frederic's arrival with his boatload of New England ice, except to create in Martinique a state of incredulous anticipation.

Next year Frederic Tudor did better, this time shipping to Havana, while he sent William faraway to England and France to secure permission to sell ice in their colonies. In December, 1807, however, came Jefferson's embargo proclamation. Stymied by this, Frederic began what he should have undertaken before: experiments at Rockwood in model icehouses designed to keep ice in tropical heat. Just as he entered into this period of his novel enterprise, he was suddenly confronted with a major catastrophe, the substantial loss of the family fortune. This occurred when Colonel William Tudor, the father, a well-known lawyer who had been judge advocate-general in Washington's army, suffered the complete loss of his investment in a Boston land development scheme. Harassed by debtors and threatened with imprisonment, the family head lived the remaining years of his life on his small salary as clerk of the Massachusetts Supreme Court; while Frederic Tudor, more and more resentful of his literary brother, deeming him to be an extra burden rather than a help, imposed upon the almost stillborn ice trade not only the hope of his personal financial success but his family's economic salvation.

At the same time, money became harder and harder for him to get; thus he could not operate, as some Boston merchants did, in defiance of the Jeffersonian trade restrictions. At length in 1810, even though he lacked passage money and was "so poor, so discouraged I felt indifferent about life," he made his way to Havana. Once there he managed to raise enough money to set up a storage house, one that would keep ice through the hottest months from April to September. From the Cuban authorities, moreover, he secured the exclusive privilege of

39

selling ice in Havana for the next six years. Immediately he decided to cover one risk with a greater one by extending the ice trade to Jamaica. This venture went so poorly he was lucky when his second cargo to Port Royal was lost at sea. He was saved a freight bill. Tudor was not so lucky when a "villainous" agent cheated him out of most of his Havana profits. As debts piled on debts, Tudor was hounded by creditors. When the War of 1812 began, bringing additional vexations, he thought he saw an opportunity in privateering and designed, patented, and built the *Black Swan*, a ship with a new type of hull. On the day she was launched, a sheriff boarded her and took Frederic off to the Cambridge jail for nonpayment of a $300 note. A few weeks before, he had been in the Boston jail, and he would be in prison again. At the end of the war with England, Tudor raised the bare sum necessary to make another shipment of ice to Havana, where his exclusive right of sale had only one more year to run. "Pursued by sheriffs to the very wharf," he reached Havana, only to find that the support of the ice trade he had won from the Cubans had been undermined by a confidence man who had convinced the Cuban authorities he could manufacture ice.[7] Tudor reestablished faith in his business and at last built what proved to be a genuinely efficient icehouse for the Cuban climate. Although he had to hide from his creditors each time he came back to the United States, his business slowly improved. It was to improve more rapidly when Tudor began to ship ice to Charleston and New Orleans, cities with more lucrative markets for ice than he had found in the West Indies.

At this juncture in his hectic career he received, ironically, from his useless literary brother what he always needed most, the help of the "ready money race." When William showed up in Frederic's counting room in October, 1820, Frederic

7   *Ibid.*, 182.

thought he had come to borrow money. Instead William had come to offer to obtain a loan for his brother if Frederic would become his patron in the literary project he was then working on, a life of James Otis. In effect William's scheme amounted to using his influence to persuade two or three wealthy Bostonians of literary inclinations to lend Frederic $3000. The interest on the loan would go to William instead of Frederic's creditors; thus endowed he could work on his book. The scheme worked; William wrote his biography, and Frederic built an icehouse in New Orleans.

After this, Frederic was frequently in financial trouble, but the ice trade grew steadily. A risky enterprise became one of reasonably calculable risks. In 1834 Frederic Tudor achieved his long dreamed of passage to India and set up his Calcutta "plantation." ("Plantation" was the term used for an icehouse.) The ice trade with Calcutta, according to Samuel Eliot Morison, was the salvation of New England's East India trade and a vital factor in the flowering of New England commerce in the mid-nineteenth century. Although the voyage, which crossed the equator twice, required four months, it sold ice. Between 1836 and 1846, the year he harvested the ice on Walden Pond, Tudor increased his overall sales from 12,000 to 65,000 tons. Ten years later Tudor shipped 146,000 tons of ice from Yankee ponds in 363 cargoes to fifty-three different ports. He reached markets in the West Indies, the East Indies, China, the Philippines, and Australia as well as domestic markets. Until the manufacture and marketing of ice became common a generation after the Civil War, ice from the ponds of New England remained an important commodity in world trade.

What sustained Frederic Tudor in his lengthy and lonely struggle for success in the ice trade? The fundamental answer: his conviction, at first simply entertained but rapidly devel-

41

oped into an absolute in his mind, that money is worth everything. This motivating conviction can be studied in his diaries and letters—especially in Tudor's "Ice House Diary," which reveals the inner as well as the outer history of how the Ice King won his crown in Boston's economy of speculation.

Here is Tudor on March 4, 1812, "locked-up as a debtor in Boston jail" for the first time: "On this memorable day in my little annals March 9th 1812 I am 28 years 6 months and 5 days old. It is an event which I think I could not have avoided; but it is a climax which I did hope to have escaped, as my affairs are looking well at last after a fearful struggle with adverse circumstances for seven years—but it has taken place and I have endeavoured to meet it as I would the tempest of heaven which should serve to strengthen rather than reduce the spirit of a true man." [8] Here is Tudor about two years later, his head bloodier but still unbowed, talking about a creditor: "[He] has driven me to immense sacrifices and great exertions, and when neither could obtain I have given him the body." He continues:

One instance of getting the amount of the bond and the pound of the flesh also I must forever remember. He had obtained judgement and ex[ecution] on me and my Father. On the day before the return day I went into the limits. In the evening and without previous notice my Father was arrested also, and was about giving bonds for limits also when . . . [his] attorney offered to release my Father provided I would give up my watch, a very favorite one, and agree to have it sold at auction unless redeemed in 60 days. This I did, handing my watch warm from my pocket to the sheriff and remaining myself imprisoned. I did it, I thank God, with indignation! [9]

And here is Tudor in seven more years:

8 *Ibid.*, 180.
9 *Ibid.*, 181.

January 7th 1821. The commencement of a new year, as all new years have for the last 15, finds me How I need not say—this book [his diary] will tell. Look back, Mr. Frederic, and wonder how so sick and weakly constituted a man as you could have sustained what is written down. In the very onsett, the result of the first year, you were ruined; the silver spoon with which you were born was torn from your mouth; and you were at once put upon your sole and unaided ability to fight your way through the world. You have fought, but are yet in the midst of the war. You have been rather of the complaining sort, if this book records your feelings; but I must admit that you have had difficulty; and although you have seen hardship and have sorrowed in the midst of it, I will admit you have manfully followed up your early determination. Well, heaven will prosper you at last; but you have yet to see much of difficulty. More than you have, you cannot; your gray locks forbid. I pray for you. Last night in a state of hallucination I asked of God his kindness. I solicited some relief from this continuation of excessive anxieties which harass your very soul. Exert yourself a little longer, cherish hope, and spare no cost of care or time or thought, and the victory shall be yours.[10]

In 1822, it is not surprising to learn, Tudor had a nervous collapse. He soon recovered however, and with the success of his trade in New Orleans, he was beginning to smell the "delicious essence" of victory and wealth. The pattern of all his striving was to be fulfilled: he was to be "inevitably and unavoidably rich."

Eventually Tudor had a town house on Beacon Street and an estate at Nahant. He indulged himself in benevolences, such as building tree-shaded roads and draining marshes; on Sundays he went to church in a blue frock coat, and everybody looked at him. When he died at the age of eighty, his life was already a legend of the "rugged individualist." In truth he had lived the legend. Ruthless, irresponsible, grasping, and self-

10 *Ibid.*, 194.

43

righteous, he regarded a competitor as the enemy who must be eliminated. "All opposition," he exults in one entry in his diary "has been met and overthrown—the field is won and now very little more than the shew of weapons and readiness for defense, I trust will be necessary. It has cost some wear and tear of muscle and nerves besides . . . $12,000 in money. A dear victory: but probably thorough. If there are any unslain enemies, let them come out." [11] Tudor subscribed wholly to the profit motive. A commodity he traded in might bring advantage to someone besides the money it brought to him—a chunk of New England ice might relieve a fevered throat in Calcutta —but this incidental benefit had nothing to do with his intention in selling ice. Except out of economic necessity, Tudor took no interest in scientific improvements in the techniques of cutting and storing ice. And he showed little concern for the incipient science of refrigeration. When he learned from experiments that oranges could be kept in ice, he hastily packed a shipment of fruit in ice and hay and sent it to the United States. But in his desire for a quick profit, he had failed to confirm by experiment his method of packing fruit for shipment, and the cargo was destroyed when the hay caught fire. "When will you learn to lay the foundations before raising the roof?" his cousin James Savage asked him.[12] Indignant when he was called by someone "a wild projector without stability of calculation or correctness of judgment," Tudor's resentment was hardly justified.[13] An incarnation of the nineteenth-century speculative spirit, he lived far outside the world of the proverbially shrewd and cautious Yankee. Once he accepted a bet that he could not sell warming pans in the

11 *Ibid.*, 199.
12 *Ibid.*, 176.
13 *Ibid.*, 185.

Caribbean and won it by filling the pans with ice and selling them as "cooling pans."

Tudor developed unshakeable arrogance of will. Whatever he did was right. "Success," he said, "is virtue." Whatever he did, furthermore, became his idea, even if, as in the case of the ice trade, it had not been. He broke off completely with the R. H. Gardiners, his sister and brother-in-law, after Emma Gardiner mentioned—and this in the privacy of a family correspondence—that William Tudor had first proposed the ice trade. Gardiner, who had been Tudor's close friend and financial angel for over thirty years, told the Ice King that the execution of the idea, not the idea itself, had counted. This was to no avail. A forbidden subject had been brought up; minor as it was, Tudor could not forgive the threat to his crown. Years later when Edward Everett observed in a public address that William Tudor "was one of the first who went largely into this [the Ice] business," Frederic replied that "the Ice trade was originated by and solely by me" and that Everett "spoils the whole thing." [14] This statement is found in Tudor's own handwriting on the copy of his pamphlet entitled *Frederic Tudor's Letter on the Ice Trade and Payment of Great Losses* (1849) in the library of the Massachusetts Historical Society. The letter is also printed in the *Proceedings* of the Society, which elected Frederic Tudor to membership in January, 1858, when he was seventy-four years old. Thereupon Tudor promptly invited the Society to hold a meeting at his home in Nahant, where a group photograph was taken, and his colleagues were shown the wonders of his estate.

Forty-two years before, in 1816, his brother William had been elected to membership. In the broad sense in which the term *literary* was still understood, the Massachusetts Historical

14 *Ibid.*, 212, n.

Society was a literary society, and one of its meetings a literary occasion. Like his brother William, Frederic Tudor now played the double role of man of commerce and man of letters. Unlike William, he had waited until he could afford to. If William had waited, the literary history of New England and that of the nation might be different.

II

In his *History of the Boston Athenaeum*, Josiah Quincy characterizes the career of William Tudor as one in which "the qualities of the gentleman and the man of business, of the scholar and the man of the world, were . . . manifestly and happily blended. . . ." [15] This is a genteel misstatement of fact. Tudor failed to achieve the image of himself he obviously attempted to realize—that of the eighteenth-century "commercial cosmopolite," the "trafficker in trade and letters," whose supreme American example is Benjamin Franklin and whose most successful representative in Tudor's day was Joel Barlow. (In general, one can easily see, Tudor's career resembles Barlow's: he combined business speculation, politics, diplomacy and letters; he traveled widely and died in a foreign land on a mission for his government; a citizen of the cosmopolitan literary world, he endeavored to promote the interests of

15 Josiah Quincy, *History of the Boston Athenaeum, with Biographical Notices of Its Deceased Founders* (Cambridge, Mass., 1851), 63. As is the case with his brother Frederic, there is no adequate biography of William Tudor. In addition to Quincy, see Pearson's essay on Frederic Tudor. Other useful sources are: E. A. and G. L. Duyckinck, *Cyclopaedia of American Literature* (New York, 1855), II, 268–71; Charles Francis Adams (ed.), *Memoirs of John Quincy Adams, Comprising Portions of His Diary from 1795 to 1848* (Philadelphia, 1874–77), VIII, 223–24, 430–31, and *passim*; Lewis P. Simpson (ed.), *The Federalist Literary Mind: Selections from the Monthly Anthology and Boston Review, 1803–1811, Including Documents Relating to the Boston Athenaeum* (Baton Rouge, 1962), *passim*. William Tudor was born in 1779 and died in 1830.

literature in his own country.[16]) Following a period of early schooling at Phillip's Academy at Andover, William Tudor went to Harvard, where he was graduated in 1796. Destined for a mercantile career by his father, he entered the counting room of John Codman, who sent him to Paris as his confidential agent. He was not especially successful in his post, but he made a firsthand acquaintance with the world of European art and letters. When he returned to Boston, Colonel Tudor furnished him the capital to undertake a trading adventure in Europe. He sailed to Leghorn and thereafter made the Grand Tour, once again paying more attention to letters than to commerce. This continued to be the pattern he followed. Although he, rather than Frederic, conceived the ice trade, this failed to divert him from the projects then uppermost in his mind, the conduct of the always insolvent *Monthly Anthology* and the founding—with only minimum financial support—of the Boston Athenaeum. These interests he combined to some extent with politics, winning a term in the legislature of Massachusetts. In 1809 he was invited to deliver the annual Fourth of July oration in the Old South Church. Before a distinguished audience, including John Quincy Adams, he was so successful that his oration was printed and reprinted. On at least three other occasions Tudor was chosen to deliver public orations: twice, in 1810 and 1815, before the Phi Beta Kappa Society of Harvard, and once, in 1817, before the Massachusetts Humane Society. The first Phi Beta Kappa oration reached its audience only in print, for Tudor sailed for England before the yearly Phi Beta Kappa festival. He had become the agent for the wealthy Boston merchant, Stephen Higginson, who was trying to ship products manufactured in England into France under the nose of Napoleon. When Tudor was

16 See Joseph Dorfman, "Joel Barlow: Trafficker in Trade and Letters," *Political Science Quarterly*, LIX (March, 1944), 83–100.

unsuccessful, he made an effort to salvage his fortunes by entering into an arrangement with some other Americans in London to set up a nail factory in Birmingham. This enterprise failed. Back in Boston, Tudor was confronted with the news of his father's financial disaster. He apparently kept out of debtor's prison by practicing law and serving as clerk of the Suffolk County Court. Throughout his hapless business career his love of letters remained the one constant inspiration of his life. This is why in 1815, virtually as alone as Frederic was in his commercial ventures, William Tudor began a new literary venture, the *North American Review*. Somehow he managed to issue it once every two months (writing most of the contents of early numbers himself) until 1818, when it was acquired by a group of Bostonians and made into a quarterly.

During the year 1818 William Tudor wrote the valuable *Letters from the Eastern States*, a book of essays in epistolary form on varied aspects of New England life during the first years of the nineteenth century. This book was published in 1819 and reached a second edition in 1821. In 1821 he published his *Miscellanies*, a book of selections drawn mostly from the *Monthly Anthology* and from the *North American Review*. Turning to the field of American biography he wrote his best book, *Life of James Otis*, which came out in 1823. While he was working on the biography of Otis, Tudor conceived the idea of a monument on Bunker Hill to the memory of the Revolutionary heroes and inaugurated a drive to secure support for the project. Before very much had been accomplished, he was appointed by President Monroe, upon the recommendation of John Quincy Adams, to be consul of the United States for Lima and other ports of Peru and left Boston for the last time.

President Adams made him charge d'affaires of the United

States at Rio de Janeiro in 1827, and the Jackson administration continued him in this position. His services in settling American financial claims against Brazil were gratifying to Adams, not an easy man to please. Having become engrossed in matters of foreign policy and international politics, Tudor spent a part of his time at Rio de Janeiro writing an allegorical poem dealing with the United States and the European powers. This work, called *Gebel Teir*, was published anonymously in 1829. One year after its publication, William Tudor contracted a fever and died from its effects at the age of fifty-one.

William Tudor left no literary diary comparable to his brother's business diary, but the motives that sustained his literary career are manifest in the pages of the *Monthly Anthology* and other documents of Federalist Boston. Generally speaking, these express the struggle of William Tudor and his friends for literary values in two ways: through direct attacks on the obsession with money; and in a search to bring the patronage of wealth to the cause of letters.

In their attacks on the love of money the writers for the *Anthology* were severe. James Savage, himself a youthful speculator, comments on the character of American merchants: "The English have been contemptuously denominated by their old enemies a nation of shopkeepers; and, as we are descended from them, and are thought to have degenerated the French will soon call us a community of hucksters. The notion often entertained of us is, that, when incited by prospect of gain, nothing is too dangerous for us to attempt, nothing too infamous for us to perform." [17] The passion for money

17 James Savage, "Silva, No. 22," *Monthly Anthology and Boston Review*, III (December, 1806), 629. Many of the authors of pieces in this magazine are identified in M. A. DeWolfe Howe (ed.), *Journal of the Proceedings of the Society Which Conducts the Monthly Anthology & Boston Review* (Boston, 1910), 317–28.

49

like the passion for democracy, the Federalist literati argued, was creating a cultural wasteland. One poet in the *Anthology* says of Boston's huckstery:

> 'Tis Merchant land! Here genius never sprung,
> Nor flourish'd friendship, nor the sons of song;
> For such *vile* weeds, why turn the wealthy soil?
> When *golden apples* grow with half the toil.[18]

Reviewing Hugh Henry Brackenridge's *Modern Chivalry*, Alexander H. Everett calls his country a "land of cent, per cent." [19] Another Anthologist, Winthrop Sargent, playing the role of a wanderer from the mythical land of Latinguin in the East, remarks that the Americans "have a national maxim which the infant is taught to lisp in its nurse's arms; it is very long, and I do not recollect it; but I know it is equivalent to 'get money'; and I believe this useful lesson is never taught in vain." He observes, "In such a country, genius is like the mistletoe on the rock; it seems to exist upon the barren and unyielding surface only by its own resources, and the nourishment it receives from the dews of heaven. The progress of literature has therefore been very slow. . . ." [20] Still another Anthologist, Arthur Maynard Walter, sketches a picture of the literary wasteland:

We may say, that we have spice ships at the Phillipines, and that our cannon has echoed among ice islands, at either pole. This is honourable and tells our enterprise; but here the story ends, nor will I busily ask, if there are no spots and stains on our flag, which the waters of the oceans we traverse, could not efface. For myself, I think we ought to have produced a few scholars; in this opinion, however, all are not unanimous, but if they agree that poetry is

18 Lucius Manlius Sargent, "To W————C————, Jun., Newport," *Monthly Anthology*, III (November, 1806), 587.

19 Alexander H. Everett, review, *ibid.*, V (September, 1808), 498.

20 Winthrop Sargent, "Letters to Leinwha," *ibid.*, II (January, 1805), 16.

natural to any country, we must be ashamed of our own. We boast of no epick, tragedy, comedy, elegies, poems, pastoral or amatory . . . [*sic*] but this field is all desert, a wide African sand garden, showing brambles, and rushes, and reeds.[21]

The compulsion to avarice in America, William Tudor asserts, is a consequence of the leveling of society. The increasing importance of wealth, he points out, has been evident in the modern histories of all nations.

Wealth is power. Do not let me be misunderstood. I am not degrading my country. Mere wealth has not a very powerful influence. But the absence of all political distinctions, of all privileged orders gives wealth, in the hands of talent, accumulated weight. Hence the desire of distinction, in many minds capable of feeling it, is enticed into this as a primary pursuit, and commonly persisted in, till the taste or the capacity for other employments is weakened or extinguished.[22]

As a result of this situation, John Sylvester John Gardiner, the president of the Anthology Society, says: "Everything smells of the shop. . . . We seldom meet here with an accomplished character, a young man of fine genius and very general knowledge, the scholar and the gentleman united."[23]

The Boston literati continued to hold to the ideal of the gentleman scholar—one who would maintain "that the little volume of Collins' poetry is worth all the 'negotiations of Walsingham'"—but they felt the suspicion of the ideal in their society.[24] The attitude of John Quincy Adams, the first

21 Arthur Maynard Walter, "Silva, No. 21," *ibid.*, III (November, 1806), 579.

22 William Tudor, "A Discourse, Intended to Have Been Delivered before the Society of Phi Beta Kappa on Their Anniversary, the Day after Commencement at Cambridge," *ibid.*, IX (September, 1810), 157.

23 John Sylvester John Gardiner, "Silva, No. 11," *ibid.*, III (January, 1806), 18.

24 Introductory note to "Ode to Spring," *Literary Miscellany*, II (Cambridge, Mass., n.d.), 404.

Boylston Professor of Rhetoric and Oratory at Harvard, toward the necessity of protecting his anonymity as a contributor to Joseph Dennie's *Port Folio* is illuminating. He is not, he observes, "ashamed of the occupation." Yet he says that "there is no small number of very worthy citizens among us irrevocably convinced that it is impossible to be at once a man of business and man of rhyme, and who, if they knew me for instance to be the author of the two pieces inclosed, would need no other proof that I ought immediately to be *impeached* for incapacity as a public servant." Significantly, Adams granted the worthy citizens their prejudice toward the literary vocation. If it exhibited "some Cherokee contempt of literature, some envious malignity toward mental accomplishments," it nevertheless had "much foundation . . . from experience." [25]

Adams' uncertain compromise between money and letters seems to document more ominously than the uninhibited strictures of Sargent, Walter, and other youthful literati, the precarious hold the life of letters had on Bostonians in the early nineteenth century. Business, Adams says in effect, is first.

There was, however, another, more positive and more important side to the struggle by the Bostonians to assert literary values. Regardless of what they said in protest against commerce from time to time, they were not alienated from it. In their imagination the wasteland was the corruption of an ideal commercial civilization, which they loudly proclaimed in the midst of the age of Jefferson and John Taylor of Caroline. Thus James Savage who condemned the hucksterly of American merchants also saw foreign trade as the best hope of his country. Commerce is a greater civilizing agency than the

25 John Quincy Adams to Thomas Boylston Adams, March 21, 1801, in *Writings of John Quincy Adams,* ed. Worthington Chauncy Ford (New York, 1913–17), II, 523.

printing press. "To the invention of printing has often been ascribed the transformation of society, but to another art we think may be attributed most of the change in the moral habitudes of man. . . . The experience and reflection of all preceding ages had never supplied such improvement to political science, as it gained in the fifteenth century from the enterprises of commerce." With implied opposition to Jeffersonian agrarian insularity, Savage contends that America's mixing with the world is decreed by nature. To thwart this decree would directly result in a cultural decline.

Some have seriously regretted that America has interfered in foreign trade, but we believe that nature intended the inhabitants of our sea coast for the merchants of the world; and that every navigable river, every bay, and every indentation in our shore, confirms her intention. In a country fertile as ours, only one third of the population need be employed in agriculture to raise sufficient for the sustenance of the whole. If foreign commerce were interdicted, we should have an immense surplus of useless commodities, and most of the incitements of industry would be lost. The whole time of half our citizens might then be wasted in the indolence of independence, or all of them might waste half of it. But if all are constrained to daily labour with their hands, there can be no cultivation of mind: and without intelligence there will be few delights of society and little interchange of benevolence. *Man in such a state ceases to be sociable, and becomes only gregarious. So that from gradual degeneration to barbarism we shall best be preserved by commerce.*

Commerce is the gateway to a rich and polished civilization comparable to that of Athens. Savage calls on the authority of the ancients: "Cicero informs us it was a maxim of Themistocles, one the most profound statesmen of antiquity, that the nation, which possesses the sea, must enjoy everything."[26] Lest anyone fear that the enjoyment brought by commerce

26 James Savage, "The Remarker, No. 27," *Monthly Anthology,* IV (November, 1807), 576–77.

need be evil, Joseph Stevens Buckminster, brilliant young minister of the Brattle Street Church in Boston and a leading Anthologist, was concerned to show how Christianity had refined trade: "Tell me not of Tyre, and Sidon, and Corinth, and Carthage. I know they were commercial and corrupt. But let it be remembered that they flourished long before the true principles of honorable trade were understood, before the introduction of Christianity had given any stability to those virtues of conscientious integrity, and strict fidelity in trusts, which are not indispensable to commercial prosperity."[27] A commercial economy, Buckminster contends, will steadily increase virtue. Quite illogically, in view of the desperate fear of the spread of Jacobin philosophy in Boston, he argues that the "state of a people cannot be unfavorable to virtue, which provides such facilities of intellectual communication between remotest regions, so that not a bright idea can spring up in the brain of a foreign philosopher, but it darts like lightning across the Atlantic. . . ."[28] The Boston men of letters held to the faith that commerce makes mankind an intellectual and spiritual community. This was a powerful ideal in Western civilization, the fundamental basis of all the coming American literary voyages to India.

Seeking to realize their vision of a unity of commerce and letters, William Tudor and his friends explored the possibilities in their world of the patronage of letters. Some of the Boston literati were skeptical that the possibilities existed. Although none of them seems to have felt as bitterly despondent over the lack of patronage in America as Joseph Dennie, most of the Anthologists would have sympathized with him when he complained to his mother: "In my Editorial capacity, I am

27 Henry Ware, Jr. (ed.), *The Works of Joseph S. Buckminster, with Memoirs of His Life* (Boston, 1839), II, 382.
28 *Ibid.*

obliged to the nauseous task of flattering republicans; but, at bottom, I am a malcontent, and consider it a serious evil to have been born among the Indians and Yankees of New England. Had it not been for the *selfish* patriotism of that hoary traitor, Adams [Samuel Adams], and the bellowing of Molineux . . . I might now, perhaps, in a Literary Diplomatic, or lucrative Situation [have] been in the service of my rightful King and instead of shivering in the bleakness of the United States, felt the genial sunshine of a Court." [29] Even William Tudor, less narrow in his political and social instincts than some of his friends, qualified his hope for the effective patronage of literature in a country which, following the lead of Jeffersonian liberalism, had done away with the right of primogeniture:

The equal division of property among children is a considerable disadvantage [to the progress of letters], though of a negative kind. Whatever value it may possess in perpetuating republican forms of government, or claim upon the feelings as doing justice towards offspring, for whom equal affection is felt, it has doubtless a pernicious effect in regard to literature and the arts. . . . It is seldom that any family retains affluence through four generations. No family is perpetuated, no man comes into life free from the solicitude attending the acquisition of property. No one inherits independence in this respect, and with it, that species of fame, of taste, and inclination, for which many families in Europe have been celebrated age after age. A splendid gallery of paintings, a magnificent library, descend to the inheritor, with the virtual obligation to cheer genius, to support science, to protect art. The fame of a family is entailed with its estate. The lot is enviable to an elevated mind, but obnoxious to our institutions; yet, looking at the succession of ages, such establishments are the property of the publick, of which the apparent possessor, is only the hereditary keeper.[30]

29 Joseph Dennie to Mary Dennie, April 26, 1797, in *Letters of Joseph Dennie, 1768–1812,* ed. Laura Green Pedder (Orono, Me., 1936), 159.

30 William Tudor, "Discourse . . . before Phi Beta Kappa," 157–58.

In some remarks on patronage by the Boston literati we encounter an unsentimental approach to the problem. Sidney Willard, who seems to have had a penchant for pricking myths, was of the opinion that altogether too much was being made of the lack of patronage of genius in America. The universal complaint that genius in this country has been killed by "the coldness of neglect," he observes, is disgraceful if true. "But," he continues, "admitting it to be well supported, it is still a question, whether neglect has that deletereous [sic] influence on the progress of genius, which it has been so fashionable to believe." First, genius must actually appear if it is to be patronized. "Without Virgil and Horace what occasion for Maecenas?" Willard argues that genius will make its way against all obstacles, converting "indifference into favor, and opposition into patronage." No amount of encouragement, on the contrary, can make a mediocre man into a genius. True genius, he contends, will sooner or later "discover itself, without being drawn into light by the force of patronage." "Genius is independent, and active, and persevering; neither perishing with indigence, nor decaying by neglect, nor yielding to opposition."[31] According to the implications of Willard's concept, the literary genius in America would force his way into prominence with the indomitable perseverance of a Frederic Tudor. This was a refreshing, if naive, idea in the welter of pessimism about patronage.

Yet it was an extreme view and served no direct purpose in finding the answer to the genuine problem of how to divert a portion of the increasing wealth of the country to literary ends. What could be done to create in the rich the desire to participate in cultural improvements? We find in the *Anthology* and

31 Sidney Willard, "Patronage of Genius," *Literary Miscellany*, I (Cambridge, Mass., n.d.), 262.

elsewhere evidence that a strategy of securing patronage was being worked out in the Boston community.

The central tactic was the appeal to social pride. This argument could be stated in many ways, so that it would play upon more than the emotion of pride alone. The encouragement of letters and the arts, one writer in the *Anthology* argues, is essential to the protection of the wealthy class from barbarity. This is only one aspect of his argument. More important, he contends, is the necessity of cultivating taste and fostering genius as a means of maintaining social order. If the affluent would do this, "they would be looked up to with that veneration, which is due to accomplished minds, superior talents, and legitimate grandeur: the genial rays of polished life would be reflected and diffused through every subordinate class of society; the mechanick, the labourer, the hind that clears the forest and first opens the bosom of the earth, would catch the softening gleam of humanity, and when the hours of toil were over, would learn to be satisfied with innocent recreations, rather than seek the inebriety of taverns, or the tumultuous discord of popular meetings."[32]

Variations of this general argument are numerous. One instance of its employment in a specific cause should be cited, this in the promotion of the Boston Athenaeum, the largest cultural project begun in the Boston community during the Federalist era. In part the plea is to pride, social and intellectual, saying in effect that when a patron hands over to the Athenaeum a sum of sound Boston money, he is by this simple act making himself both intellectual and immortal. At the same time he is protecting his fortune by helping to insure social order: "In proportion as we increase in wealth, our ob-

32 Robert Field, "An Essay on the Liberal Arts," *Monthly Anthology*, III (June, 1806), 300.

ligations increase to guard against the pernicious effects of luxury, by stimulating to a taste for intellectual enjoyment; the more we ought to perceive and urge the importance of maintaining the laws by manners, manners by opinion, and opinion by works, in which genius and taste unite to embellish the truth." [33]

In sum, whether they condemned the money economy or sought to woo its resources for literary uses, Boston men of letters like William Tudor, uncertain and confused as they often were, brought the literary resources of their community into action against the raw economics of a Frederic Tudor.

III

Underlying this antimercenary impulse was nothing less than the formidable culture of Puritan unworldliness. But the transformation of this historical culture into the primary literary resource of nineteenth-century New England was not an axiomatic process. It was a result of a conflict in values.

This struggle shaped a literary development of critical importance in American cultural history: the representation of the literary life became more definite and more coherent in Boston than in any other American community. It was as though Frederic Tudor had deliberately dedicated himself to creating in the Boston of Jeffersonian America an economy of speculation, while William Tudor had given himself to creating a countereconomy of profitless literary pursuits. By the end of the first four decades of the Republic, an economy of money and a humanistic economy of letters were separate and distinct powers in the Boston community. This distinction hardly obtained elsewhere in America. Not in Philadelphia, declining in its role as a literary center, and certainly not in

33 "Boston Athenaeum," *ibid.*, IV (November, 1807), 601. Author unidentified, probably William Smith Shaw.

New York. There a rising literary market tended more strongly than in Boston to make literature a commodity in a trade as bustling and inhumane as that in Wall Street or on the Boston Exchange. In Boston there was effected a kind of balance of power—a conciliation partly owing to the strategy of patronage —between the community's dynamic commercial ambitions and its literary aspirations. This conciliation, to be sure, did not provide a sure flow of "ready money" in the form of patronage from the money to the literary economy. The most original literary ideas—those comparable in audacity to the China trade or the ice trade—repelled rather than attracted patronage. When William Tudor's wealthy friends made a deal to loan Frederic Tudor money if he would pay the interest on the principal to William in support of a literary project, they were subsidizing a thoroughly "respectable" venture, a biography of James Otis, not a *Walden*. Boston wealth paid tribute to letters as an institution of social order. The Boston conciliation between money and letters, nonetheless, was broad and deep enough to provide a world in which the literary vocation, even in its singularities, enjoyed a patronage of respect. William Dean Howells, having transferred his own literary life from Boston to that "great mart" New York City, doubted if there was ever in the world "so much taste and feeling for literature" as in the Boston he had left. In the New England capital the circulation of books and magazines and the interplay of ideas assumed a marked degree of independence from money negotiations. The Boston-Cambridge-Concord community—and the union of rural and city life in the Boston community must be emphasized in any accounting of its literary character—had a literary economy in which a writer could claim an exemption from incessant commercial busyness and, what is more important, from the equation of book sales and "success."

He could speculate in the Emersonian realm of "the leisures of the spirit." Of the mid-nineteenth-century Boston community, T. S. Eliot said: "One distinguishing mark of this distinguished world was very certainly leisure; and importantly not in all cases a leisure given by money, but insisted upon. There seems to be no reason why Emerson or Thoreau or Hawthorne should have been men of leisure; it seems odd that the New England conscience should have allowed them leisure; yet they *would* have it sooner or later." [34] Literary leisure, Eliot failed to realize, imposed itself with the authority of a duty upon New Englanders who felt a vocation to letters. Thoreau going to Walden Pond to conduct his experiment in living—"to front only the essential facts of life"—seized on his obligation to leisure in a more stringent manner than most of his contemporaries. No doubt he acted in a way that would have been regarded as socially irresponsible by William Tudor, or any of the Anthology circle, who would likely have agreed with James Russell Lowell's charge of misanthropy against Thoreau. But according to the logic of New England's literary history, Thoreau fulfilled the idea of leisure that the literary generation before him had established in the Boston community in their opposition to the goal of sheer money making. The economy Thoreau had set up in the Walden woods when Frederic Tudor's ice crew intruded upon it represented a romantic extension of the Boston economy of letters, which may

34 T. S. Eliot, "Henry James," in Edmund Wilson (ed.), *The Shock of Recognition: The Development of Literature in the United States Recorded by the Men Who Made It* (New York, 1943), 859. Originally in *The Little Review*, August, 1918. Misleading statements about the economic status of New England men of letters are unfortunately rather common. A flagrant one occurs in Martin Green, *The Problem of Boston: Some Readings in Cultural History* (New York, 1966), 56: "William Tudor founded *The North American Review* after making a fortune selling ice." This not only confuses William Tudor with his brother but gives a thoroughly false impression of the literary economy of the Boston community.

more aptly be called an economy of leisure. Thoreau's economy, in other words, was a radical version of an existing economy.

Thoreau was far bolder in adventuring in the possibilities of a literary life than William Tudor; indeed in the ruthless emphasis he placed on individualism, he was more like Frederic Tudor. In fulfilling their "passages to India," Thoreau and Frederic Tudor may both be said to have been heroic voyagers, one exemplifying the heroic in letters and the other the heroic in commerce. It is a fine historical irony that Frederic Tudor's voyage to India is now remembered mostly because Thoreau made it into a symbol of a great voyage of the literary imagination—Thoreau who capitalized transcendentally upon what Frederic Tudor regarded as the literary improvidence of his "worthless" brother William.

✍ Emerson's Early Thought: Institutionalism and Alienation

> This is the amount of all our insight into nature, the discovery of the purpose; and wherever we are at fault in our search our whole views become loose & unsettled; the fact where the study fails is regarded as monstrous.
>
> Emerson, Journals (1823)

EMERSON PUBLISHED *Nature* in his thirty-third year. Until this event in the fall of 1836, he had offered no unusual promise to the world. When he had graduated from Harvard fifteen years before, he had won a place no higher than the dead center of mere competence. He was number thirty in a class of fifty-nine; and if his deportment had not been exemplary, he probably would have been lower in the standings. Following this undistinguished entry into the world, he had, quite reluctantly, done a little school teaching. Subsequently he had attended the Harvard Divinity School, had been licensed to preach, and eventually had been ordained. Accepting a call to the Second Church in Boston, he had within less than four years announced that he could no longer celebrate the Lord's Supper and had resigned his pastorate. This had caused a small stir, but he had soon left the scene for an extended European journey. In 1836 he issued a dramatic manifesto asserting the radical freedom of the "new consciousness." What had happened? A man well past thirty who had never seemed to be more than a mild and somewhat uncertain rebel, Emerson appears to have experienced an illumination or a revelation.

In a way he had. But students of Emerson are coming to understand that in its apparent uncertainty and tentativeness his early career is deceptive. During this period his "Foundation and Ground-Plan," as Carlyle called *Nature*, was thoroughly meditated. Indeed, in his youthful years Emerson himself experienced an interesting and critical episode in what he once called "the interior and spiritual history of New England": its coming into the modern philosophical and poetic sensibility. Properly speaking, *Nature* does not record a beginning. It marks the climax and the resolution of a long crisis in the mind of a precocious seeker struggling to discover and to come to grips with a central modern problem: the relationship between knowledge as an institution and knowledge as consciousness. Or, it may be said, between knowledge as doubt and knowledge as wonder—in some ultimate sense between knowledge as Appearance and knowledge as Being. If this is the case, I cannot describe Emerson's early mentality in a short essay. I can attempt to do no more than suggest the importance of recognizing a broad, dramatic configuration in the story of Emerson's thought and emotion in the 1820s. I shall be especially concerned with the time of the mid-1820s, after Emerson had settled on a ministerial career and had not yet conceived of any other way of life.

I

As it comes to us in his *Journals* and letters, the story of Emerson's mind before the publication of *Nature* is a drama (and the dramatic quality must be emphasized) interwoven with and intimately related to poverty, illness, and death. When the Reverend William Emerson died in 1812, his family was left in a state of genteel poverty. Glimpses of the consequences of this deprivation are detailed in Ralph L. Rusk's biography of Emerson: the necessary sale at auction of the father's small but treasured library; Waldo as a little boy seeking desperately among fallen poplar leaves for a lost dollar bill he had been given to buy shoes; Waldo and his brother Edward forced to share a single coat and to face the taunt of their schoolmates, "Whose turn is it to wear the coat today?"; the Emerson boys heroically giving their last loaf of bread to one even poorer than they. Later on poverty forced Emerson to tax his precarious health and to delay his preparation for the ministry by becoming a "hopeless," "droning" schoolmaster in his brother William's finishing school for young Boston ladies. "Hope, it is true, still hangs out, though at a further remove, her gay banners," he confided to his *Journals* at this period of his life, "but I have found her a cheat once, twice, many times, and shall I trust the deceiver again?" Bad health and recurrent serious sickness hampered the life of the young Emerson more than lack of money. Tuberculosis ("the mouse in my chest," he called it) was a family curse that threatened his life for years. In addition, he suffered severely from other ailments, particularly rheumatic pains and, occasionally, from decided impairment of vision. At times he was seriously ill; at other times he was "not sick, not well," just irritatingly "luke-sick." In either case, as with poverty, "the worst part of sickness was the deferring of hopes," which made him "heart sick." Emerson's spells of "heart sickness" bordered on what today might be diagnosed as spells of psychic depression, when he had agonizing doubts about his personality.

Neither poverty nor illness were as hard on young Emerson as several intense bereavements: the death of Ellen Tucker Emerson, his first wife, and of his two beloved brothers, Edward and Charles. Within eighteen months after his marriage to Ellen in 1827—during which Emerson says his bride was "plaful & social" even when "her sociability" was "imprisoned in whispers"—she was dead of the common scourge, tuberculosis. Emerson was never to be released from the presence of the "one person in the world in whose separate existence as a soul" he "could so readily and fully believe." The early deaths of Edward and Charles were scarcely less difficult for him than Ellen's. Edward died of tuberculosis in Puerto Rico in 1834, concluding, Emerson said, "the short life of a silent poet & silent orator." Two years later tuberculosis took the life of Charles, who was on the verge of what might well have been a distinguished career in law and politics. In terrible loneliness, Emerson asked, "When one has never had but little society—and *all that society* is taken away—what is there worth living for?" At the moment it seemed to him that if poverty and illness had chastened him, death had confounded him.

Yet out of unpropitious beginnings, and from low states of spirit, close at times to despair, Emerson came forth to proclaim in *Nature* a vision of the autonomy and power of the individual consciousness that can only be compared to celebrations of the creative force of the individual will in Blake, Kierkegaard, Nietzsche, and in Emerson's own disciple Thoreau. How did Emerson overcome the critical deprivations of his childhood and early manhood? Part of the answer at least lies in the ethic of ambition to which he subscribed. Emerson was born into the discipline of what Oliver Wendell Holmes called the "Academic Races" of New England. This was a class of men of letters—drawn heavily from the ministerial families like Emerson's but representing the professions of teaching and law as well as the ministry—who assumed responsibility for the moral and intellectual and literary condition of their culture. Guided by an amalgam of classical and Christian virtues—the compound of values young Emerson called "Virtue"—the members of the Academic Races were given to translating the ills of life from deprivations into positive resources of the spirit. Virtue demands that one triumph over unfortunate circumstances. Virtue's commandment is what Emerson felt when, in his mature years, he refused to waste sympa-

65

thy on a poor boy, as poor as he himself had once been, who hesitated to go to college. "Go to Cambridge & eat bread & water & live to *think*," Emerson told the boy. Virtue sustained Emerson when, alone in faraway Florida on what seemed to be an almost desperate mission to restore his sick lungs, he wrote to his Aunt Mary: "He has seen but half the Universe who never has been shown the house of Pain. Pleasure and peace are but indifferent teachers of what it is life to know."[1]

We find nonetheless that young Emerson did not altogether accept the official ethic of ambition in his world. His knowledge of pain and death qualified as well as stimulated his eagerness for success. A reflection from his *Journals* in March, 1824, is of interest.

Shall I embroil my short life with a vain desire of perpetuating its memory when I am dead & gone in this dirty planet? I complain daily of my world, that it is false, disappointing, imperfect, & uncomfortable; & reason would that I should get thro' it as silently & hastily as I can & especially avoiding to tie any hopes or fears to it. I make it my best boast that I am the citizen of a far country far removed from the low influences of earth & sea, of time & change; that my highly destined nature spurns its present abode & aspires after a mode of existence & a fellowship of beings which shall eclipse & efface the gaudy glory of this. When my body shall be in the clods my triumphant soul, glad of any deliverance, will think no more of it or its habitation. Am I then to give my days and nights to a gnawing solicitude to get me a reputation, a fame,

1   For information on the experiences of poverty, illness, and death in Emerson's early life, see the following: Ralph L. Rusk, *The Life of Ralph Waldo Emerson* (New York, 1944), 1–151; Ralph L. Rusk (ed.), *The Letters of Ralph Waldo Emerson* (6 vols.; New York, 1939), II; William H. Gilman and others (eds.), *The Journals and Miscellaneous Notebooks of Ralph Waldo Emerson* (Cambridge, Mass., 1960–), I, II; Edward Waldo Emerson and Waldo Emerson Forbes (eds.), *The Journals of Ralph Waldo Emerson* (Boston and New York, 1909–14), I, II. See also Lewis P. Simpson, "Joseph Stevens Buckminster: The Rise of the New England Clerisy," an essay in the present volume; and Lewis P. Simpson (ed.), *The Federalist Literary Mind* (Baton Rouge, 1962).

forsooth among these worm-eaten, worm-eating creatures of clay, these boys of the universe, these infants of immortality as they all must be while they live on earth? Virtue says Go beg the impartial goddess to enrol your name on her historic scroll. Why? Because if you toil & deserve to write your name there, you will effectually contribute by the same efforts to the good of yourself & your species. The attempt is very laudable, even if it fail of success. The "ambition of immortality is chimerical" to all but a few. But in many instances doubtless the silver trumpets of angels will answer to the flourishes of earthly fame. As in case of Newton, Socrates, Howard, & more—[2]

Worldly fame is the instrument of virtue in perpetuating and extending knowledge for the good of the individual and the race. This was a standard attitude in the humanistic value system of the Academic Races. But in the somber meditation I have quoted, Emerson questions as well as upholds the validity of the quest for fame. He is drawn to the Christian rejection of the world, conceiving himself to be a stranger and a pilgrim on "this dirty planet," and fixing his vision on his citizenship in "a far country." Underlying Emerson's desire to reject the world we detect a degree of physical and emotional exhaustion; poverty, illness, and death—particularly illness—seem to have taxed Emerson's capacity to respond to the ethic of the Academic Races. But in entertaining the vision of a beatified citizenship in a far country, Emerson is not simply failing to respond to this ethic; at the same time he responds, I think, to a growing anxiety rising from intimations of doubt about the value of the institutional concept of knowledge. Forced by deprivations into the role of the introspective observer of his age, young Emerson indicates his experience—intimate and graphic if indecisive—of the modern breakdown of the Renaissance and Enlightenment assurance that the ac-

---

[2] Gilman and others (eds.), *Journals and Miscellaneous Notebooks,* II, 231–32.

cumulation of knowledge is the true vocation of the mind. The best way to understand this is to approach Emerson's early thought not in the conventional way through his break with Unitarianism but through the wider drama of his later thought when his estrangement from the "liberal religion" or the "rational religion" or the "Boston religion" (as it was variously labeled) is considered in the light of the character of the Boston literary mind. I mean especially its domination by one of the historic, controlling notions of Western civilization, the concept of "the progress of letters."

I I

The emergence of this idea in the Boston-Cambridge world, which goes back to the founding of Harvard, reveals its relation to a complex of attitudes. These include the ancient concept of the transfer of letters and learning from pre-Athenian seats of learning to Athens, to Rome, to Paris, to London, to America (not least to Boston). John Adams spoke for the general educational experience of his community when he observed, "There is nothing in my little reading, more ancient in my memory than the observation that arts, sciences, and empire traveled westward; and in conversation it was always added since I was a child, that their next leap would be over the Atlantic into America." [3] Another attitude strongly present in the theme of the progress of letters is the preservation of society from the effects of the love of money and luxury. Perhaps the most important attitude in the theme of the progress of letters derives from its association with the eighteenth-century metaphysic of linear progress. This is the idea that human knowledge (knowledge as conceived before the age of specialization) is a perfectible institution. This attitude is strikingly

3 Quoted in Benjamin T. Spencer, *The Quest for Nationality* (Syracuse, 1957), 22.

illustrated in a plea made in 1807 for the patronage of the newly established Boston Athenaeum. This was an enterprise of the Boston-Cambridge literati, including Emerson's father, the Reverend William Emerson, the first president of the Anthology Society and a dedicated man of letters.

Among the many literary and scientifick establishments, which have been thought worthy of the patronage of influence and wealth, that of large repositories of books has justly been considered as most illustrious for its dignity, its importance, and its pleasures. The history of learned libraries is the history of power consecrated to learning. It celebrates the patronage of monarchs, the munificence a splendid nobility, the support of a lettered clergy, and the liberality of cultivated gentlemen. The generous aid of rank, opulence, and influence proceeds from the intrinsick excellence of the subject. Whatever is intellectual is a portion of the supreme reason, and proportionally as it is free from corruption, approaches nearer the fountain. The operations of this principle are recorded in volumes. The earliest of these is almost coeval with the primary institutions of society, and from that period to the present the mass of human knowledge, notwithstanding the diminutions it has suffered, and the obstructions it has encountered, has accumulated from age to age, and has descended from generation to generation, till its present possessors are captivated in admiring the variety of its parts, the beauty of its materials, or are lost in contemplating its extensive magnitude, its diversified splendour, and its irresistible power.[4]

This kind of excited devotion to the institutional power of letters and learning—embodied in the library, the university, the literary society—was an intimate part of the education of Emerson. Young Emerson accepted as germane to the literary life the crucial necessity his father's generation felt in their literary endeavors: the preservation of civilization against barbarism. As he puts it in "Wide World XIII," he accepted as

[4] *Monthly Anthology and Boston Review,* IV (November, 1807), 600.

axiomatic "the superiority of a civilized to a savage nation & of the educated to the uneducated part of a community." How "discouraging to the cause of Education" it would be, young Emerson ponders, "if Newtons, Bacons, & Lockes were as often bred in shops & stables as in colleges." Such, however, is not the case; for "the fact is that *all* genius has owed its development to literary establishments." Self-made Benjamin Franklin, Emerson recognized, had formed himself on the institutional character of knowledge. What if Franklin had been born a New Zealander? It may be that he "would have been a clever swimmer, boatman & weather prophet . . . but he would certainly not have left an institution or a name." [5] He would not have left the American Philosophical Society and other institutions to represent the progress of letters in the new nation—institutions which had taken their place in the advancement of knowledge Emerson saw continuing, according to divine purpose, into the present late age.

All objects in the universe, far as the eye can reach & thought can comprehend them, fulfill some purpose, and are parts of some plan; and whatsovever things the infancy of knowledge once regarded as exceptions to this prevailing order, the advancement of knowledge has brought in to fill a chasm in the regular series of things & beings. Mind, which in human nature creeps on its long journey [he first wrote "on its progress"] to the source of things with a snail's pace, (compared with the intellects he is fond of imagining,) by the excellent necessity of its nature, *expands*, as it proceeds; and, in this late age, when it looks no longer with the timid glance of a child, but with the experienced eye of centuries into the bosom of nature, it is able to unite things severed by long intervals, to compare mean beginnings with remote & mighty results, & thus to restore order to a Chaos of mighty things, where, in time past the grandeur of the object outwent the capacity of the

5 Gilman and others (ed.), *Journals and Miscellaneous Notebooks*, II, 231.

Observer; so that even the slow & halting march of human science continually discovers the divine adjustment to circumstances to fulfill purposes.[6]

Yet in his youthful years when Emerson was inescapably drawn toward the unqualified acceptance of the progress of letters, both as a metaphysic and a value system, he was asking deep questions about the validity of the concept. This questioning, implied and overt in his writings in the 1820s, grew out of and was an extension of his questioning of the adequacy of Unitarianism. But only partly. With his propensity always to enter upon wide speculation, Emerson was an inquirer into universal problems as much or more as he was into particular Unitarian doctrines. This tendency is apparent in the passage from his *Journals* just given; it still more apparent in what immediately follows in the same entry:

This is the amount of all our insight into nature, the discovery of the purpose; and wherever we are at fault in our search our whole views become loose & unsettled; the fact where the study fails is regarded as monstrous. Now, in all the varieties of this investigation the question recurs to the investigator—What is the purpose of Man? Or is all nature, from sun & stars, to the root & the clod— instinct & dignified with design, & Man alone, the thinking inhabitant & the peerless Lord of all—an insulated & casual creation? In this vast theatre of being, in the tremendous uncertainity that shuts up the future around the present activity of Nature's immense family of worlds & beings; what, & where, I pray you, is his security from its possible convulsions? Is his lot cast upon the waters of chance? Is he unallied to Nature & independent of God? Then when Change & Destruction, those terrible agents in the Universe, obey their lord, & take hold on life & matter & dissipate the parent elements, when Thought is gathered through all its infinite channels to its Divine Fountain, & Goodness to its reward, & Matter is dissolved—then can his will bridle the ministers of

6 *Ibid.*, 140–41.

the Universe, & stop their almighty operation? But the man who denies a moral design to his existence, thus sets himself adrift upon wild & unknown seas.[7]

We think of Pascal "swallowed up in the infinite immensities of space," feeling himself "terrified" and "astonished" at his condition. To believe in the "moral design" of the "vast theatre of being" so conceived required more than a rational faith in the advancement of knowledge. I think we may refer to two letters, broadly speculative in import, Emerson wrote to his Aunt Mary in the 1820s. In them we see the more overt beginnings of his rebellion against the institutional sensibility of knowledge. The importance we may attach to these letters is increased by the fact that they were written to his Aunt Mary; a person of remarkable intellect and "faithful lover" of the "mysteries of Providence," she was a doubter who, Emerson realized later, refused to admit to doubt. She was, it is significant, the only confidant Emerson had in his younger days who was his intellectual peer. What, he asks Aunt Mary in one letter written in 1823, is the purpose served in making the mysteries of Providence inexplicable? "Does the Universe great & glorious in its operation aim at the slight of a mountebank who produces a wonder among the ignorant by concealing the causes of unexpected effects?" Emerson pushes on through a series of momentous questions, centering on the problem of why a benevolent God allows evil and punishes it by death. He works up to the "Gordian knot" of freedom of the will, and finally reveals a strong influence that had worked on him even in his undergraduate days, the writings of David Hume. "Who is he that can stand up before him [Hume] & prove the existence of the Universe, & of its Founder? He hath an adroiter wit than all his forefathers in philosophy if he will confound this Uncircumcised. The long & dull procession of

7 *Ibid.*

Reasoners that have followed since, have challenged the awful shade to duel, & struck the air with their puissant arguments. But as each new comer blazons 'Mr. Hume's objections' on his pages, it is plain they are not satisfied the victory is gained."[8] If Emerson's throwing up Hume to his Aunt Mary was to some extent prankish, he was taunting his own mind more than hers. He was challenging himself to transform his dissatisfaction with rational Christianity into a comprehensive inquiry into the whole rationalistic approach to knowledge. The challenge is still more insistent in another letter to Mary Moody Emerson in 1824:

No fashion is so frantic as to depreciate thought. No change of times or minds has ever occurred to throw too much intellect on the market. The world is very poor amidst the rich library of all knowledge its vaunting children have bequeathed it. Now, in its ripe and learned old age, come I, its docile child, to be pleased and instructed by its abundant wisdom; but when I open its accepted gospels of thought and learning, its sages and bards, I find they were all fain to spin a spider thread of intellect, to borrow much of each other, to arrive at few results, and to hide or supply meagreness by profuse ornament. I am therefore curious to know what living wit (not perverted by the vulgar rage of writing a book) has suggested or concluded upon the dark sayings and sphinx riddles of philosophy and life. . . . Why is the fruit of knowledge sorrow? I have, it may be, a pleasant poetical cast of thought—because I am ignorant. I had a pleasanter and more romantic existence (for such is childhood) whilst I thought the rainbow a symbol and an arch in heaven, and not necessary results of light and eyes, whilst I believed that the country had more essential sacredness, some nobler difference from the town than that one was builded, t'other not. A flower and a butterfly lose every charm when poring science discloses lobes and stomachs, acids and alkalies in their delicate beauty. I dislike to augment my slender store of chemistry and astronomy, and I think I could have helped the monks to belabour

8 Ralph Waldo Emerson to Mary Moody Emerson, October 16, 1823, in Rusk (ed.), *Letters of Ralph Waldo Emerson*, I, 137–38.

Galileo for saying the everlasting earth moved. Now these lines are an epitome of the history of knowledge. Every step Science has made ["science" has a more general signification here than it would have in another generation]—was it not the successive destruction of agreeable delusions which jointly made up no mean portion of human happiness? In metaphysics, "the gymnastics of the soul," what has reason done since Plato's day but rend and tear his gorgeous fabric. And how are we the wiser? Instead of the unmeasurable theatre which we deemed was here opened to the range of the understanding, we are now reduced to a little circle of definitions and logic round which we may humbly run. And how has Faith fared? Why, the Reformer's axe has hewed down idol after idol, and corruption and imperfection, until Faith is bare and very cold. And they have not done stripping yet, but must reach the bone. The old fable said Truth was by gods or men made naked. I wish the gods would help her to a garment or make her fairer. From Eden to America the apples of the tree of knowledge are but bitter fruit in the end.[9]

We are struck by Emerson's reversal of the progress of letters. If he were merely saying that knowledge is bitter because in the form it takes in science it forces us to acknowledge that a rainbow is a natural phenomenon and that butterflies have stomachs, we might pass over his complaint: it had become conventional by this time for poets to say that science destroys "agreeable delusions." The implication of Emerson's lament runs deeper, down indeed to the center of modern thought. In repudiating the value of accumulated knowledge and, at the same time, the triumphant movement of letters and learning from the East (Eden) to America, he indicates in his attitude toward rational knowledge that he realizes its fundamental basis in doubt. The tree of knowledge—of rational letters and learning—bears only bitter fruit, for its source of inspiration is not wonder but doubt. In *The Human Condition*, an erudite

9 Ralph Waldo Emerson to Mary Moody Emerson, March 24, 1824, in Emerson and Forbes (eds.), *Journals of Ralph Waldo Emerson*, I, 356–59.

and imaginative explanation of the situation of modern man, Hannah Arendt points out that modern philosophy began when doubt became fully operative as a "critical method in scientific inquiry and philosophic speculation." That is, with Descartes' *de omnibus dubitandum est*, with doubt conceived as the replacement of "the Greek *thaumazein*, the wonder of everything that is as it is." According to Hannah Arendt, "Descartes was the first to conceptualize this modern doubting, which after him became the inaudible motor which has moved all thought, the invisible axis around which all thinking has been centered. Just as from Plato and Aristotle to the modern age conceptual philosophy, in its greatest and most authentic representations, had been the articulation of wonder, so modern philosophy since Descartes has consisted in the articulations and ramifications of doubting." [10]

In other words, with the acceptance of Cartesian doubt as the way to knowledge, Western man began to know his existence only through doubt. Emerson not only recognizes this situation but points out its origin almost explicitly when he says, "I dislike to augment my slender store of chemistry and astronomy, and I think I could have helped the monks to belabour Galileo for saying the everlasting earth moved." The *idea* that the earth might move was no novelty to intellect in Galileo's time. But Galileo truly disturbed the universe by making an instrument, the telescope, which broke asunder forever the assumed relationship between what appears to be so and what the telescope says is actually so. What is actually so ("the new reality") may be grasped only when the mind, refusing all that seems to be to the senses, adapts a cosmic point of view *outside* the world. The telescope established a

10 Hannah Arendt, *The Human Condition* (New York, 1959), especially 225 ff. My indebtedness to Hannah Arendt is general throughout this essay.

cosmic standpoint, creating, Hannah Arendt says, the "new science of the Archimedean point." The ancient philosopher Archimedes dreamed of putting enough distance between himself and the world that he could secure the leverage to lift it. As long as this kind of dream of universal power remained a dream, it had no influence on the trust in the senses and the confidence in what they reveal. Galileo's invention made it possible for the mind to act on the world from outside the world, making it necessary to doubt the validity of anything not confirmed from the Archimedean point. The world—our home—ceased to be our home and became an object of our desire to know. The cost of such detachment proved to be the loss of the certainity of the world, even the certainty that the world has an objective existence. For the senses (sight, smell, touch, hearing, taste) do not comprehend the world: it can be conceived only in the processes of cognition within the individual consciousness. There is no "given truth." Truth does not reveal itself; nothing has existence save in the constant flow of process.[11]

If young Emerson by no means explicitly comprehended all the implications of the unfolding Cartesian age, he was fully aware of the mood that attended the destruction of the control man had formerly had over nature when he had apprehended it through trust in his natural senses. Inherent in this trust was the power of wonder as contrasted with the power of doubt. Let me appeal to yet another entry in the *Journals* for 1824 (realizing that I am quoting too much but fearing not to do so lest we lose the flavor and tone—the poetry—of Emerson's thought):

To deny a Providence with Epicurus & a God with the Atheist, is a mournful speculation. It is depriving Nature of that kindly

11 See *ibid.*, especially 234 ff.

sympathy, that majestic society it held with us whilst we thought it instinct with divine life. It is casting man back into a cold & comfortless solitude. You leave him alone in a Universe exposed to the convulsions of disorder & the wrecks of systems where man is an atom unable to avert his peril or provide for his escape, you leave him destitute of friends who are able to control the order of Nature. While he feels himself backed by Omnipotence he can approve the nobility of his origin, can do the deeds of a godlike nature—but if you put out the eye of the Universe, if you kill that life to which all his hopes, his virtues, his affections essentially attach themselves—that being is ruined. He thought his virtue was known & acknowledged by an omniscient & benevolent Mind; Night & Morning he lifted his hands to bless him that had admitted him to this glorious society of intelligent beings; his heart yearned after that blissful communion which he hoped to enjoy with the Divinity—and now he learns there is no God, that virtue & vice are sick men's dreams and his heart sinks within him & hope dies. Why should he live longer in this infinite wilderness of suns & stars; he has no security, no interest, no love, in this dire dominion of Chance.[12]

Through the power of wonder—we may say, devising a gloss on this homily—man controlled nature by reliance on the supernatural. He was in rapport with the supernatural, himself thus godlike, in no way more so for one of Emerson's spiritual inheritance than in an intimately felt relation to Divine Providence. Underlying Emerson's reaction to atheism was not a simple, outraged response to the sacrilege of rejecting the omnipotence of God, but a complex and paradoxical response to the deprivation of man's power accompanying the loss of faith in the divine arrangement of the universe. He does not think of atheism as a specific philosophy but as a convenient label for the general rule of doubt, constantly expanding its sway in the eighteenth and nineteenth centuries—the bitter

[12] Gilman and others (eds.), *Journals and Miscellaneous Notebooks*, II, 252.

and novel fruit of the tree of knowledge transported into the modern world by the long progress of letters.

At times young Emerson effectively put down the radical novelty of the Cartesian condition. He does this vividly in 1826 in a rather lengthy meditation on the principle of compensation. Written after a very severe illness, this meditation invokes the house of the past as the proper and continuing home of the mind.

> I rejoice that I live when the world is so old. There is the same difference between living with Adam & living with me as in going into a new house unfinished, damp and empty, and going into a long occupied house where the time and taste and its inhabitants has accumulated a thousand useful contrivances[,] has furnished the chambers, stocked the cellars, and filled the library. In the new house every comer must do all for himself. In the old mansion there are butlers, cooks, grooms & valets. In the new house all must work, & work with the hands. In the old one there are poets who sing, actors who play & ladies who dress & smile. O ye lovers of the past, judge between my houses. I would not be elsewhere than I am.[13]

Emerson pursues his meditation into a discussion of the vanity of living for wealth and prestige. Those who do so secure their fate in "the history of retributions," which "more than any other [is] fit to establish the doctrine of Divine Providence." Not the least aspect of their destiny is that they go "unrecognized by the great brotherhood of intelligent minds who are penetrating into the obscure on every side & adding new provinces to the kingdom of knowledge."[14] This brotherhood—the community of letters and learning—Emerson says in effect is an institution of the wondrous operation of God's Providence. Thus he returns to the Christian-humanistic value

13 *Ibid.,* 340.
14 *Ibid.,* 341–42. Cf. Sheldon W. Liebman, "Emerson's Transformation in the 1820's," *American Literature,* XL (May, 1968), 133–54.

system ingrained in him by inheritance. The assumed vocation of the man of letters is the fulfillment of the sense of wonder through the progressive discovery of the purpose of all things.

But the progress of the principle of doubt had entered too powerfully into Emerson's view to allow him to rest in such an assumption. If the progress of letters had become the progress of doubt, he had to find a way to break his allegiance to the received theory of the advancement of the mind in his community. Nor would a compromise with doubt—the compromise that was the rationale of Unitarianism—for long satisfy a mind so zealous for the comprehensive and the absolute as Emerson's.

In the crisis of his early thought, which was the crisis of his age, Emerson derived a great deal from Coleridge. While reading *The Friend* in 1829, Emerson told his Aunt Mary, "I like to encounter these citizens of the universe, that believe the mind was made to be spectator of all, inquistor of all, and whose philosophy compares with others much as astronomy with the other sciences, taking post at the centre and, as from a specular mount, sending sovereign glances to the circumference of things." [15] This comment with deceptive casualness announces Emerson's initial discovery of the Archimedean point. The poet-philosopher must peer into a universe in which what appears to be is no guide to what is. He finds a model in the astronomer, a leading figure of the scientist. Through the instrumentation of the normal power of perception, defying the limits of the senses, the astronomer, Emerson suggests, stands outside the world; taking his stance upon the Archimedean point—not merely spectator but ruthless inquisitor—he learns that all appearance is false, that noth-

15 Ralph Waldo Emerson to Mary Moody Emerson, December 10, 1824, in Emerson and Forbes (eds.), *Journals of Ralph Waldo Emerson,* II, 277.

ing given to us by the senses is true. By means of mind-devised
instruments his mind fabricates—his mind makes—the world
and the universe. Through the telescope, he becomes the "Eye
of the Universe."

I am exaggerating, yanking and tugging at strands and implications in Emerson's early thought, but I think not overstating
the crisis which is its basic pattern. He entered early into the
anxiety of "world alienation"—the apprehensive sense of estrangement from the earth homeland that began to arise when
Galileo's ingenuity confirmed the speculation of Archimedes.
If this estrangement carried in its nature the possibility of a
complete and even necessary surrender to doubt, it also—
before the destruction of the classical physics in the second
half of the nineteenth century—offered the possibility of a
freshness of wonder comparable to Adam's in the Garden. One
romantic reaction to the progress of doubt—and the institu-
tionalization of doubt in the corporate body of letters and
learning—was the assertion of the power of a faith inspired by
radical novelty. When things become new again, faith makes
its own forms. This would be the Emersonian dictum. "Faith,"
he set down in 1824, "is a telescope." He hardly grasped what
he was saying, but affirmed as a methaphor of faith, instead of
doubt, the telescope transformed the anxiety of alienation
from the world home into a tremendous sense of pyschic
power. The telescope conceived poetically was a projection of
the consciousness into the universe (instead of the reverse); it
became an instrument which conferred upon man, quite directly, godlike capacities of perception and opened to him
tantalizing prospects of his universal dominion. And yet the
telescope was in effect a projection of the universe into the
consciousness. Dominion over the world and the universe
achieved by the telescope was in and of the consciousness—in
and of the individual consciousness so completely that, as

Hannah Arendt points out, "the inner sense with which one senses his senses" is "found to be the only guaranty of reality." How to be conscious of consciousness—this imperative problem makes the modern philosopher and poet into an experimenter with the self. Philosophers and poets experiment "with their own selves no less radically and perhaps even more fearlessly than the scientists have experimented with nature." [16]

On the basis of what I have attempted to set forth about the nature of the crisis in Emerson's early thought, I suppose we might say that he was from the commencement of his development as a poet and thinker irresistibly attracted to the potential power of, as Perry Miller says, "the mighty Self." This figure, the presence of which in philosophy and literature from the early nineteenth century on is so marked, we might designate with some degree of poetic license as the Archimedean Self. By the time he wrote *Nature*, Emerson was in the grip of a sense of amazement deriving from the daring possibilities of the Archimedean Self as the omnipotent source of all knowledge. He had begun to see the traditional man of letters deriving from the concept of the "progress of letters" as useful only in the realm of the "Understanding." He already felt, and almost distinctly, the conviction expressed a few years later during the agitation over the *Divinity School Address*, when he said, "A believer, a mind whose faith is consciousness, is never disturbed because other persons do not yet see the fact which he sees." [17] In *Nature* he sets forth an ecstatic image of the potentiality of consciousness: "Standing on the bare ground,—my head bathed by the blithe air and uplifted into infinite space,—all mean egotism vanishes. I become a transparent eyeball; I am nothing; I see all; the currents of the Uni-

16 Arendt, *The Human Condition*, 267.
17 Stephen E. Whicher (ed.), *Selections from Ralph Waldo Emerson* (Boston, 1957), 119.

versal Being circulate through me: I am part or parcel of God. The name of the nearest friend sounds then foreign and accidental: to be brothers, to be acquaintances, master or servant, is then a trifle and a disturbance. I am the lover of uncontained and immortal beauty." [18]

The famous image of the transparent eyeball—inspired by an indescribable experience of wonder—is a radical metaphor of the power of the consciousness of consciousness. It represents Emerson's full apprehension of the Archimedean point conceived spiritually and poetically. The mind aware of itself comprehends all facts, and in the comprehension finds no fact monstrous. The mind reflecting on the mind is a study that never fails, a source of "perpetual revelation" (replacing historical revelation and, for that matter, the agency of Providence). In the metaphor of the transparent eyeball the issue of the crisis in Emerson's early thought is made dramatically plain: the restoration of wonder by the transforming of the radical objectivity of the rational and experimental point of view into a radically subjective or introspective one. The telescope becomes the transparent eyeball; faith is a transparent eyeball. Out of this transformation arises the novel and tremendous sense which excites Emerson—the capacity of the mind to transfer the universe into a pure inner vision and thus locate it in the mind and to control and direct it. This capacity is what Emerson in his retrospective "Life and Letters in New England" calls the "new consciousness." (It is the response he made to the necessity of finding a "new reality" to replace the "old reality" lost through the separation of Being and Appearance.) In Nature the enraptured "contemplation of the whole"—that is to say, "the wonder at everything that is as it is"—is restored. In this vision one can again exist in a pre-

18 *Ibid.,* 24.

Cartesian (and pre-Christian) unity and harmony with the All, no longer threatened by estrangement from Being, the lover of "uncontained and immortal beauty."

But there are other implications in Emerson's exuberant vision of consciousness. There are implications he did not grasp, though they haunted him and are reflected in the decline of his spiritual arrogance in the 1840s, when he came to recognize that vision is mediate and that the mind cannot look directly upon the mind. Ironically, the expense of being a lover of transcendent beauty is essentially the same one imposed upon the disciple of doubt. It is alienation from the world homeland of man and the community of men who make the world a household. Implied in the godlike capacity of controlling the universe as a transparent eyeball is not only an aspiration to the dimensionless character of God and the denial of any fixity of time and space, but the desertion of the community of human relationships. Family, friends, servants —all fade as the Self in the flow of the currents of the Universal Being becomes part and parcel of God. The flow of Being is away from the human community of the world and never toward it. There is no returning stream. In 1838 Emerson had his most ecstatic, austere, and chilling vision of the destiny of the Self:

The things we now esteem fixed shall, one by one, detach themselves like ripe fruit from our experience, and fall. The wind shall blow them none knows whither. The landscape, the figures, Boston, London, are facts as fugitive as any institution past, or any whiff of mist or smoke, and so is society, and so is the world. The soul looketh steadily forwards, creating a world before her, leaving worlds behind her. She has no dates, nor rites, nor persons, nor specialities nor men. The soul knows only the soul; the web of events is the flowing robe in which she is clothed.[19]

19 *Ibid.*, 93.

83

Believing explicitly in the ultimate morality of all things and in the absolute moral character of the consciousness that is the soul, Emerson contemplated the wonder of sheer Becoming—the infinite progress of consciousness from that mere fugitive fact, the world—as the perfection of knowledge that came with "the action of man upon nature with his entire force,—with reason as well as understanding." He was willing to accept, in states of ecstasy at any rate, the consequence of the progress of consciousness, which is the utter loss of the human world.

So Emerson followed the logic of the moral analogy he saw between faith and the telescope; never, however, clearly discerning its precarious nature. The uncontained and immortal beauty Emerson dared to love and the solitudes of space Pascal feared share a common source: alienation from the household of the world originating in the action of the mind upon nature from a perspective outside that which shaped man's sense of actuality before Galileo. Without the moral and mystical assumptions of Emerson, the control of man over nature is open to the ruthless, merciless, dehumanizing exploitation of the world that has attended its perception from the "specular mount" of ceaseless doubt. The technological desecration of a great symbol of wonder like the moon is only the latest testimony to the failure of Emerson's heroic attempt to restore wonder to its ancient place in the modern psyche.

❧ The Treason of William Dean Howells

In the early 1890s, William Dean Howells began writing a series of reminiscences about American men of letters he had known in New England twenty to thirty years earlier. He did not finish these memoirs until 1900, when (having first appeared in *Harper's* and, in the case of his memoir of James Russell Lowell, in *Scribner's*) they were collected and republished by Harper's under the title of *Literary Friends and Acquaintance: A Personal Retrospect of American Authorship*. One explanation of Howells' long delay in the completion of his remembrances lies in the pressures of the numerous tasks he had assumed in the same period. Another surely lies in the doubts and uncertainties, half-conscious or unconscious inhibitions, Howells felt about the meaning of his New England experience. It was a life he experienced intimately but always as an outsider. He appears to have been struggling between a desire, on the one hand, to give form and expression to the past he had known in the Boston community and, on the other, a wish to suppress it. But to write about the New England he knew was a compulsion. When he was seeing *Literary Friends and Acquaintance* to the printer in 1900, he confessed to his friend Thomas Bailey Aldrich: "In these days I seem to be all autobiography; but I thank heaven I have done my reminiscences of literary Cambridge and Boston, and they

85

are to be booked for oblivion next fall. How gladly I would never speak of myself again! But it's somehow always being tormented out of me, in spite of the small pleasure and pride the past gives me. 'It's so damned humiliating,' as Mark Twain once said of *his* past." [1]

To understand the psychic demands *Literary Friends and Acquaintance* made on Howells—to gauge the pressures hidden by his unassuming manner and genteel politeness—we have to recognize its place, emotional and thematic as well as chronological, in the Howells canon. The book has a complex inner dimension of meaning, belying its simple appearance as a pleasant, nostalgic recollection of the golden New England world of the author's early and middle-aged successes. *Literary Friends and Acquaintance* is a chief aspect of a larger story Howells was engaged in writing much of his life. This story— told in letters, essays, reviews, editorial columns, short stories, novels, and memoirs—constitutes an irregular history of literary and intellectual life in America for a period of sixty or more years. Taken altogether—in both its direct and implicit dimensions—it is one of Howells' major achievements, having a significance comparable to the lifelong records of the literary and intellectual life in America afforded in the writings of an Emerson or, in our own day, of an Edmund Wilson.

As in the case of an Emerson or a Wilson, we may read the Howellsian record as a major imperative of an American literary career. It is the necessary account of a complex, at times tortuous, quest for the meaning of the vocation of an American man of letters. The crucial theme of Howells' quest became a suspicion—irrational but compelling—that in the very midst of success and power he had betrayed the ideal of literary life in America. Howells' sense of his betrayal is subtle;

1 Howells to Aldrich, June 10, 1900, in Mildred Howells, *Life in Letters of William Dean Howells* (New York, 1928), II, 129.

but it appears, when we examine his feeling for his vocation in some detail, that it centered in his relation to New England.

I

To suggest that Howells had a mind dark and intricate enough even for a mild treason is by one standard of judgment to take his creativity too seriously. In an influential opinion, delivered two or three years before Howells died in 1920, H. L. Mencken declared that the "Dean of American Letters" had written "a long row of uninspired and hollow books, with no more ideas in them than so many volumes of the *Ladies' Home Journal*." Several years later, Sinclair Lewis, speaking from the Nobel Prize rostrum, improved on Mencken, asserting Howells had followed a literary creed as insipid as that of "a pious old maid whose greatest delight is to have tea at the vicarage." [2] Fierce denunciations of Howells for triviality, for sheer mindlessness, were so effective in the 1920s and 1930s that his massive literary career came to seem an irrelevance. By the 1950s and 1960s Howells had fallen into such discard that combat critics, like Leslie Fiedler, were giving him no more than a short burst or two, if in fact they bothered to point a typewriter in his direction.

But through the years Howells has had, and continues to have, more discerning critics. Although in the midst of declarations about the pertinence to American literature of his two close friends Henry James and Mark Twain the discussion of Howells' significance has seemed to attract scarcely more than incidental attention, it has yet been substantial. Howells criticism indeed has followed the same tendency we see in the arguments for the importance of James and Mark Twain: it

---

2   H. L. Mencken, "The Dean," in Kenneth E. Eble (ed.), *Howells: A Century of Criticism* (Dallas, 1962), 95; E. A. Karlfeldt, *Why Sinclair Lewis Got the Nobel Prize* (New York, 1931), 20–22.

has assumed an ever increasing sophistication and subtlety. We can follow a line of development in the interpretations of Howells, leading from an emphasis on his relation to ideas and ideals—his power as literary and social critic—to a stress on his affinity for the irrational. A few years ago Newton Arvin and other sympathetic critics set forth an anti-Menckenian view of Howells—a Howells who, granting his neurotic tendencies, had a strong capacity for rational democracy; a writer who critically surveyed his world and deliberately sought to improve it. This programmatic, up-to-date Howells of the 1930s, has undergone considerable modification in the last twenty years or so. In a study by George C. Carrington, Jr., entitled *The Immense Complex Drama: The World and Art of the Howells Novel* (1967), we have an interesting attempt to portray, if not a fully existentialist Howells, a definitely Heideggerian Howells. Presented purely in the role of literary artist (as a satirical novelist, not as a "man of letters," a focus Carrington elects not without being aware of other choices), Howells' artistic motivation is seen as a search after the knowledge that is not in any idea or idealism but is in the knowledge that is "a quality of being." This near-existentialist Howells (whose neurosis is inseparable from his quality as an artist) is full of uncertainties and anxieties, and he is the familiar of the alien and the demonic. He may hardly be relevant to the interpretation of certain sophisticated problems seized upon in our present-day literary criticism, but the existentialist or near-existentialist Howells seems not much farther away from us than James or Mark Twain. He is somewhere in our neighborhood; he speaks, as we say, to our condition.

Although nothing is likely to produce the Howells revival predicted by a small band of present-day enthusiasts, the effective description of a definite existential impulse in Howells will perhaps widen his twentieth-century audience. At the same time, let us hope that the Howells whose imagination of life was to a degree in the existential mode will not obscure the Howells whose imagination of the possibilities of life was thoroughly idealistic. We have reached the interesting point in the evolution of Howells studies where a more understanding and comprehensive inquiry into his significance as a man of letters—Howells the literary and social critic, the editor, the literary businessman, the fictionist, the memoirist—is possible. This will involve us in a study of the intricate, shifting relationship between the existentialist or near-existentialist Howells and the ideological Howells—an uncertain but compelling drama in which we detect the central motivation of his lifelong history of American literary life.

Perhaps the basic document in the Howellsian history is a single letter, one he wrote to Henry James on March 17, 1912, not long after he had been honored on his seventy-fifth birthday at the famous dinner given by his publisher, Colonel George Harvey, head of Harper and Brothers. With the President of the United States and hundreds of personages in attendance, the dinner had the air of a state occasion. Publicly the "Dean of American Letters" took the affair with the modesty he was so well known for, yet inwardly he was more than a little vexed by it all. He confides his experience of the dinner and its aftermath in the letter to James. It begins casually with acknowledgment of two letters he had received from his friend—one personal, and one a birthday tribute designed for public reading. But Howells' letter turns into a psychological horror story.

I owe you an answer for two letters, or two answers. The first, the public one, I do not know how to acknowledge. It almost convinced me that I had really been some help or service to you, at any rate, I am going to believe it as a pleasure to which I can turn in the night when I wake to the sense of what a toad I am and always have been. Your letter, so fully, so beautifully kind, will help to take away some of those dreadful moments of self-blame, and I can think, "Well, there must have been something in it; James would not abuse my dotage with flattery; I was probably not always such a worm of the earth as I feel myself at present." Your letter, meant for the public eye, brought before mine the vision of those days and nights in Sacramento Street, "when my bosom was young," and swelled with pride in your friendship and joy in sharing your literary ambition, as if it were the "communion of saints." I do thank you for it, and I am eager for all men to read it in the *North American*, to which, as alone worthy of reporting it, it has been transferred from the *Weekly*. I was rather glad it was not in our host's scheme to read it at the dinner, where the best, the finest effect of it would have been lost. No letters were read, but all will be printed in the *Review*—quaint enough, as I feel, since they were some of them personally addressed to me, who may be supposed to smuggle them into print for the gratification of my vanity. But I believe it is the convention to ignore that sort of ostensibility; at any rate, I found the matter past my control. It is at the worst, part of the divine madness of an affair in which I still struggle to identify my accustomed self. It was really something extraordinary. Four hundred notables swarmed about a hundred tables on the floor, and we elect sat at a long board on a dais. Mrs. Clifford was among us, two elbows from the President of the United States, and she can tell you better about it than I, who remained for the whole time in a daze from which I wrenched myself for twenty minutes to read my farrago of *spropositi*; it was all, all wrong and unfit; but nobody apparently knew it, not even I till that ghastly waking hour of the night when hell opens to us.[3]

The anguish of Howells' "crisis of identity" is authentic; this is all the more confirmed by the tone of half-whimsical indulgence in neurotic self-contempt and self-blame. In James's reply to his old friend, he is sensitive to Howells' suffering, without, however, detecting precisely the source of it. James scolds Howells for talking so deplorably "about the figure you

3   Howells to James, March 17, 1912, in *Life in Letters of Howells*, II, 316–17.

make to yourself in the watches of the night," and demands to know how he could take anything "but a friendly and understanding and acceptingly 'philosophic' view" toward a career marked by devotion, self-sacrifice, labor, courage, and "admirable and distinguished production." James continues: "We all fall short of our dreams—but of what can you have fallen short unless of some prefiguring delirium? In that case it hasn't been you but the delirium that was wrong."[4] The question James asks is right: in a sense Howells had fallen short, almost a whole lifetime short, of a prefiguring dream of the literary vocation—a dream that he, or James for that matter, could not have dismissed as mistaken. Reading James's tribute to him, Howells experienced a moving recollection of a moment when this dream (a "delirium," in the sense of "transport") had, he thought, been an actuality. In his memory he had a vision of the time in Cambridge thirty-five years earlier, when he and James had shared a literary friendship "as if it were a communion of saints." By implied contrast this poignant sharing of the pure literary spirit is joined in Howells' letter to the unanticipated, demonic, three-o'clock-in-the-morning metamorphosis of his birthday dinner in his emotions. His retrospective glimpse of a brief time of happy literary community (when Howells had been assistant editor of the *Atlantic Monthly* and James was writing his first stories) and the transformation of the birthday dinner into a vision akin to that of a descent into hell were responses to opposing images deeply entangled in his consciousness: a vision of an ideal and sacred American literary order and a counter, nightmarish vision of the actual, corrupt disorder of the American literary life. On the one hand, Howells was compulsively drawn toward idealizing the vocation of the American man of letters, feeling a sacerdotal obligation to represent the literary life as a transcendent, re-

4 James to Howells, March 27, 1912, *ibid.*, 318–19.

deeming spiritual order; on the other hand, haunted from the beginning of his career by intimations of doubt about this kind of idealism, he was increasingly disturbed by the feeling that a transcendent frame of reference for American literary life was a meaningless illusion. It was, no less than other ways of the national life, subject to the limits of actual possibility. The result was that, for all his amazing community with American writers and for all his authority for many years as the leader of the American profession of letters, Howells found it impossible to satisfactorily define the nature of his vocation, or to establish securely his concept of himself as an American man of letters. Simply put, Howells could never reconcile his ideal of being a writer in America with the realities—the contingencies—of being one.

This situation in his thought and emotion, growing more complicated as he became older, is the shaping force in his diverse account—in his fiction, nonfiction, and in the memorializing that is somewhere in between—of the drama of literary life in America as he knew it.

II

The background of Howells' divided sensibility of vocation is to be found particularly in two books of memoirs, *My Literary Passions* and *Years of My Youth*, in which he gives us his memories of literary apprenticeship. Undertaken by his own volition and pursued under his own direction, his apprenticeship to letters was so passionate and strenuous that it bore the character of a novitiate; well before the time Howells had completed his self-imposed probation to letters, he had consecrated himself to a vision of literature as the transcendent purpose of his existence.

And yet we are not to think of his consecration as an act of isolation or defiance. Assuming alienation to be an imperative

of the literary vocation in America, we are tempted today to
see Howells' novitiate as a lonely experience under the hostile
circumstances of a crude frontier society. Some of the evidence
seems to support this interpretation. We discover the youthful
Howells reading Longfellow's "The Spanish Student" in a loft
of the log cabin, which the Howellses, in their opportunistic
migrations from one place to another in Ohio, occupied for
one year. He holds his book to catch the light from "the little
gable window that overlooked the groaning and whistling
grist mill." Or we find him meditating upon his projected life
of Cervantes while walking to and from his tasks at his father's
printing office across a bleak midwestern wintry landscape, his
head hot with Cervantes and his feet chilled in frozen boots;
or we find him, after a long day's work, poring over Shakespeare
"by night, in the narrow little space which I had for my study,
under the stairs at home." In this cubbyhole, his "workshop
for six or seven years," we attend Will Howells struggling to
learn Latin and Greek, Spanish, French, and German, reading
insatiably, and working anxiously at his own writing. He felt
"fierce to shut out" everyone from his retreat, "so that no
sound or sight should molest me in the pursuit of the end
which I sought gropingly, blindly, with very little hope, but
with an intense ambition, and a courage that gave way under
no burden, before no obstacle." [5] But the evidence of young
Howells' literary isolation is deceptive. Important though the
individualistic quality of Howells' literary apprenticeship is,
we see in it always a public and professional quality. Had he
been reared in a region farther west or southwest, in Missouri,
say, where Mark Twain was born two years before him, this
might not have been so, nor might Howells have made so con-

5 William Dean Howells, *My Literary Passions* in *Writings of
William Dean Howells*, Library Edition (New York, 1910), 31, 62–63;
Years of My Youth (New York, 1916), 84.

scious a dedication to letters. Like Mark Twain, his literary school was the country printing shop, but its context was the village life of post-frontier Ohio rather than the semi-frontier life of Hannibal, Missouri. Under the cultural conditions existing in Ohio in the 1840s and 1850s there was an intellectual life, and it aspired to some degree of community, sufficiently so to provide a boy of very strong natural literary instincts with an environment in which to nourish them. If with more gentility than sophistication, the society in which Howells lived subscribed to letters and the literary vocation as constituting a superior moral and spiritual order. In his desire to become a fit representative of this order, he was attracted to no strange faith; he had been born among believers, and he lived among them, his memoirs generally emphasize, a youth respected for his devotion to the literary ideal. Meanwhile, he took advantage of whatever visible realization there was of the literary profession in the places where he lived in Ohio, notably in the little town of Jefferson in the Western Reserve (a cultural colony of New England) and in Columbus. Outside of the printing shop, Howells' prime schoolroom, literature was attended to mostly in combination with the other professions— medicine, the ministry, teaching, and especially the law. This was the kind of combining that had formed the practice of the American clerisy—the intellectual patriciate—now declining but still influential after conceiving the new nation and ruling it for three generations. Howells experienced the spirit of the old order of intellect directly when the post-frontier clerisy dropped into his father's office "to stand with their backs to the stove and challenge opinions concerning Holmes and Poe, Irving and Macaulay, Pope and Byron, Dickens and Shakespeare"; or when they congregated to debate scriptural inspiration, Free Soil principles, or more purely literary matters. Howells knew the influence of the American clerisy, too,

94

in his delight in the great English literary reviews of the nineteenth century—the *Edinburgh*, the *Westminster*, the *North British*, and the *London Quarterly*—magazines that were principal elements in the cosmopolitan literary community which New England intellectuals like William Tudor, who founded the *North American Review*, endeavored to represent. "We got them in the American editions," Howells explains in *My Literary Passions*, "in payment for printing the publisher's prospectus, and their arrival was an excitement, a joy, and a satisfaction with me, which I could not now describe without having to accuse myself of exaggeration." He adds, "The love of literature, and the hope of doing something in it, had become my life to the exclusion of all other interests, or it was at least the great reality, and all other things were as shadows." [6]

Judging from the testimony in *My Literary Passions*, the reviews contributed more than anything else to impress upon the literary novice his sense of a calling to letters and his sense of literature as an order. His sensibility of vocation was so confirmed that in his mind it became an assumption he might contradict but not question:

If I thought of taking up some other calling it was as a means only; literature was always the end I had in view, immediately or finally. I did not see how it was to yield me a living, for I knew that almost all the literary men in the country had other professions; they were editors, lawyers, or had public or private employments; or they were men of wealth; there was then not one who earned his bread solely by his pen in fiction, or drama, or history, or poetry, or criticism, in a day when people wanted very much less butter on their bread than they do now. But I kept blindly at my studies, and yet not altogether blindly, for, as I have said, the reading I did had more tendency than before, and I was beginning to see authors in their proportion to one another, and to the body of literature. [7]

6 *My Literary Passions*, 91.
7 *Ibid.*, 92. See also *Years of My Youth*, 87–89 and *passim*.

95

III

During the years of young Howells' literary apprenticeship, the order of authors and the body of literature were represented in the new nation by Boston. Well before the time Howells commenced his apprenticeship to letters, the capital of the "American province of the republic of letters" (to use Howells' phrase) [8] had shifted its center from Philadelphia to Boston. Here for the first time, and no doubt the last, the logic of American cultural history brought into being a literary community (Boston, Cambridge, and Concord) in the image of the humanistic ideal of literary order.

With "his being" already "wholly in literature," as he says in *Literary Friends and Acquaintance*, Howells came to the Boston-Cambridge-Concord world for the first time in 1860. As "the passionate pilgrim from the West approached his Holy Land," [9] he was confidently prepared to find what he expected to find: the detailed, living embodiment of the literary order which he had already been called to represent; and, in spite of some fear and trembling about how he would be greeted, his appropriate reception into that order. (His prospect of being duly received had been considerably enhanced some time before when the *Atlantic Monthly* accepted and paid for one of his poems. "I was glad of the pay," he recalled, "but the gain was nothing to the glory; and with the letter which Lowell wrote me about it in the pocket next my heart, and felt to make sure of its presence every night and morning

8 William Dean Howells, *Literary Friends and Acquaintance: A Personal Retrospect of American Authorship*, ed. David F. Hiatt and Edwin H. Cady (Bloomington and London, 1968), 14. (Note: This volume constitutes Volume XXXII of *A Selected Edition of William Dean Howells* now being issued irregularly under the general editorship of Edwin H. Cady by the University of Indiana Press and the Center for Editions of American Authors.)

9 *Ibid.*, 7, 16.

and throughout the day, I was of the potentiality of immeasurable success." [10] The way in which Howells' expectations of the American seat of letters were rapturously fulfilled gives us some of the most charming pages in *Literary Friends and Acquaintance*. When James T. Fields, the distinguished publisher, had him to breakfast in his "friendly home of lettered refinement" situated "beside the Charles, and in the close neighborhood of Dr. Holmes," he sat amid the autographed books and pictures of famous contemporary authors and "breathed in" the atmosphere "as if in the return from lifelong exile." Recently the Fieldses had been with Tennyson in England, Howells recalls, "and Mrs. Fields had much to tell of him, how he looked, how he smoked, how he read aloud, and how he said, when he asked her to go with him to the tower of his house, 'Come up and see the sad English sunset!' which had an instant value to me such as some rich verse of his might have had." [11] The visit to Fields's home is not so well known as another episode in the story of Howells' first visit to Boston which he records in the early part of *Literary Friends and Acquaintance*. This is the story of the intimate dinner in an upper room of the Parker House during which Dr. Holmes (who with Fields and Howells was the guest of Lowell) looked at the youthful poet from the West and said to his host, "Well, James, this is something like the apostolic succession; this is the laying on of hands." Holmes intended to be funny, but the likely young man from the far provinces recognized the great secret concealed in the little joke, even if thirty years later he was reticent to be explicit about it. ("I took his sweet and caressing irony as he meant it; but the charm of it went to my head long before any drop of wine, together with the charm of hearing him and Lowell calling each other James and Wen-

10 *Years of My Youth*, 180–81.
11 *Ibid.*, 40.

97

dell, and of finding them still cordially boys together.") [12]
More on the strength of a literary preparation manifest in his
very presence than in his as yet small literary achievement, the
youthful Howells had been admitted by an act of literary and
social grace to the awesome intimacy of the inner circle of the
American clerisy. He had been ordained, perhaps not yet to
the priesthood, but surely to the diaconate. Priesthood and
bishopric would follow six years later when, after his period of
diplomatic service in Italy and a brief career in New York on
the *Nation*, he was appointed first to the assistant editorship
of the *Atlantic Monthly* and subsequently to the chief editorship. At the early age of thirty-four, Howells had come into a
position through which, it would seem, he could fulfill his
vocation to the rising American dominion of letters with a
maximum influence.

And yet by the time he became editor-in-chief of the *Atlantic*, Howells' piety of vocation had become subject to a
progressive doubt of Boston's place in this dominion. This
occurrence in the thought and emotion of Howells is difficult
to define. It did not occur suddenly, nor (contrary to the tendency of literary historians to overdramatize his removal to
New York in 1890) did it eventuate in his entire falling off
from Boston. If he came to resent the stuffiness of the elite
humanism of Boston, Howells had a compulsive regard for
what he assumed to be the truth Boston represented: the
transcendent consecration of the literary life. But in the expansion of his general social perspective in the 1870s and 1880s,
he experienced a need to accommodate the sacramental sense
of the literary vocation to the imperative of equality unfolding
in American history. In a summation of his vision of the
American equalitarian principle he said in 1888:

12 *Ibid.*, 36.

Somehow, the idea that we call America has realized itself so far that we already have identification rather than distinction as the fact which strikes the foreign critic in our greatness. Our notable men, it seems, are notable for their likeness to their fellow-men, and not for their unlikeness; democracy has subtly but surely done its work; our professions of belief in equality have had their effect in our life; and whatever else we lack in homogeneity, we have in the involuntary recognition of their common humanity by our great men something that appears to be peculiarly American, and that we think more valuable than the involuntary assumption of superiority, than the distinction possible to greatness, among peoples accustomed to cringe before greatness. . . . We have been now some hundred years building up a state on the affirmation of the essential equality of men in their rights and duties, and whether we have been right or been wrong, the gods have taken us at our word, and have responded to us with a civilization in which there is no distinction perceptible to the eye that loves and values it.[13]

What concept of the literary vocation could express the American consciousness of equality Howells thus idealizes?

In his disjointed manifesto against the "vested interests of criticism" entitled *Criticism and Fiction* (to which he later adapted the above remarks), Howells repudiates the hierarchical basis of fraternity and order among writers and proclaims a democratic ethic of literary order. "The time is coming, I hope, when each new author, each new artist, will be considered, not in his proportion to any other author or artist, but in his relation to the human nature, known to us all, which it is his privilege, his high duty, to interpret."[14] In the argument bearing on this statement Howells misinterprets Edmund Burkes' idea that "the true standard of the artist is in

13 William Dean Howells, "Editor's Study," *Harper's Monthly,* LXXVII (July, 1888), 315–16, 317.
14 William Dean Howells, *Criticism and Fiction* in *Writings of William Dean Howells,* Library Edition (New York, 1910), 196.

every man's power." Burke assumed the eighteenth-century concept of universal taste, which meant that the true standard of art is in every *lettered* man's power; in other words, art was within the province of every man who belonged to what Basil Willey calls the "closed and interlocked system" of the eighteenth-century literary order.[15] Burke belonged to a world in which the difference between civilization and barbarism was still carefully discriminated on the basis of literary standards and in which literary rank and distinction were conferred within the literary realm. He would not have approved, or understood, Howells' notion of the literary judgment of "the common, average man." But Howells makes his own use of Burke. He sets Burke, a figure revered by the American clerisy, in opposition to the contemporary English critic Matthew Arnold and his scorn of American leveling. "Matthew Arnold complained that he found no 'distinction' in our life," Howells says, "and I would gladly persuade all artists intending greatness in any kind among us that the recognition of the fact pointed out by Mr. Arnold ought to be a source of inspiration to them, and not discouragement." [16]

In Howells' ideally homogeneous America—"the new order of things"—there will be no arrangement of classes or realms of existence. All existence, literary and otherwise, will be comprehended in one scheme of democratic identification, the source of all fraternity and authority, political, religious, literary. The time of literary legalism when "certain authors were considered authorities in certain kinds, when they must be accepted entire and not questioned in any particular" is going. Howells sees the patrician American literary order pass-

15 *Ibid.* See Basil Willey, *The Eighteenth-Century Background* (London, 1940), 122.
16 *Criticism and Fiction*, 257.

ing through a process of decentralization, literature at length to become integrated with society, acknowledging only the authority of what he would call in his birthday address in 1912 the "high average which reigns . . . in all American things." [17] A withering away of the literary estate will occur; what Howells terms "the communistic era in taste foreshadowed by Burke"(!) will come about. Describing how this happened in his native land, Homos, the Altrurian, says: "The artist, the man of genius, who worked from the love of his work, became the normal man, and in the measure of his ability and his calling each wrought in the spirit of the artist." [18]

When he identified the vocation of the American writer with the achievement of an ideal "communistic" order of letters—implicitly if not overtly rejecting the ideal of literary order represented by Boston—Howells moved out onto the dangerous frontier of the American psyche, where the mind is fully exposed to the difference between America as a pure and incorruptible idea and America as the United States—this is to say, as a rough and unpredictable, as an ambiguous, even as a deceptive, day-to-day historical reality. For so long as he believed that the ideal of the order of letters—the community of the "Republic of Letters"—was the spiritual homeland of the American writer, and that the American writer properly should serve this transcendent polity, Howells could see his faith made flesh in the Boston-Cambridge-Concord world. When he attempted fully to embrace the imperatives of literary equalitarianism, he was subject to the traumatic experience resulting from an intensified consciousness of the chasm between the literary life conceived under the aspect of ideal order

17 William Dean Howells, "Literary Recollections," North American Review, CXCV (April, 1912), 556.
18 William Dean Howells, A Traveler from Altruria (New York, 1894), 278–79.

and the problematical, formless, literary condition of the nation perceived in its actuality. Howells was in more danger of exposing his idealization of the literary life to his faculty for the perception of unadorned contingency than ever before in his career. He could hardly avoid recognizing the discrepancy between his idealistic commitment and the imprecision and nastiness, the general messiness of the "facts"; and in recognizing this difference, feel that it was a treachery in which he himself was somehow involved because he could not control his own way of seeing things.

This recognition is documented in the basic distinction Howells makes between Boston and New York in *Literary Friends and Acquaintance*: New York is "a mart" and Boston "a capital" in literature.[19] In his "Essay on American Literary Centres" Howells comments:

Boston, in my time at least, had distinctly a literary atmosphere, which more or less pervaded society; but New York has distinctly nothing of the kind, in any pervasive sense. It is a vast mart, and literature is one of the things marketed here; but our good society cares no more for it than for some other products bought and sold here; it does not care nearly so much for books as for horses or for stocks, and I suppose it is not unlike the good society of any other metropolis in this. To the general, here, journalism is a far more appreciable thing than literature, and has greater recognition, for some very good reasons; but in Boston literature had vastly more honor, and even more popular recognition, than journalism. There journalism desired to be literary, and here literature has to try hard not to be journalistic. If New York is a literary centre on the business side, as London is, Boston was a literary centre, as Weimar was, and as Edinburgh was. It felt literature, as those capitals felt it, and if it did not love it quite so much as might seem, it always respected it.[20]

19 Hiatt and Cady (eds.), *Literary Friends and Acquaintance*, 221.
20 William Dean Howells, "Essay on American Literary Centres," *Literature and Life* (New York, 1902), 179–80.

102

More succinctly, in the same essay, Howells says:

> I doubt if anywhere in the world there was ever so much taste and feeling for literature as there was in that Boston. . . . New York, I am quite sure, never was such a centre, and I see no signs that it ever will be. It does not influence the literature of the whole country as Boston once did through writers whom all the young writers wished to resemble; it does not give the law, and it does not inspire the love that literary Boston inspired. There is no ideal that it represents.[21]

Among all the asides and qualifications of the Howellsian nostalgic manner, the flat condemnation of New York is unusual. It hints at the anxiety we find more definitely expressed in another essay Howells wrote on the literary situation in America, "The Man of Letters as a Man of Business," surely a key document in the history of the literary profession in this country. The writer in America, Howells argues, is a stranger— an alien alike to the business class and to the working class. His proper identity should be with the workers, for he is an artist in the sense of an artisan, "allied to the great mass of wage-workers . . . who live by doing or making a thing, and not by marketing a thing after some other man has done it or made it." Writers ought to take a glory in their vocation because they "bring into the world something that was not choately there before. . . ." Thus writers "ought to feel the tie that binds" them "to all the toilers of the shop and field, not as a galling chain, but as a mystic bond also uniting us to Him who works hitherto and evermore." But to the multitude of their fellow working men writers are what? "Shadows of names, or not even the shadows." The literary artist is nowhere, yet "he has to be somewhere, poor fellow. . . ." He is "in a transition state," Howells says vaguely, waiting for the coming in "the flesh" of "that human equality of which the instinct has been

21 *Ibid.*, 184.

divinely planted in the human soul." [22] Groping to define the
actual situation of the American writer in "The Man of Letters as Man of Business," Howells remains the idealist of the

22 William Dean Howells, "The Man of Letters as a Man of Business," *Literature and Life*, 33–35. I would not argue that the conflict
between existential awareness and idealism in Howells can be isolated
from his intimate personal stake in American society. In his efforts to be
democratic, as Kermit Vanderbilt points out in *The Achievement of
William Dean Howells* (Princeton, 1968), Howells was greatly inhibited
by his "natural conservatism," by his yearning (which he shared with the
Boston patricians) for a preindustrial, agrarian America, and by his satisfaction in the very considerable wealth he accumulated from his literary
career as time went on. The conflict in Howells' mind between being a
"theoretical socialist" and a "practical aristocrat" unquestionably contributed to his existentialist mood—promoting his inability to maintain a
consistent faith in the vision of an ideal democratic literary order in America—and produced in him feelings of guilt about betraying his equalitarian
commitment. Vanderbilt gives a careful, thoughtful analysis of Howells'
"social ambivalence." Howells' dilemma concerning the relation of his
political to his economic behavior is an inextricable part of the total
problem of interpreting his career. In general Howells' social and/or
literary ambivalence is explained by his most recent biographer—Kenneth S. Lynn, *William Dean Howells: An American Life* (New York,
1971)—as the result of an extreme self-consciousness. Lynn sees Howells
as "a man of modern sensibility, whose awareness of life was rooted in
radical doubt and anxiety." Howells was "not a schizophrenic" but he
experienced "a measure of the schizophrenic's tortured and desperate
feelings of alienation." When Howells realized in the 1880s that he had
been "playing roles" to fulfill in Boston "an outlander's ferocious ambition at the cost of cutting himself off from his deepest emotional needs,"
he attempted to "unite self-consciousness and social consciousness." If
he failed in the attempt, he yet "opened the way to the wider sympathies
and broader perspective of the modern American novel." The thesis I
attempt to expound in the present essay can no doubt be accomodated
to both Vanderbilt's and Lynn's much more detailed studies. (Both of
these need to be looked at with reference to Edwin H. Cady's well-known
and less thesis-oriented biography of Howells [1956, 1958], which is a
basic source for all students of Howells.) I have chosen in my brief, quite
specialized study to let the question of Howells' perplexed allegiance to
the ideal of literary order dominate, in order to emphasize a central aspect
in his career that has been neglected in American literary history. In this
same connection I must call attention to the influence on my approach
of Lionel Trilling's "William Dean Howells and the Roots of Modern
Taste," in *The Opposing Self: Nine Essays in Criticism* (New York,
1959), 76–103.

equalitarian order. He can consider the existential condition of the writer only by reference to his vision of an ideal situation. Finding it more and more difficult to envision the ideal through the fog of the actual, he comes close in "The Man of Letters as a Man of Business" to suggesting the mood of alienation.

His inability to idealize the literary life in America in the face of his perception of the materialistic forces overwhelming it becomes manifest in three novels of the 1890s: *A Hazard of New Fortunes*, *The World of Chance*, and *A Traveler from Altruria*. Each of these stories develops the incapacity of the man of letters in the later nineteenth-century American society to relate himself to a fulfilling concept of vocation.

The drama of Basil March's hazard of new fortunes is Howells' most comprehensive attempt to dramatize the ordeal of an American man of letters up against the problem of defining his relation to the struggle for equality in the American urban and industrial plutocracy. It is not a direct attempt to transfer autobiography into fiction, for March, although he is a "Western man," is not derived clearly from Howells himself. Before he goes to New York as the editor of Fulkerson's projected magazine, he has a career in the Boston insurance business. On the other hand, he has had an early career in journalism; and he is, Fulkerson detects, a "natural-born literary man," who has "always had a hankering for the inkpots." March has hoped, moreover, with a sufficient income from his salesmanship, to find the leisure to "come more freshly to literature proper."[23] In this inclination he has followed the deadliest tendency of a patrician literary elite as exemplified by the Boston clerisy—to make literature "a high privilege, a sacred refuge." March has been reading a great deal, writing a

---

[23] William Dean Howells, *A Hazard of New Fortunes* (New York, 1890), I, 1–3.

little, and fooling himself into believing that he is pursuing the literary vocation, while progressively sealing himself in a genteel entrapment.

Does he break out of this when he goes to New York—or, we should ask, when he is thrown into New York? Unable to make up his mind about taking Fulkerson's offer, he accepts it only when he learns that his superior in the insurance business has no faith in March's ability as salesman. In his contact with Lindau, the embittered old revolutionist, March encounters in the most vivid way the drama of the desperate struggle for equality in modern society. This forces him to question the meaningfulness of the Boston society and to see its poverty of spirit. When his wife laments "the literary peace, the intellectual refinement of the life they had left behind" in the ivory tower of Boston, March agrees that it had been "very pretty" but, he says, "not life—it was death-in-life."[24] But he hardly awakens to a new sense of his moral responsibility as a man of letters. March wants to come to grips with the modern reality; what prevents him is that he cannot find it. Now and then he glimpses its ambiguous and shifting dimensions, its terrible multiplicity. If he achieves a certain degree of moral certainty when he defies Dryfoos and refuses to fire Lindau, his action accomplishes nothing. March seems to attain simply enough moral capacity to make evident his moral powerlessness. If he and his wife find in the "immense, friendly homelessness" of New York "a refuge and a consolation"[25] to make up for their lost Boston, March discovers in New York no order to replace the "pretty" literary life in Boston; he finds no democratic clerisy of the High Average. Nor does March achieve lonely independence. In an argument for "The Contemporaneity of Howells," Richard Foster surely overstates

24 *Ibid.*, II, 74.
25 *Ibid.*, 78.

the case when he says that Howells dramatizes in March "consciously and fully the isolation of the intellectual in the modern world" and that March represents "the new intellectual's education in the nature of the modern world" and the acceptance of "his responsibilities and limitations as an isolated intelligence within it."[26] There is a kind of futility about March that is akin to despair. He hardly represents the resources of literary alienation.

In *The World of Chance* the literary vocation is removed still further from the possibility of a transcendent context. Percy Bysshe Ray, an aspiring young author from Midland, comes to New York seeking a publisher for his first novel. Although he remains faithful to a certain ideal image he has of himself as an artist, his inability to locate a publisher when lesser authors do so forces him to "fall back upon that theory of mere luck which first so emboldens and then so embitters the heart."[27] The whole literary situation, Ray discovers, is dominated by the expediencies of profit; young writers devise schemes to win editorial favor like gamblers seeking to break the bank at Monaco, and publishers take each book as a bet. The notion of an overruling Providence which ultimately makes meaning out of the seemingly fortuitous is, Howells suggests, an illusion. At the end of the novel, Ray, rushing through the night in a sleeping car, entertains the idea of the subservience of chance to a larger law, but he falls asleep remembering it was the publisher Kane who once said so. Kane, George W. Carrington says, may be compared to Satan in Mark Twain's *The Mysterious Stranger.*

Because Ray is an appealing and believable young man and an idealist in spite of his lesson in the rule of chance, *The*

26 Richard Foster, "The Contemporaneity of William Dean Howells," *New England Quarterly*, XXXII (March, 1959), 63, 71.
27 William Dean Howells, *The World of Chance* (New York, 1893), 262.

World of Chance is not altogether a closed world. But in Twelvemough, the author in *A Traveler from Altruria*, we meet a writer of romantic novels who has no feeling for anything except the false world he fabricates with his literary skill and the success and money this brings him. Since he is the narrator of the story, his superficial intellect is the center of the story, ironically revealing the closed minds of the minister, the doctor, the professor, the banker, and the lawyer as they encounter the world of the Altrurian. None of them, and least of all, Twelvemough, is guided by an ideal of vocation.

The attitude toward the literary vocation in America in *Literary Friends and Acquaintance*, composed in part while Howells was writing *The World of Chance* and *A Traveler from Altruria*, is related to the ironic representation of American literary life in the novels. "At that day," Howells says of his outlook when he first saw Boston, "I believed authorship the noblest calling in the world, and I should still be at a loss to name any nobler."[28] An elevated faith declining into a muted qualification—this defines the somewhat blurred focus in *Literary Friends and Acquaintance*. Admiring, not to say reverential, Howells' depiction of Boston as an ideal literary world is reduced by a tendency, evasive and irresolute but marked, to deny it relevance or reality as a meaningful historical world. In effect he almost seals off the Boston which represented the ideal of the literary order from the present and future of American letters.

It seems to me [Howells says in a prefatory "Note" to the first edition of *Literary Friends and Acquaintance*] that if one is to write such a book as this at all, one cannot profitably do so without a frankness concerning one's self as well as others which might be misunderstood. But I wish to make of my own personality merely a background which divers important figures are projected against,

28 *Literary Friends and Acquaintance,* 39.

and I am willing to sacrifice myself a little in giving them relief. I will try to show them as they seemed to me, and I shall not blame any one who says that they are not truly represented; I shall only claim that I have truly represented their appearance, and I shall not claim that I could fully conceive of them in their reality.[29]

One motive for offering this apology at the threshold of his recollections is clearly enough Howells' continuing intimidation by Boston. He is led to erect a protective barrier against the criticism of anyone who may say that he has pictured the Boston writers falsely. He has not, Howells urges, intruded his own personality; he has rather "sacrificed" his ego, in order to use his personality as a background against which to throw his subjects into relief. He has not been confident enough, furthermore, to assume that he could fully conceive the reality of (the implication seems to be) his superiors, claiming no more than honestly to have set down his friends as they appeared to his memory. Actually Howells is intimately and pervasively and centrally present in his memoir, and indeed if we read his note carefully this is what he tells us in it. His consciousness of the significance of the past controls the work and directs the terms on which he makes his peace with Boston: recognition of the failure of the Boston ideal of the literary vocation in America; or, differently put, the recognition of the impossibility of its realization.

The strategy Howells employs is to insist that Boston is not continuous with contemporary American literary life—so largely directed, as Howells sees it, by the contingencies and expediencies of commerce. The Boston-Cambridge community was for a time a perfected literary existence. It was a patrician republic of letters to which all of the best people

29 William Dean Howells, *Literary Friends and Acquaintance* (Original ed.; New York and London, 1900), [iii].

belonged: "Literature in Boston . . . was so respectable, and often of so high a lineage, that to be a poet was not only to be good society, but almost to be good family. If one names over the men who gave Boston her supremacy in literature during that Unitarian harvest-time of the old Puritanic seed-time which was her Augustan age, one names the people who were and who had been socially first in the city ever since the self-exile of the Tories at the time of the Revolution."[30] Cambridge, less overtly concerned with family status than Boston and removed from commerce, was yet more perfect: "To my mind, the structure of society [in Cambridge] was almost ideal, and until we have a perfectly socialized condition of things I do not believe we shall ever have a more perfect society. The instincts which governed it were not such as can arise from the sordid competition of interests; they flowed from a devotion to letters, and from a self-sacrifice in material things which I can give no better notion of than by saying that the outlay of the richest college magnate seemed to be graduated to the income of the poorest." And all Cantabrigians wrote books. Howells recalls Bret Harte, newly from California, saying, " 'Why, you couldn't fire a revolver from your front porch anywhere without bringing down a two-volumer!' "[31]

Howells increases the isolation of the Boston community in the ideal by contrasting it with an oversimplified picture of New York. His impressions of literary New York are enlightened by humor but on the whole promote the notion of the city as a place of bohemian and commercial barbarism. His first brief time in New York, although he was not afterwards sure why, found him seeing mostly the bohemian side of "New York authorship." When he sat at a table in Pfaff's beer cellar, listening "to the wit that did not seem very funny, I thought

30 Hiatt and Cady, *Literary Friends and Acquaintance,* 125.
31 *Ibid.,* 153.

of the dinner with Lowell, the breakfast with Fields, the supper at the Autocrat's, and felt that I had fallen very far." In fact, he was inhibited by the feeling "that a person who had seen the men and had the things said before him that I had in Boston, could not keep himself too carefully in cotton. . . ."[32] If Howells jokes a little, the basis of his contrast between Boston and New York was genuine enough. Speaking of Edmund Clarence Stedman, he says, "In him I found the quality of Boston, the honor and passion of literature, and not a mere pose of the literary life; and the world knows without my telling how true he has been to his ideal of it."[33] Howells' feeling that New York was almost wholly a literary marketplace underlay the strongest, most explicit contrast he drew between New York and Boston, and enforced in his imagination a dream of a Boston-Cambridge-Concord world pure beyond money.

What tends most strongly, however, to remove Boston from historical actuality and make it a static ideal in *Literary Friends and Acquaintance* is, paradoxically, the decline of Howells' faith in idealizing. As a consequence, *Literary Friends and Acquaintance* does not turn, although we might expect it to do so, on a tension between Howells' ideal of a patrician literary culture and his vision of an equalitarian literary life. Such a tension is hinted at when he says that Cambridge is a society perfect enough to do until the arrival of a socialist one. It is more strongly hinted in some of the harsh things Howells says here and there about Boston. One of these, by implication, occurs in his impression of Thoreau. If Howells was uncertain how to rank Thoreau (observing that "the great New England group might be enlarged perhaps without loss of quality by the inclusion of Thoreau"), he

32 *Ibid.,* 68.
33 *Ibid.,* 74.

regarded Thoreau as a writer "who came somewhat before his time," and although he had not looked into *Walden* since 1858, judged his ideas to constitute "a drastic criticism of our expedential and mainly futile civilization"—a criticism which "would find more intelligent acceptance now than it did then, when all resentment of its defects was specialized in enmity to Southern slavery." Not even Tolstoy, Howells declares, "has more clearly shown the hollowness, the hopelessness, the unworthiness of the life of the world" than Thoreau does in *Walden*.[34] Considering Howells' reverence for Tolstoy, this is a high tribute to Thoreau. Still he fails to do much with Thoreau in *Literary Friends and Acquaintance*, not returning to him after his vivid description of an awkward visit with him in Concord in 1860. Howells ignores Thoreau's intense criticism of the hollow materialism of the Boston community.

The most significant failure to develop an effective criticism of Boston culture in *Literary Friends and Acquaintance* is to be found in Howells' equivocal essay on Lowell. When he was young, or at least until past the time when he came back to Boston to fill the assistant editorship of the *Atlantic*, Howells was worshipfully devoted to Lowell. Lowell's had been the most authoritative hand laid on Howells at the Parker House dinner, and not only because Lowell represented literary authority. Howells found in him a new kind of moral capability that, he thought, radiated throughout the national letters.

I grow [he wrote Charles Eliot Norton in 1868] more and more into the admiration of Lowell's power, or liking of it rather; for when I reflect that with his great gifts to persuade and to make afraid—his poetry and his wit—he has never used them once falsely or cruelly, I feel myself in the presence of a new kind of great man, in whom there is a perfect balance of law and strength.

34 *Ibid.*, 15, 53.

It could not be, of course, and yet I wish that there were some means for an extension of his personal influence over young men. It is vast already, and his strength is felt throughout the whole puny body of our literature, for there is no one who would not prize his praise above that of any contemporary; but it would be well for every youngster if he could see him and hear him.[35]

In the years to come his "admiration of Lowell's power" turned to partial resentment and became a burden to Howells. The full extent to which he resented the mentor he once believed should be the chief literary influence in the nation is hard to assess, but in the portrait in *Literary Friends and Acquaintance* his antipathy to Lowell comes through distinctly. To some degree, obviously, Howells reacted to Lowell in the way a bright disciple always does toward his master—in Lowell's case a master subject to a comparatively mild yet definite megalomania. We may guess how many long afternoons lengthened to tedium while Howells sat in the study at Elmwood quietly enduring the tyranny of a Lowell monologue. But on such afternoons it was not so much the discourse which held dominion over Howells; it was the symbolic quality of the Elmwood room and the dominating New England literary presence who sat in it year after year. Off and on for over twenty-five years Howells came to Lowell's study, there to sit facing an inkstand he, in his youthful eagerness to please, had brought to Lowell from Italy. Fashioned of bronze in the likeness of a lobster, it's back opened to disclose an inkwell and a sandbox. Howells suspected that Lowell thought it gauche. From the moment of the gift, Lowell kept it on his desk unused, "the inkpot . . . as dry as the sandbox."[36] It was an unintentional symbol of a relationship in which Howells, doomed

35 Howells to Norton, November 12, 1868, in Mildred Howells, *Life in Letters of Howells*, I, 135–36.
36 Hiatt and Cady (eds.), *Literary Friends and Acquaintance*, 179.

113

by origin to be an outsider, was always to feel slightly patronized. In *Literary Friends and Acquaintance*, Howells recalls the session after he gave the inkstand to Lowell:

> He lighted his pipe, and from the depths of his easy chair, invited my shy youth to all the ease it was capable of in his presence. It was not much; I loved him, and he gave me reason to think that he was fond of me, but in Lowell I was always conscious of an older and closer and stricter civilization than my own, an unbroken tradition, a more authoritative status. His democracy was more of the head and mine more of the heart, and his denied the equality which mine affirmed. But his nature was so noble and his reason so tolerant that whenever in our long acquaintance I found it well to come to open rebellion, as I more than once did, he admitted my right of insurrection, and never resented the outbreak. I disliked to differ with him, and perhaps he subtly felt this so much that he would not dislike me for doing it. He even suffered being taxed with inconsistency, and where he saw that he had not been quite just, he would take punishment for his error, with a contrition that was sometimes humorous and always touching.[37]

From such a subtle domination—a tyranny of respect and affection imposed by the deep desire, deep as childhood yearning, to belong to Lowell's world—Howells never escaped. Not even when Lowell's fastidiousness turned into downright snobbery did Howells' democracy of the heart, his disposition to the commonality of man, cause him genuinely to revolt against Lowell. Only in one notable instance in *Literary Friends and Acquaintance* is his reaction to Lowell marked. This occurs in a passage dealing with the influence upon Lowell of his service in England as the American minister to the Court of St. James:

> He could never have been anything but American, if he had tried, and he certainly never tried; but he certainly did not return to the outward simplicities of his life as I first knew it. There was

37 *Ibid.*, 180.

no more round-hat-and-sack-coat business for him; he wore a frock and a high hat, and whatever else was rather like London than Cambridge; I do not know but drab gaiters sometimes added to the effect of a gentleman of the old school which he now produced upon the witness. Some fastidiousnesses showed themselves in him, which were not so surprising. He complained of the American lower class manner; the conductor and cabman would be kind to you but they would not be respectful, and he could not see the fun of this in the old way. Early in our acquaintance he rather stupified me by saying, "I like you because you don't put your hands on me," and I heard of his consenting to some sort of reception in those last years, "Yes, if they won't shake hands."[38]

In context the devastating effect of this description, we must note, is undercut by the way Howells introduces it: "He could never have been anything but American, if he had tried, and he certainly never tried. . . ."

Nothing in *Literary Friends and Acquaintance* seriously disturbs its character as a dream of American literary order—an order achieved in a moment of cultural fruition, to be cherished in the memory but hardly of living consequence. How ells' account of the literary life in Boston is the story of a past,

[38] *Ibid.*, 207–208. Hiatt and Cady in examining a set of proofs of "Studies of Lowell" in the Charles E. Feinberg Collection discovered two significant passages omitted from the published versions of this essay. In one, in the fourth section, Howells recalls an "almost suffocating shyness in my early visits to Lowell, which was perhaps not wholly displeasing to him." He says that he would arrive at Lowell's door "with my heart beating in my throat." In the other omitted passage, at the end of the fifth section, Howells remarks about Lowell's inability at times "to keep himself from wounding," particularly in his encounters with women, and recalls a scene when he presented a feminine admirer to Lowell, only to witness Lowell receive "her compliment in freezing silence." Howells says that Lowell "had moments when the toryism of his nerves, as he called it, was too much for his head and his heart. . . ." In one other omission of interest respecting Howell's attitude toward the Bostonians, Howells recalls Lowell's advice to him about getting along with James T. Fields. "He said that I would find Fields easy to work with, though he advised me to work in entire subordination, even (I remember his word) to écraser myself if necessary." (Hiatt and Cady [eds.], *Literary Friends and Acquaintance*, 358–60).

which barely impinges upon the present and the future. His tolerant skepticism of the Boston literary vocation, even his occasional intolerances, serve Howells' motive to idealize it. Ironically, the book by contrast illuminates the anxiety and uncertainty he expresses about American literary life in the novels.

Howells' autobiographical impulse in the 1890s had strong motivation in the deeply personal question of the identity of his vocation. After a lifetime as a writer, he found himself still searching for the meaning of his career. What does it mean to be a writer in America? The meaning he found in Boston, one which fulfilled his youthful dream of vocation, he could never fully accept nor wholly reject.

IV

In the last years of his life, Howells, who remained to the end mentally vigorous, continued to struggle against the subversion of his faith in transcendent literary order. Four important documents of his latter-day struggle are the address he gave at his seventy-fifth birthday dinner, his memoir of Mark Twain, a short story entitled "The Critical Bookstore," and two unfinished essays on Henry James.

The address Howells gave before President Taft and the assemblage of dignitaries at the dinner—his "farrago of *spropositi*" to be followed by his waking nightmare of the dinner's unfitness—is an uncritical and, on the surface, magisterial survey, of the promise—no, almost of the achievement—of Howells' ideal American dominion of the High Average. Recalling his acquaintance with the American authors of the nineteenth century (Howells had known nearly all of them personally), he states that younger American writers differ from the older ones because of a "new conditioning" under "the light of equality." Writers, Howells observes, now escape the patrician bonds of New England to constitute an authentic "American authorship." And, he says, sounding like a literary Rotarian— "Indianapolis is, as Boston was, a city in which books are held dear and the art of them is prized above any other." [39]

Howells traces the service of equality by American poetry, the American novel, and the American drama; but he finds its greatest attainment in American humor. "In that American humor which within the half-century of my observation developed itself in such proportion as almost to dwarf any other growth of our air," he comments, "there was one humorist who when he died might well have given us the sense of Shakespearian loss, though we are not yet aware of a Shakespearian gain." He refers to Mark Twain, whose "soul . . . which divined and uttered the inmost and most immanent American mood has passed again so lastingly into the American consciousness that it will remain the inspiration of that high or higher average in humor which once again is the distinctively American thing." Howells says it has been "glory enough" in itself "to have lived in the same time and in the same land with the man whose name must always embody American humor to human remembrance." [40] In his idealization of American humor and of Mark Twain, Howells comes close to saying that Mark Twain is the High Average become incarnate: "But hereafter that high or higher average of our humor must always be generous and magnanimous; in its broadest clowning, its wildest grotesquery, it can never forget to be kind, to be kind to the whole world that the touch of nature makes kin, but especially kind to those that the world and the world's law seem to have kept strangers to the rest of the family." [41]

39 "Literary Recollections" (April, 1912), 553.
40 *Ibid.*, 557.
41 *Ibid.*

117

As for his own career, Howells at the conclusion of his address expresses his "poignant regret for having said so little about myself in my survey of things." He exclaims: "What has been my own influence on that time, in that land, I should like so much to say. . . ." He repeats, "so much to say!"[42] In the simple poetry of the repetition we divine not modesty, perhaps, but a lament for a massive career which lay under the censure of his self-condemnation. Howells could believe that Mark Twain had fulfilled the covenant between the American writer and American democracy when he himself could not keep the faith. Mark Twain became the embodiment of his conscience.

The reference to those estranged from society by "the world's law" recalls the conclusion of what may well be the most poignant document in Howells' lengthy record of American literary life, the famous memoir he called *My Mark Twain*, which he had published following Mark Twain's death in 1910. Howells speaks of the impossibility of conveying "the intensity with which he [Mark Twain] pierced to the heart of life, and the breadth of vision with which he compassed the whole world, and tried for the reason of things, and then left trying." And he recalls his final meeting with his friend which had been especially gratifying because with "kind, clear judicial sense" Mark Twain had "explained and justified the labor-unions as the sole present help of the weak against the strong."[43] There follows the well-known last paragraph of Howells' memoir; it is one of the great moments in American literary memorializing, with its graphic apotheosis of Mark Twain through his identification with, in Howells' conception,

42 *Ibid.*
43 Hiatt and Cady (eds.), *Literary Friends and Acquaintance*, 322. The memoir of Mark Twain was added by Howells to the Library Edition of *Literary Friends and Acquaintance* (1910).

the martyred god of American equalitarian democracy, Abraham Lincoln:

> I looked a moment at the face I knew so well; and it was patient with the patience I had so often seen in it; something of puzzle, a great silent dignity, an assent to what must be, from the depths of a nature whose tragical seriousness broke in the laughter which the unwise took for the whole of him. Emerson, Longfellow, Lowell, Holmes—I knew them all and all the rest of our sages, poets, seers, critics, humorists; they were like one another and like other literary men; but Clemens was sole, incomparable, the Lincoln of our literature.[44]

Lifted up in Howells' imagination into the Democratic Mystery, Mark Twain approximates closely the figure of the writer prophesied in "The Man of Letters as a Man of Business." He knew the "mystic bond" between the writer and "the toilers of the shop and field." He is the harbinger of the time in the future when the literary artist may "see in the flesh the accomplishment of that human equality of which the instinct has been divinely planted in the human soul."

In a way, in his exaltation of American humor and of Mark Twain, Howells was taking a final stab at Boston, where many years before at another birthday dinner, the one given in 1877 by the *Atlantic Monthly* for John Greenleaf Whittier, Mark Twain had burlesqued the vocation of the man of letters in America as this was represented by Emerson, Longfellow, and Holmes, and other Brahmins. For Howells, who served as toastmaster of the Whittier dinner, it was such an intensely painful occasion that, as Henry Nash Smith has conclusively shown, he made Mark Twain's gaucherie into a public scandal when it actually was not one and then forever kept it twisting like a cold knife in his memory—"the amazing

44 *Ibid.*

mistake, the bewildering blunder, the cruel catastrophe."[45] The way Howells held onto his sense of guilt over "that hideous mistake of poor Clemens" in defiance of all reason (for he had no power to have prevented Mark Twain from telling his burlesque story) is evidence of how strongly he was attached to Boston and at the same time how resentful of it.

Howells, we conclude, was unable to follow either the ideal of the transcendent institutionalism of letters or the ideal of the transcendent egalitarianism of letters without feeling guilty. He had, in short, the conscience of the idealist and the perception and feeling of the existentialist. He never became firmly one or the other, never being any more a solid realist than a determined idealist. In his case the ideal is invalid not so much because reality demonstrably and substantially refutes it as because it does not do so. In the Howells novel, George W. Carrington suggests, reality is as deceptive as idealism, confirming appearance, not substance. Something like the same situation occurs in Howells' response to the meaning of the literary life in America. Moved by his cultural environment, and in a negative sense by his lack of intellectual sophistication, to accept and reverence the idealistic mode of literary community, Howells found no adequate counter to his rebellion against this mode in an opposing realistic mode. Taunted in his heart by the secret, remorseless knowledge of the unreality of the ideal and the unreality (the insubstantiality) of reality, he lived with his long inner treason to the literary vocation—unwilling, uncertain, to a considerable extent unconscious, but nonetheless agonizing.

That the existential mood grew stronger in his feeling about the literary vocation in his last years is indicated by the short

45 *Ibid.*, 295. See Henry Nash Smith, *Mark Twain: The Development of a Writer* (Cambridge, Mass., 1962), 98–100.

story "The Critical Bookstore," which was published the year after the birthday dinner.[46] Slight on the surface, it is a story of substance. Altogether, it is probably Howells' bleakest look at the literary situation in America.

The setting is New York City, where Frederick Erlcort, a literary intellectual of dilettantish cast—who has long held the notion "that there might be a censorship of taste and conscience in literary matters strictly affiliated with the retail commerce in books"—sets up a bookstore offering for sale only books selected by himself as being worth reading.[47] His final decision to do this is made after he has discovered that the one thing a great modern department store refuses to take back when it does not meet the expectations of the purchaser is a book. With the help of an artist friend, Margaret Green, a charming "elderly girl," he makes an old shop among the quaint buildings on Sixth Avenue into a bookstore of "refined hospitality" and calls it "The Critical Bookstore." At Margaret's suggestion little mirrors are affixed to the shelves, so that " 'when a woman looks up and sees herself with a book in her hand, she will feel so intellectual she will never put it down.' " [48] Erlcort's patronage turns out, in fact, to be mostly feminine; it is especially strong among members of a woman's society called The Intellectual Club. Making selections to sell in the Critical Bookstore by an arduous process of discrimination involving volunteer judges but ultimately resting in his own judgment, Erlcort succeeds, at least among a host of women, in selling the books he himself deems worthy of being read. When a slump in business sets in after Christmas, he decides at the suggestion of Margaret, who has always been

46 *Harper's Monthly*, CXXVII (August, 1913), 431–42.
47 *Ibid.*, 431.
48 *Ibid.*, 434.

skeptical of the wisdom of Erlcort's enterprise and of her part in it (she takes down " 'those immoral mirrors,' " as she calls them), to offer the leading magazines (the "Big Four") as well as his self-chosen books in his store. " 'You could keep them with a good conscience, and you could sell them without reading,' " she advises her friend; " 'they're always good.' " [49] When some of his customers nonetheless complain about the nature of various selections in the magazines, Erlcort forthwith carries his principle of critical discrimination into downright censorship. He begins to blot out portions of the magazines with a roller blacked with printer's ink "the way the Russian censorship blots out seditious literature before it lets it go to the public." [50] Finding him so engaged one day, Margaret tells him he is going crazy. Suddenly, in a moment of self-realization, Erlcort admits doubts about his motives. " 'I've sometimes thought so: crazy with conceit and vanity and arrogance. Who am I that I should set up for a critical bookstore-keeper? What is the Republic of Letters, anyway? A vast, benevolent, generous democracy, where one may have what one likes, or a cold oligarchy where he is compelled to take what is good for him? Is it a restricted citizenship, with a minority representation, or is it universal suffrage?' " He has, he says, made a mistake: " 'Literature is the whole world; it is the expression of the gross, the fatuous, and the foolish, and it is the pleasure of the gross, the fatuous, and the foolish, as well as the expression and the pleasure of the wise, the fine, the elect. Let the multitude have their truck, their rubbish, their rot; it may not be the truck, the rubbish, the rot that it would be to us, or may slowly and by natural selection become to certain of them. But let there be no artificial selection, no survival of the fittest by main force—the force of the spectator,

49 *Ibid.*, 440–41.
50 *Ibid.*, 442.

who thinks he knows better than the creator of the ugly and the beautiful, the fair and foul, the evil and good.' " [51]

Margaret is lost in admiration. If only the Intellectual Club could hear Erlcort now! And what will he do with his Critical Bookstore? Erlcort declares he has made arrangements to sell it to the author of a bestseller, an uninhibited, merry fellow who scoots around in an electric runabout. " 'He's got an idea,' " Erlcort tells Margaret. " 'He's going to keep it a critical bookstore, but the criticism is to be made by universal suffrage and the will of the majority. The latest books will be put to a vote; and the one getting the greatest number of votes will be the first offered for sale, and the author will receive a free passage to Europe by the southern route.' " [52] Whereupon Erlcort asks Margaret to marry him and take a trip to Europe by the southern route.

In "The Critical Bookstore" the satire is double-edged. The story ridicules not only the idea of prescriptive literary order in the depiction of the absurd genteel authoritarianism of Erlcort, it also in effect ridicules the notion of an ideal equalitarian community of letters. Erlcort's democratic vision of literature as the whole world is confused. Rubbish in letters is not rubbish to everyone, Erlcort says. Then again, he says, perhaps some process of natural selection operates to reduce the spread of bad books. In either case the sacramental concept of the High Average is denied in Erlcort's impassioned acceptance of literary democracy. The denial is complete when Erlcort announces how his successor will fulfill the critical function of the bookstore. Books will be selected for sale by crude majority vote with a voyage to Europe as a prize to the author of the book winning the most votes. In embracing democratic commercialism, Erlcort not only gives up literature

51 *Ibid.*
52 *Ibid.*

123

as a vocation, he denies that it can be one. Presided over by a clever bestselling novelist, it becomes a game of chance not subject even to the possibility of "a larger law."

V

In spite of the pessimism of "The Critical Bookstore," Howells ultimately had a commitment to the idea of the sacred character of the vocation of the American man of letters too compelling to be betrayed by existential impulse. The most powerful motive of this commitment remained fundamentally his experience of New England. This is well illustrated in his three late ventures into memorializing: his essay on Charles Eliot Norton and the two essays on Henry James left uncompleted when he died.

Like the memoirs of New England men of letters in *Literary Friends and Acquaintance*, the remarkable essay on Norton is as much about Howells as it is about its subject. In it he makes still another attempt to compose a valedictory to the literary culture of nineteenth-century New England and at the same time to define his own relationship to it. He creates a masterly portrait of Norton, worthy to stand beside the one of Lowell, as a perfect figure of resolution and finality in the deep autumn of the New England patrician culture: a member by birth "of the Brahaminical caste . . . marked equally by the Calvinistic severity . . . and by the Unitarian lenity," but no longer able to believe even a Christianity limited to the four gospels; a lover of beauty who "imagined himself Hellenic" and yet was "in his heart Hebraic," so that "when he thought he was supremely loving beauty, he was supremely loving duty"; a critic of American culture whose "working hypothesis" seemed to many to be a "dialectic of despair," and yet, Howells says, in his "practical wisdom was radiant with welcome for any good thing said or done."[53] The "last of the great group of Cambridge men," Norton was

the youngest of the group; the years counted ten between him and Lowell, and twenty between him and Longfellow; after they were gone he grew into contemporaneity with them, and then into a seniority which could judge them paternally, as the present can always judge the past. But in him, beyond all other men, the child was father of the man, and his relation to his fellow citizens of that ideal commonwealth was filial as well as paternal. I think that his sense was not only the just measure of it, but was also the perception of its significance in contrast with the vast, sprawling, unwieldy Republic of Letters and Laws which has replaced it.[54]

To a marked degree, Howells knew, Norton's perception of the contrast between the "ideal" New England literary order of the past and the national literary disorder of the present was in truth despairing; and that in his sense of despair Norton, more than Lowell, was drawn toward congenial refuge in English culture. It is noteworthy that Howells, as in the less difficult case of Lowell, insists on Norton's Americanness against his Anglophilia. Howells recalls making a challenge to Norton after Norton had been praising England: " 'Well, after all, if you could change, would you rather have been an Englishman than an American?' " According to Howells, Norton replied: " 'No, if I could choose I would rather have been an American,' as if here was still the world's home of Opportunity."[55] What Norton despised in American life, Howells says, was not the common but the vulgar.

He was very inflexible concerning principles; he would have none of my doctrine that in equality was the only social righteous-

---

53 "Charles Eliot Norton: A Reminiscence," *North American Review*, CXCVIII (December, 1913), 836, 841, 846.
54 *Ibid.*, 846.
55 *Ibid.*, 843.

ness and happiness; and I felt that in his relentless difference from me he was putting a strain on his unbroken kindness, which was all it could bear. I am not saying or meaning that he was an aristocrat, or was so much 'a Tory in his nerves' as Lowell. With less profession of democracy he was quite as near a realization of it; he could not so much as Lowell love the common or commoner man for his humorous originality, but he could as truly fellowship what was good in him. I cannot claim that I knew him very well on this side, but it appeared to me that there was light on it in the passionate regret with which a very common man spoke of his death to me on the sunny bench in the Public Garden the day after he died. I wish I could remember the words; they implied and revealed a brotherly relation to such men which I had not imagined of him.[56]

In his remembrance of Norton, Howells maintains the controlling point of view in *Literary Friends and Acquaintance;* observing of the New England men of letters, "it was my good fortune to be among them as I could never be of them," and, again, "I was the latest if least citizen of the world which he [Norton] had known for great and beautiful, that wonderful Cambridge world of poets and scholars which many centuries will not see again." [57] Still, in a subtle way his point of view has altered. In his struggle against his existential vision of American literary life suggested in "The Critical Bookstore," Howells has come not only to idealize the nineteenth-century New England literary world more than ever, but to make it more clearly a sacramental mystery—one all the more powerful because he could never be of the essence of the mystery like those born in it but had experienced its grace with the pure perception of the pilgrim.

Faith in the relationship of this mystery to the American literary vocation illuminates the two essays on Henry James which Howells, in extreme pain and dying, endeavored vainly

56 *Ibid.,* 843.
57 *Ibid.,* 845, 846.

to complete in 1920. Both pursue the basic argument that James was "American to his heart's core to the day of his death." One (Howells was doing it for "The Easy Chair" in *Harper's*) is devoted specifically to the charge of treason lodged against James when during World War II he renounced his American citizenship to become a British subject. The long years James had been in England, Howells contends, had not corrupted his incorruptible Americanism. "Through all the perversities of his expatriation, and his adoration of foreign conditions and forms," James had remained "an inalienably American soul." Treated rudely and harshly by America, James never changed in his allegiance to his native country. James, Howells asserts, "may have made the English think him English; he may have made himself think so; but he was never anything but American." [58]

The basis of such an essentially metaphysical assertion is developed in the other essay on James which Howells was writing at the time of his death. Called "The American James," it locates the source of James's inalienable American identity in the sacramental literary life of New England. In "The American James" Howells recalls the literary suppers when he and his wife and James sat down to table in the quiet Cambridge evenings; James, because of chronic indigestion, foregoing even the simple meal before them for a crumb of biscuit ordered by doctor's prescription and carried in his pocket. After table they would sit and talk. Whatever of strangeness James brought to Cambridge by reason of his earlier life in France disappeared as they "joined in an American present around the airtight stove which no doubt over heated our little parlor." [59] Since Howells did not live to finish "The American James," we can only conjecture how it might have turned out.

58 Mildred Howells, *Life in Letters of Howells*, II, 394–95.
59 *Ibid.*, 398.

But the conjecture can be made with assurance on the basis of what he did write. Out of his recollection of the years he spent with James in the early afternoon of the New England world, he would distill James into an American authorial essence—into a pure idea of the American literary vocation. Howells would have made James's vocation into an idea so pristine that it could not have been betrayed, not even by James himself. And is this not what Howells had for so long wanted somehow to establish about his own career? That he had lived for a calling he had never deceived, because the vocation to American authorship he had long ago assumed when the New England hands were laid on him was transcendently undeceivable? Could James have read what Howells was trying almost with his last breath to write about him, James, out of his refined sense of irony, might have said that his old friend had a complex and most exquisitely American sense of treason.

128

II

THE SOUTHERN QUEST
FOR LITERARY AUTHORITY

It was just as hard to attain to salvation in the 13th century as it is now (perhaps harder), although the results in literature were grander and more coherent. That was largely because salvation was common, not personal.

Allen Tate (1929)

The general intelligence is the intelligence of the man of letters. . . . His critical responsibility is . . . what it has always been—the recreation and the application of literary standards, which in order to be effectively literary, must be more than literary. His task is to preserve the integrity, the purity, and the reality of language wherever and for whatever purpose its may be used. He must approach his task through the letter—the letter of the poem, the letter of the politician's speech, the letter of the law; for the use of the letter is in the long run our one indispensable test of the actuality of our experience.

Allen Tate (1952)

The South, however defeated it may feel in other areas, has triumphantly taken possession of the American literary world. . . . [The Southern] body of writers is unrivalled in a single region of America since the New England transcendentalists in the second third of the last century made Concord, Massachusetts, for a while the intellectual capital of the nation.

C. Hugh Holman (1960)

✑ Poe's Vision of His Ideal Magazine

"Touching 'The Stylus':—this is the one great purpose of my literary life."

Poe to Philip Pendleton Cooke, 1846

LET US begin somewhat indirectly by looking at two pictures. One is the daguerreotype portrait made of Edgar Poe during the autumn of 1848 at Providence, Rhode Island, where on November 15, 1848—if we can believe his own testimony—Poe attempted to end his life by taking an overdose of laudanum. In this representation Poe appears as a rather seedy gentleman, with his right hand thrust pretentiously into an untidy waistcoat. His haunted, unfocused stare indicates he may have been at the time drunk, doped, or as mad as Roderick Usher.[1] To say how many persons have been influenced in their conception of Poe by this daguerreotype would be impossible. But does it not resemble the dominant image in our memory of Poe more than any other depictions we have of him? It is the image of the demon-ridden "man apart" that Poe's bohemian followers have made into a holy comforter of the alienated— the Poe to whom Baudelaire prayed and Mallarmé celebrated in his sonnet "Le Tombeau D'Edgar Poe." Looked at in this way the Providence picture symbolizes a dominant conviction

---

1 The history of the portraits and daguerreotypes of Poe is, like almost anything connected with his biography, complicated and uncertain. See Amanda Allan Poe, "Portraits and Daguerreotypes of Edgar Allan Poe," in *Facts about Poe* (Charlottesville, 1926), pp. 35–38. The Providence representation of Poe is reproduced in Hervey Allen, *Israfel: The Life and Times of Edgar Allan Poe* (New York, 1934).

131

of the modern literary temper, the isolation or alienation of the literary artist.

The other picture is a group one which first came to my attention when I saw it used to illustrate a review of a collection of letters written by various authors to James T. Fields, successor to James Russell Lowell as editor of the *Atlantic Monthly.* Done by the American portrait painter, Thomas Hicks, it is a stylized representation of a group of American writers whose careers spanned the first half of the nineteenth century. To us today, although probably not to people of the time, it seems grossly indiscriminate. Present are not only Cooper, Bryant, Irving, Emerson, Lowell, Holmes, Poe, Hawthorne, and Whittier (Thoreau, Melville, and Whitman are to our present-day eyes conspicuously absent), but also Mrs. Sedgwick, Mrs. Welby, Mrs. Sigourney, Mrs. Southworth, and others of that subliterary "d—d mob of scribbling women" Hawthorne complained about. The general idea of the painting, however, is more interesting than the writers who appear in it. The setting is a classic rotunda. On either side are steps mounting to a spacious platform surrounded by columns crowned by Ionic capitals. In the center of this are three larger-than-life statues, representing, as I interpret them, Petrarch, the restorer of the classics, Homer (the central figure), the great original poet, and Dante, the hero of the vernacular tongues. In Olympian tranquillity these literary immortals gaze out over the American authors, who are depicted in various seated and standing postures on the flanking staircases and in the area below. Thus the writers of the new nation are viewed in an idealized relationship to the Western literary tradition, and the painting manages to suggest, if somewhat ludicrously, the continuity, authority, fraternity, and not least, the public importance and dignity of the literary life.[2] We see in Hicks's work a symbol-

2 See *New York Herald Tribune Book Review,* January 31, 1954,

ism belonging more to another age than to ours. It is a representation of literature as a constitutive and central order of civilization.

Poe, many of us would be inclined to say, does not belong in this second picture at all; the image of him is so strongly that of the alienated artist. Interestingly enough, Thomas Hicks seems to have had some reservations about Poe's place in the American literary world. He depicts him wearing a black cloak, standing with his back to Hawthorne and gazing downward, withdrawn and introverted.[3] Is Hicks merely presenting the romantic poet of popular legend, or is he trying to convey a sense of a special relationship Poe had to the world of letters, to say in effect that Poe was both of the public dominion of writers and not of it?

This question, I think, suggests the basis for a study of Poe's whole literary career as a quest for an authoritative literary community in America. The intense desire Poe felt to impose order on the disorder of America's literary situation is a discernible motive in his *Marginalia*, in his *Literati of New York City*, and in his proposed broader work, *Literary America*. I should like here only to offer some speculative and somewhat random notes on what I take to be always the center of Poe's vision of literary order: his ideal magazine, the establishment of which he declared to be "the one great purpose of my literary life." I shall be concerned with the ideal goals of the never-to-be-realized magazine Poe first named the *Penn Magazine* and later called the *Stylus* and with the context of these goals in the American literary environment.

To be sure, I must readily admit that Poe had strong, purely personal motives in his drive to found his own magazine. He

---

p. 1, for a reproduction of an engraving by A. H. Ritchie after the painting by Thomas Hicks.

3 Hawthorne is depicted in the same pose, but I do not wish to become involved with Hawthorne's case in this discussion.

knew the literary situation of his day not as a dispassionate observer but as a desperately involved participant; and the aspirations which prompted his literary adventures were always intensely self-serving. In fact, the story of his ideal magazine can be read simply as the history of a frustrated private ambition that persisted beyond the possibility of realization into illusion and finally perhaps into hallucination. But granting that it may be uncommonly difficult to distinguish between an ideal and a selfish aim in Poe, we hardly do justice to the acknowledged scope and complexity of Poe's career if we fail to seek the meaning of his fruitless endeavors to publish his own magazine under the aspect of a broader and more profound motive than that of an individual literary ambition. In our search we may discover that the *Penn* and the *Stylus* are more significant in American literary history as dream works than many periodicals are as actualities.

I

On the basis of documentary evidence it is impossible to say exactly when the story of Poe's ideal magazine began. Poe must have begun to think about having his own magazine in the earliest days of his literary career. And after he left his first editorial post with the *Southern Literary Messenger* in 1837, his ambition to establish and control a magazine undoubtedly acquired a central importance in his plans. The first definite mention of it occurs two years later, when we find him remarking to Philip Pendleton Cooke, "As soon as Fate allows I will have a Magazine of my own." [4] In a few more months he was boldly courting Fate by issuing in the Philadelphia *Saturday Courier* a "Prospectus of the Penn Magazine, a Monthly

4 Poe to Cooke, September 21, 1839, in John Ward Ostrom (ed.), *The Letters of Edgar Allan Poe* (Cambridge, Mass., 1948), I, 119. Hereinafter referred to as *Letters of Poe.*

Literary Journal, to be Edited and Published in the City of Philadelphia, By Edgar A. Poe." Because this is the chief document in the history of Poe's illusory magazine, I will quote from it at some length:

To those who remember the early days of the Southern periodical in question [the *Southern Literary Messenger*] it will be scarcely necessary to say that its main feature was a somewhat overdone causticity in its department of Critical Notices of new books. The Penn Magazine will retain this trait of severity in so much only as the calmest yet sternest sense of justice will permit. Some years since elapsed may have mellowed down the petulance without interfering with the rigor of the critic. Most surely they have not yet taught him to read through the medium of a publisher's will, nor convinced him that the interests of letters are unallied with the interests of truth. It shall be the first and chief purpose of the Magazine now proposed to become known as one where may be found at all times, and upon all subjects, an honest and a fearless opinion. It shall be a leading object to assert in precept, and to maintain in practice the rights, while in effect it demonstrates the advantages, of an absolutely independent criticism—a criticism self-sustained; guiding itself only by the purest rules of Art, analyzing and urging these rules as it applies them; holding itself aloof from all personal bias; acknowledging no fear save that of outraging the right, yielding no point either to the vanity of the author, or to the assumptions of antique prejudice, or to the involute and anonymous cant of the Quarterlies, or to the arrogance of those organized *cliques* which, hanging like nightmares upon American literature, manufacture, at the nod of our principal booksellers, a pseudo-public-opinion by wholesale. These are objects of which no man need be ashamed. They are purposes, moreover, whose novelty at least will give them interest. For assurance that I will fulfill them in the best spirit and to the very letter, I appeal with confidence to the many thousands of my friends, and especially of my Southern friends, who sustained me in the Messenger, where I had but a very partial opportunity of completing my own plans.

In respect to the other features of the Penn Magazine, a few words here will suffice. It will endeavour to support the general interests of the republic of letters, without reference to particular regions; regarding the world at large as the true audience of the author. Beyond the precincts of literature, properly so called, it will leave in better hands the task of instruction upon all matters of very grave moment. Its aim chiefly shall be to *please*; and this through means of versatility, originality, and pungency. It may be as well here to observe that nothing said in this Prospectus should be construed into a design of sullying the Magazine with any tincture of the buffoonery, scurrility, or profanity, which are the blemish of some of the most vigorous of the European prints. In all branches of the literary department, the best aid, from the highest and purest sources, is secured.[5]

Norman Foerster calls this prospectus—it has the ring of a manifesto—the best statement Poe made of his "ideal in criticism." But its chief significance, I conjecture, lies in the implications of the divided purposes Poe pledges his magazine to. In the first place, Poe declares his magazine will devote itself to "an absolutely independent criticism; a criticism self-sustained; guiding itself only by the purest rules of Art." In the second place, he asserts it will "support the general interests of the republic of letters, without reference to particular regions; regarding the world at large as the true audience of the author." If at first glance we do not see division between these intentions, in a closer study of Poe's prospectus we uncover a fundamental discrepancy. The implied image of the man of letters playing the role of arbiter in the world of letters is subordinated to a more strongly implied image, which is not that of a human arbiter at all but that of a "criticism self-sustained." We are reminded of Allen Tate's remark that no

5 The entire "Prospectus" is reprinted in Arthur Hobson Quinn, *Edgar Allan Poe: A Critical Biography* (New York, 1941), 306–308. It originally appeared in the Philadelphia *Saturday Courier*, X (June 13, 1840), 2.

136

writer in the United States, England, or France during the nineteenth century went so far in "his vision of dehumanized man" as Poe.[6] Tate is showing how Poe's view of the cosmic destiny of man in *Eureka* is an extension of his vision of the ordering of human existence through sheer mechanical sensation and will. Is his vision of literary order in the statement about the *Penn* likewise an extension of his vision of dehumanized man? As such can it be related to the total complex of motives which drove Poe to reject life in favor of death?

These questions go beyond my intention. I want simply to suggest that in his vision of bringing literary order to the literary situation in the United States, Poe creates an almost complete split between alienation and community. Essentially he posits two symbolic literary realms. There is, Poe fails to realize, no easy nor even necessary relation between his absolutely autonomous, depersonalized if not dehumanized, realm of Pure Art and the Republic of Letters—the traditional public dominion of letters. The sensibility controlling Poe's realm of Pure Art is not different in degree but different in kind from that governing the more generous conceptions of the literary republic. The two realms are discontinuous.

This does not exhaust the unresolved conflicts in Poe's vision of the function of his ideal magazine. A further complication is introduced when we consider his inclination to accept the spirit and techniques of nineteenth-century journalism. This is implied in the prospectus of the *Penn* and emerges plainly in a series of almost identical letters Poe wrote to prominent American men of letters, including Washington Irving, John Pendleton Kennedy, Henry Wadsworth Longfellow, and Fitz-Greene Halleck, on behalf of the *Penn*. An extract from the letter to Irving will suffice for illustration:

6 Allen Tate, "Our Cousin, Mr. Poe," *Essays of Four Decades* (New York, 1970), 395.

I need not call you [*sic*] attention to the signs of the times in respect to Magazine literature. You will admit the tendency of the age in this direction. The brief, the terse, the condensed, and the easily circulated will take the place of the diffuse, the ponderous, and inaccessible. Even our Reviews are found too massive for the taste of the day—I do not mean for the taste of the merely uneducated, but also for that of the few. In the meantime the finest minds of Europe are beginning to lend their spirit to Magazines. In this country, unhappily, we have not any journal of the class, which either can afford to offer pecuniary inducement to the highest talent, or which would be, in all respects, a fitting vehicle for its thoughts. In the supply of this deficiency there would be a point gained; and the project of which I speak has originated in the hope of supplying it.[7]

In the *Marginalia* Poe makes the same point more explicitly:

The increase, within a few years, of the magazine literature, is by no means to be regarded as indicating what some critics would suppose it to indicate—a downward tendency in American taste or letters. It is but a sign of the times, an indication of an era in which men are forced upon the curt, the condensed, the well-digested in place of the voluminous—in a word, upon journalism in lieu of dissertation. We need now the light artillery rather than the peacemakers of the intellect. I will not be sure that men at present think more profoundly than half a century ago, but beyond question they think with more rapidity, with more skill, with more tact, with more of method and less of excrescence in the thought. Besides all this, they have a vast increase in the thinking material; they have more facts, more to think about. For this reason, they are disposed to put the greatest amount of thought in the smallest compass and disperse it with the utmost attainable rapidity. Hence the journalism of the age; hence, in especial, magazines.[8]

Apparently Poe, who liked to call himself a "magazinist," had glimpses of creating a literary dominion in America differ-

7 Poe to Irving, June 21, 1841, in *Letters of Poe*, I, 162.
8 James A. Harrison (ed.), *Complete Works of Edgar Allan Poe* (New York, 1902), XVI, 82.

ent from either the transcendent realm of Pure Art or the comprehensive Republic of Letters. Both of these assume leisure. Poe was drawn toward a pragmatic compromise with the dynamic "time spirit" of the New World, where the present threatened to overwhelm not only the past but the eternal as well. At least he was so drawn in certain moods. He would never have joined those who, like Cornelius Matthews and other "Young Americans," were seeking virtually to isolate American letters in the humming present.

II

If Poe's vision of directing and organizing American letters was divided, it was based on a central assumption: the necessity of literary order in America. His vain and torturous efforts for a decade to see his ideal magazine into print illustrate graphically the difficulties of realizing such an assumption in the literary environment in which he existed.

The date of the first issue of the *Penn* was supposed to be January, 1841. When this date came around, Poe announced publication would be delayed until March, 1841. By the end of this month he was writing to his friend Dr. J. E. Snodgrass: "The Penn, I hope, is only 'scotched, not killed.' It would have appeared under glorious auspices, and with capital at command, in March, as advertised, but for the unexpected bank suspensions." [9] Whether Poe's explanation of the failure of the *Penn* to materialize is correct or not is uncertain. Likely he considerably exaggerated the extent of the backing he had for it. In any event he suspended his project while he went back to editing a magazine for someone else, in this case the owner of *Graham's Magazine*.

In January, 1843, after changing the punning title of his proposed magazine from the *Penn Magazine* to a deeply sym-

9 Poe to Snodgrass, April 1, 1841, in *Letters of Poe*, I, 157.

bolic one, the *Stylus*, Poe entered into an agreement with Thomas C. Clarke, a Philadelphia publisher, to bring out his long-delayed periodical. A prospectus was issued and Poe sketched a title page for the *Stylus*. This second prospectus which Poe wrote for his ideal magazine places a greater emphasis on the Republic of Letters than the first one:

> The new journal will endeavor to be at the same time more varied and more unique;—more vigorous, more pungent, more original, more individual, and more independent. It will discuss not only the Belles-Lettres, but, very thoroughly, the Fine Arts, with the Drama; and, more in brief, will give, each month, a Retrospect of our Political History. It will enlist the loftiest talent, but employ it not always in the loftiest—at least not always in the most pompous or Puritanical way. It will aim at affording a fair and not dishonorable field for the true intellect of the land, without reference to the mere prestige of celebrated names. It will support the general interests of the Republic of Letters, and insist upon regarding the world at large as the sole proper audience for the author. It will resist the dictation of Foreign Reviews. It will eschew the stilted dulness of our own Quarterlies, and while it may, if necessary, be no less learned, will deem it wiser to be less anonymous and difficult to be more dishonest, than they.[10]

The general tone of this is about the same as that in the earlier prospectus, but, we note, Poe announces a greater variety of subject matter for the *Stylus* and does not insist upon the limitation to "literature, properly so called." Consequently, he is more in harmony with the traditional image of the Republic of Letters. Yet Poe concludes the second prospectus, as he commenced the first one, with a firm appeal to "a criticism self-sustained; guiding itself only by the purest rules of Art." Thus the second statement reveals more sharply

[10] Quinn, *Poe*, 376. The "Prospectus" appeared originally in the Philadelphia *Saturday Museum*, March 4, 1843, p. 3.

than the first the split in Poe's literary sensibility between alienation and community.[11]

Again fate blocked Poe's magazine. It did not come into being even briefly, as had James Russell Lowell's *Pioneer* the same year. By June, 1843—the *Stylus* was scheduled to make its debut in July, 1843—Poe was writing to Lowell: "I received your poem, which you undervalue, and which I think truly beautiful—as, in fact, I do all you have ever written—but alas! my Magazine scheme has exploded—or, at least, I have been deprived, through the imbecility, or rather through the idiocy of my partner, of all means of prosecuting it for the present. Under better auspices I may resume it next year."[12]

Although feasible "auspices" did not appear again, Poe never ceased to seek them. The next year he wrote to Lowell, who had cooled toward him, suggesting "that the elite of our men of letters should combine secretly" and each subscribe two hundred dollars to establish a monthly literary magazine. No reply came from Lowell. Poe figured some more and wrote to Lowell again a few months later, urging that twelve "influ-

11 Poe, however, did not abandon the idea of "literature proper." The title page he designed for the *Stylus* describes it as a "Monthly Journal of Literature Proper, the Fine Arts and the Drama." (The title page is reproduced in Allen, *Israfel*, 589.) We must recognize with Robert D. Jacobs (*Poe: Journalist and Critic* [Baton Rouge, 1969], 249) that, as in all the magazine prospectuses of the time, the element of "tall talk," is present in Poe's presentation of the aims of his ideal magazine. (In this connection also see Frank Luther Mott, *A History of American Magazines* [New York, 1930], 340–41.) I must gratefully acknowledge that Mr. Jacobs has kindly called my attention to the distinct possibility that Poe's apparent broadening of the scope of his proposed magazine was influenced by his desire to secure the backing of the administration of President Tyler. He eagerly sought articles from Robert (Rob) Tyler, the son of the President, and from Judge Abel Parker Upshur, evidently being willing to allow Whig politics to intrude to some extent upon the literary character of the *Stylus*. See Poe to Frederick W. Thomas, February 3, 1842, February 25, 1843, in *Letters of Poe*, I, 191–93, 223–25.

12 Poe to Lowell, June 20, 1843, in *Letters of Poe*, I, 234.

ential men of letters" form a corporation to get out a magazine, each one buying a share of stock at one hundred dollars.
The results would be salutary: "The work should be printed
in the very best manner, and should address the aristocracy of
talent. We might safely give, for $5, a pamphlet of 128 pp. and,
with the support of the variety of our personal influence, we
might easily extend the circulation to 20,000—giving $100,000.
The expenses would not exceed $40,000—if indeed they
reached 20,000 when the work should be fairly established.
Thus there would be $60,000 to be divided among 12—$5000
per an:apiece." [13] The plan was not entirely fantastic; but Poe
by now was beginning to sound like the tracts being issued by
the multifarious tribe of American schemers and promoters.

Month after month, year after year went by. The possibility
of Poe's magazine became more illusory, the dream more
grandiose. In 1846 we find him, following the demise of the
Broadway Journal, with which he had been associated, writing
to Sarah J. Hale: "The B. Journal had fulfilled its destiny—
which was a matter of no great moment. I have never regarded
it as more than a temporary adjunct to other designs. I am now
busy making arrangements for the establishment of a Magazine which offers a wide field for literary ambition. Professor
Chas. Anthon has agreed to take charge for me of a Department of Criticism on Scholastic Letters. His name will be
announced. I shall have, also, a Berlin and a Parisian corre-
spondent—both of eminence. The first No. may not appear
until Jan. 1847." [14] Professor Charles Anthon, an acquaintance
of Poe, might conceivably have agreed to work with him. The
Berlin and Paris correspondents were almost surely fictitious,
though they may have been real enough to Poe. January, 1847,
came and went. The *Stylus* did not appear.

13 *Ibid.*, October 28, 1844, I, 265–66.
14 Poe to Sarah J. Hale, January 16, 1846, *ibid.*, II, 312.

Finally, in the last year of his life, Poe once again saw "auspices," this time in the person of one Edward H. N. Patterson of the semifrontier community of Oquawka, or Yellow Banks, located on the Mississippi River in Illinois. Here the story becomes ludicrous, for Patterson, it seems, wanted to publish the *Stylus* in Oquawka, an impractical, not to say ironic, location from which to consider "the general interests of the Republic of Letters," not to mention those of Pure Art. But Poe seemingly was willing to try St. Louis, if he could not get Patterson to agree to New York, and, still confident that he could muster twenty thousand subscribers for the magazine, told Patterson that he proposed

to take a tour through the principal States—especially West & South—visiting the small towns more particularly than the large ones—lecturing as I went, to pay expenses—and staying sufficiently long in each place to interest my personal friends (old College & West Point acquaintances scattered all over the land) in the success of the enterprize. By these means, I would guarantee, in 3 months (or 4) to get 1000 subs. in advance, with their signatures—nearly all pledged to pay on the issue of the first number. Under such circumstances, success would be certain. I have now about 200 names pledged to support me whenever I venture on the undertaking—which perhaps you are aware I have long had in contemplation—only awaiting a secure opportunity.[15]

Negotiations continued with Patterson, who held out for a three-dollar instead of a five-dollar magazine. "The mere idea of a '$3 Magazine' would suggest namby-pamby-ism & frivolity," Poe exclaimed indignantly to his potential sponsor, who agreed to the five-dollar magazine if Poe could raise a thousand subscribers. An arrangement was made for Poe to meet Patterson in St. Louis during October, 1849. Poe planned, lectured to try to raise money to get to St. Louis, al-

---

15 Poe to Patterson, April 30 (?), 1849, *ibid.*, II, 440.

though he likely never really meant to go, and continued to drink. He died in Baltimore on October 7, 1849. A few months before he had written to George W. Eveleth: "Touching 'The Stylus' . . . I am awaiting the *best opportunity* for its issue—and if by waiting until the day of judgment I perceive still increasing chances of ultimate success, why until the day of judgment I will patiently wait." [16]

III

If through some combination of fortuitous circumstances, Poe had actually managed to publish the *Stylus* for a decade, would it have influenced the course of American literary history to any extent? Would it have become, as Poe dreamed it would, an organizing locus, an intellectual capital, of American letters? Even if we grant Poe more temperamental stability as an editor and man of letters than he seems to have had, this is doubtful. His ambiguous juxtaposition of the Republic of Letters, the realm of Pure Art, and the realm of Journalism in his vision of literary order is symptomatic of an intangible yet definite truth: in the culture in which Poe lived the literary mind of the Western tradition was undergoing a radical process of displacement.

At this point it will be helpful to recall an important comment on Poe in 1845 by the youthful James Russell Lowell. At the time Lowell had not met Poe personally (an experience that later proved not to be a very happy one) but had corresponded with him, and had been gratified to publish him in Lowell's short-lived magazine, *The Pioneer*, and had acquired a familiarity with Poe's desire for the achievement of an ordering criticism in America. Being, as he puts it, "naturally led into some remarks on American criticism by the subject of

16 *Ibid.*, August 7, 1844, p. 457, also 458; Poe to Eveleth, June 26, 1849, *ibid.*, 449–50.

the present sketch," Lowell prefaces his essay on Poe with a graphic, and hyperbolic, depiction of the chaotic provinciality of the American literary condition.

The situation of American literature is anomalous. It has no center, or, if it have, it is like that of the sphere of Hermes. It is divided into many systems, each revolving around its several suns and often presenting to the rest only the faint glimmer of a milk-and-watery way. Our capital city, unlike London or Paris, is not a great central heart, from which life and vigor radiate to the extremities, but resembles more an isolated umbilicus, stuck down as near as may be to the center of the land, and seeming rather to tell a legend of former usefulness than to serve any present need. Boston, New York, Philadelphia, each has its literature almost more distinct than those of the different dialects of Germany; and the Young Queen of the West [Cincinnati] has also one of her own, of which some articulate rumor barely has reached us dwellers by the Atlantic. Meanwhile, a great babble is kept up concerning a national literature, and the country, having delivered itself of the ugly likeness of a paint-bedaubed, filthy savage, smilingly dandles the rag baby upon her maternal knee, as if it were veritable flesh and blood, and would grow timely to bone and sinew.[17]

To resolve the American literary chaos Lowell appeals in consonance with Poe for the centering of American literature in criticism. "But, before we have an American literature, we must have an American criticism." The nation must "seek a profound, original, and aesthetic criticism." In contrast to the "'American Macaulays,' the faint echoes of defunct originalities" who impede rather than further this search, Lowell holds up Poe as "the most discriminating, philosophical, and fearless" American critic. And he asserts: "Had Mr. Poe had the control of a magazine of his own, in which to display his critical abilities, he would have been as autocratic, ere this, in

17 James Russell Lowell, "Edgar Allan Poe," in Edmund Wilson (ed.), *The Shock of Recognition: The Development of Literature in the United States Recorded by the Men Who Made It* (New York, 1943), 5.

America, as Professor Wilson has been in England; and his criticisms, we are sure, would have been far more profound and philosophical than those of the Scotsman." [18] Now Lowell's image of Poe as an American version of John Wilson, the noted critic of *Blackwood's Magazine*—which was published in Edinburgh, a literary center virtually as important to Americans in the nineteenth century as London—must have been gratifying to Poe. Clearly in his criticism he essayed the role of the literary autocrat or dictator in the tradition descending through such figures as Ben Jonson, John Dryden, Alexander Pope, and Samuel Johnson. This role was an integral part of the tradition of the Republic of Letters. Yet it may well be that Lowell's interpretation of Poe's role, or potential role, in remedying the disorder of American letters reflects Lowell's image of himself rather than an accurate image of Poe. When we examine Lowell's diagnosis of the anomalous situation of American literature, we discover, I would suggest, that it is a kind of ironic inversion of the ideal of literary community in the Western tradition. A calculated exaggeration of the decentralized state of American literary existence, its inspiration lies in what it pointedly, if implicitly, repudiates, namely, Lowell's deep feeling for the literary centripetalism of the Boston-Cambridge world. Lowell, in other words, had been reared in an environment in which the centrality of literary expression—of the assimilating discipline of letters—in civilization was present as an assumption to a greater degree than it was elsewhere in the new nation. To the literati whom it accepted, and who accepted it, the Boston-Cambridge environment afforded a sense of belonging to the public place of letters—to a place of men of letters, of literary societies, of magazines and publishers. Existing for the nation in its own self-image as the "American Athens," the New England city

18 *Ibid.*, 7.

of letters represented to Americans generally the realm of letters. As Van Wyck Brooks says somewhere, the Boston writers
became spokesmen of the universal Republic of Letters, at the
same time making their own part of it known in the consciousness of the world. In picturing an America in which the literary
mind has no city of letters to which to look, Lowell hardly
rejects his fundamental attachment to the Boston center. Employing the strategy of irony, he makes an association between
an ordering critical authority in America and the traditional
representation of literary order. He conceives Poe as America's
most promising figure in this representation.

Lowell never grasped the sense of alienation in Poe, the
sense that (among other motives in a complex of motives)
urged upon Poe the conception of "a criticism self-sustained."
Lowell never experienced the sense Poe had of the dislocation
of the literary mind in America. This mind—British and, overall, European in its origins, the inheritor of the whole Western
humanist literary corpus and sensibility—instinctively sought
a place of letters to gravitate toward, a London or a Paris. Like
Lowell, Poe shared deeply in the traditional literary mind. All
educated Americans shared in it, or in the longing for it. It was
there, you might say, in the books. But the possibility of an
American coming into a tangible community with it, outside
of going to Britain or the Continent, was virtually restricted
to those who were accepted into the realm of Boston.

Since Poe was unable to accept Boston any more than Boston was able to accept him, the possibility of his identifying
himself with the only coherent literary culture in American
was nullified early in his career. Instead, he participated constantly in the life of America's Grub Street. He lived more
intimately in the America where literature was product and
commodity than any other major writer of the nineteenth century. As a literary contributor, editor, and critic, he was par-

147

ticularly involved in the New York version of Grub Street, probably in the mid-nineteenth century the grubbiest Grub Street in the world, a "literary butcher shop" Perry Miller calls it.[19] In this world of quackery, Poe was fully exposed to the loss in America of the ideal of the civilizational power of the literary order.

This loss which could neither be resolved nor transcended seems of major significance to Poe's vision of the *Stylus*. The story of Poe's ideal magazine documents the history of a lost cause, that of bringing literary order to the anomalous condition of American letters. To be sure, the condition was not unique to America. In his *Journals* for 1835, Emerson records without comment the following remark Samuel Taylor Coleridge had put down in his *Table Talk* in 1832: "Three silent revolutions in England; first, when the professions fell from the Church; 2. when literature fell from the professions; 3. when the press fell from literature."[20] By the time Coleridge made this shrewd observation, the first silent revolution, the falling off of the professions from the Church, had long been accomplished. But the other two, we can see from our perspective today, were not yet complete. The second, the falling off of literature from the professions, was well underway; the third, the falling off of the press from literature, was just getting underway. Both the second and third revolutions were still being held in restraint in the British and European worlds by the perpetuation of a strong sensibility of literary and intellectual community which had informed them for centuries—the sensibility which found its symbolic expression in the concept of the Republic of Letters. But in America the forces antitheti-

19 Perry Miller, *The Raven and the Whale: The War of Words and Wits in the Era of Poe and Melville* (New York, 1956), 7.

20 Edward Waldo Emerson and Waldo Emerson Forbes (eds.), *The Journals of Ralph Waldo Emerson* (Boston and New York, 1909–14), III, 494.

cal to the humanistic idealism of literary order operated with comparatively little check. In the thin cultural atmosphere of a democratic, capitalistic, and increasingly technological society—one going all out for the steamboat, the railroad, and the six-shooter—Coleridge's second and third revolutions worked more nakedly and more rapidly than in the Old World. Clearly Poe's career illustrates the falling off of the press from literature. In pursuing his dream of the *Stylus*, Poe was attempting to reverse history. But then this has been the attempt of the whole modern effort in "literature proper."

149

⤳ Mark Twain:
The Pathos of Regeneration

> "What are the Great United States for, sir," pursued the General, "if not for the regeneration of man? But it is nat'ral in you to make such an enquerry, for you come from England and you do not know my country."
>
> *Charles Dickens,* Martin Chuzzlewit

> "The angels are wholly pure and sinless, for they do not know right from wrong, and all the actions of such are blameless."
>
> *Mark Twain, "That Day in Eden"*

WHEN IT first made its appearance, Maxwell Geismar's big, ill-organized, clumsily written—but in its way important—book* was taken by academic students of Mark Twain (like Brom Weber, writing in the *Saturday Review* for February 27, 1971) to be a more advanced stage of an "ugly political attack" Geismar had launched against "American literary intellectuals" a few years before in his *Henry James and the Jacobites* (1963). *Mark Twain: An American Prophet* is, Weber declared, "an apocalyptic New Left tract, replete with all the fever, anti-intellectualism, psychosocial fantasy, and messianism considered requisite nowadays to explode a reader's mind and send him off on a rampage." Now that the initial period of reaction to Geismar's treatise on the significance of Mark Twain is well past, we may wonder if it was not marked, to use the jargon of the age, by an overreaction. An impression of Geismar's book may have been created that its character under more

---

* Maxwell Geismar, *Mark Twain: An American Prophet* (Boston, 1970).

150

deliberate consideration does not substantiate. Some passages in *Mark Twain: An American Prophet*, notably those indicting American critics and scholars for in effect being tools of the official American culture of the Cold War times and suppressing some of Mark Twain's writings, do smoke a little (although not as acridly as several of the voluminous passages Geismar quotes from Mark Twain, for example, those on the Spanish-American War). But that Geismar's work could trigger an explosion even in a mind with a short, fast fuse is in fact unlikely. Its militancy is erratic and unsustained, and the messianic note is struck sporadically and unconvincingly. The temper of the book is almost constantly cooled by Geismar's longing evocation of a far distant American past. If Geismar often insists on Mark Twain's relevance to the present moment, he tends to appeal not to the image of a Mark Twain standing alongside a Mark Rudd, but to the image of an aged prophet speaking to us out of the depths of the Old Republic about an American pastoral destiny that could never be.

It is this tendency, more than any call to action, that relates Geismar's book to the politics of the New Left—that is, to the New Left's association of a hatred of present-day society with a love for the aborted promise of pre-industrial America. This association, romantic and wistful, possibly encourages violent apocalyptic deeds. Blowing up symbols of the Establishment may be an expression of a fierce nostalgia for agrarian simplicity and the restoration of the fabled American innocence. But protestors' symbolic expressions of the wish for the destruction of the industrial-technological culture are more frequently passive. They include back-to-nature gestures, such as wearing Indian garb, or taking up residence in a rural hippie commune and subsisting on organic squash and hemp. In this respect we see in the amorphous New Left movement a resurgence of the pastoralism that has been consistently expressed in American literature since the Republic began its existence coincidentally with the commencement of the machine age. And this in the face of its ideal conception of itself according to the large and golden doctrine of a new redemption of man through his relationship with "the fresh, green breast of the New World." The poignant phrase occurs in Nick Carraway's vision of the meaning of the Republic at the end of *The Great Gatsby*. Carraway experiences the dead Gatsby's need, or compulsion, to believe that America is a redemption from the past and that the American is in fact a novel moral being, for whom the light is always green. Carraway has discovered the difficulty of believing this; and he has discovered the greater difficulty of not believing it. In his story about Gatsby, as told by Nick Carraway, Fitzgerald dramatizes the primary shaping force in the American existence: the complex psychic struggle of faith and doubt concerning the American condition as regenerate.

This was the conflict that was first specifically experienced in the American consciousness as it sought to become distinct from its origins in the European imagination of America. What is the essence of the American identity? St. Jean de Crèvecoeur put the question into its classic form in 1782. "What, then, is the American, this new man?" he asked in his *Letters from an American Farmer*. The question assumed the answer: the American is a novel creation. But the question ironically echoed a desire for the renewal of the original condition of man. This was a desire rooted deeply in the whole Western mythic imagination, pagan and Christian. Did the possibility exist that man could somehow find his way back to a prehistorical earthly paradise? By the time of the American Revolution the assumption of the American as either a new or a renewed version of man—having formerly seemed incredible—had become, it seemed, quite credible. The notion that the part of the New World which had become the New Republic, the Great Experiment, constituted either a new creation or a re-creation came to dominate the opposing conviction of man's innate depravity and historical inability. It became the major premise of the condition of life in the new nation. The American must believe it, and, regardless of logic or fact, he must seek to reconcile theology and history to the vision of American regeneration. Under pressure of this necessity, the American consciousness has typically been characterized by a pathos of regeneration. Charles Dickens strikingly recognized the ironic power of the American pathos in the satirical episode in *Martin Chuzzlewit* about General Cyrus Choke, U.S.M., and the Eden Land Corporation, developers of the Valley of Eden. By the second and third generations of the Republic, the pathos of regeneration had, it appeared to a shrewd if not dispassionate observer, become the heart of Americanism.

As with all powerful, commonplace cultural motives, this phenomenon remained unexamined by critical analysis until it began to lose its assimilating force. As it has weakened in the twentieth century, especially since the end of the Second World War, American literary critics—Henry Nash Smith, R. W. B. Lewis, Charles L. Sanford, Leo Marx, and others—have made a determined effort to define it, and in doing so, to place it in historical perspective, saying with Leslie Fiedler, "an end to innocence." But it is difficult to transcend a fundamental premise of the very culture the critic lives and writes in even though it may be declining in power. The assumption of the redemptive ethos by American critics colors their analysis of it and makes impossible a clear-cut repudiation of it. The critical inquiry into the regenerative nature of American existence as this is expressed in the American literary imagination is itself an expression of the motive it seeks to explain.

In the inquiry, Henry James and Mark Twain are central subjects, their works centering so clearly in the drama of the response to the question, What is America for if not for the regeneration of man? If we can generalize about a highly involved argument, it would appear that James comes off better in the critical discussion than Mark Twain. Critics find that he came to grips with the nature of American innocence in relation to the evil of the European establishment and eventually developed a mature understanding of the "complex fate" of being an American. But critics have tended to discover that for various reasons—including family tragedies, business failures, and a recognition of the ever increasing corruption of the national life—Mark Twain quit trying to believe in any possible regeneracy of man; and, consequently, in his later career he became a frustrated, embittered, and despairing writer, seeking to write off the "damned human race." Geismar contends that this is a spurious judgment. His struggle to prove why it is, and to project what he conceives to be the true image of Mark Twain, notably of the older Mark Twain, reflects directly Geismar's total involvement in the pathos of regeneration. Geismar, to be sure, occupies a virtually singular position among American critics in yet standing, or attempting to stand, on the doctrine of regeneration. This nativistic doctrine is, it would seem, fundamentally more significant to Geismar, a socialist, than Marxism. It is a received truth on which he has sought in a series of books on American literature to base a radical American literary and cultural politics. In his studies Geismar has made a strong effort to define and defend a tradition of American regeneracy; and he has, one might say, named a succession of regeneracy, consisting most prominently of Emerson, Whitman, Mark Twain, and Dreiser. Critics who doubt the efficacy of the tradition of regeneracy are in Geismar's outlook traitors to true Americanism and conspirators

154

against it. Thus when the "New Criticism" (a term Geismar uses very loosely) reached its apogee in the oppressive 1950s, the American academic literati became entangled in a gross betrayal of their literary heritage. They did so, Geismar says in his book on Henry James, because of their deference to "a formidable body of 'received opinion' about good writers and bad writers." Accepting a canon of "good writers" which emphasized James, Eliot, and Pound, they declared anyone who spoke against the canon a fool. "Well, then," Geismar exclaims, "thank God . . . for the Fools; who in ancient culture were viewed as emissaries of the Lord."

This zealous spirit informs the whole of *Henry James and the Jacobites*. Looked at in the light of the progression of his critical studies, Geismar's bumptious, evangelical negating of Henry James and his disciples represents a preparation for his depiction of the genuine American writer in Mark Twain; it is a necessary putting down of the false idol and of heretical doctrines. It is a study of a fallen American writer and a condemnation of the equally fallen critics who have falsely celebrated his fall as a victory. It is, in short, a study in American literary degeneracy.

In his version of the fall of the American writer as exemplified in the case of James, Geismar harps on the power of three evils to be seen at work in James's career. One is nostalgia for Europe. James early drank of the poisonous cup of nostalgia and was so overcome that he never sought an antidote. James also lacked the capacity to resist another insidious evil, finance capitalism, although he never realized to what extent he was the novelist of the Veblenian leisure class. There was, however, a deeper evil at work in the case of James, one more difficult to describe, and Geismar does not succeed in doing so with precision. He indicates it as something like a fall into the self, the absorption in the image of the self, captivation by

155

narcissism. James, that is, presents us with an early instance of the modern writer who suffers from solipsism. Afraid of the unconscious, he developed into "pure manners and pure consciousness." He became an inhabitant of an unreal world; the vision of life in his novels is "all vision," containing only "illusion, or enchantment, or magic." It is a vision alien to life and a perversion of art as the representation of reality. As an artist James was thus a pretender. "Indeed perhaps never in the history of humane letters had a novelist done so much with so little content as Henry James ... the Dark Prince of the American leisure class, the self-made orphan of international culture, the romantic historian of the *ancien régime*, the European inheritor, the absolute esthete, the prime autocrat of contemporary (and contrived) art." So Geismar summarizes the degeneracy of Henry James. As an artist James was the pretender and all his followers are Jacobites.

The premise underlying Geismar's attack on James and his admirers is that civilization is the fall of man. As an epigraph to *Henry James and the Jacobites*, Geismar quotes from *To the End of Thought*, the work of a disciple of Otto Rank, Jack Jones: "In the course of evolutionary development, the profound tragedy in the human heritage (and the base of culture) was the loss of the Plenary-Pagan state—which became the trauma of 'original sin' in the dialectical manner of human thought, and from whence came the Edenite memory and dream. And it appears to become increasingly clear that this was also, inevitably, the moment of an evolutionary self-destruction. For how can modern man understand the 'meaning of life,' when the meaning is steadily decreasing with each 'advance' of modern civilization." This is the anti-Freudian (and anti-Aristotelian) argument, associated with the Rankian school, which holds that civilization, an order achieved by the repression of the instinctual basis of life, has not fulfilled the

meaning of life but has increasingly in its "progress" estranged
man from the source of meaning. The "pleasure principle" of
the "Plenary-Pagan state" was so suppressed in James that he
became "quite morbid or even deeply neurotic" and developed
a "pathological complex of anxiety, fear and aversion." Geismar suggests that underneath the aspect of James's pretense,
his guise as a "romantic medievalist," he was a "literary monster." He represents the full and terrible consequences of the
subversion of the "Edenite memory and dream" by modern
civilization.

The subversion of Eden is a theme that is more explicit in
Geismar's study of Mark Twain than in his work on James.
Employing the Rank-Jones thesis as the scientific rationale of
the myth of American regeneracy, Geismar holds that in spite
of all the contrary opinions of Mark Twain scholars (and these
become associated in his mind with the false notions of the
New Critics, the pretenders), Mark Twain did not in the
final phase of his career experience frustration and despair, nor
did he decline in his literary capacity. Although sorrow was
abundant in the fifteen years before his death, it was in these
years that he came into full possession of his genius and his art.

There is no question [Geismar states] that the decade of the
nineties was one of trauma and disaster in Mark Twain's life, finan-
cially and domestically. It did indeed *appear* to split his life in two;
and life for him would never be the same again. Yet he emerged on
the other side of the chasm bloody and beaten in spirit, but un-
conquered—unconquerable. He had added a dimension of tragic
experience to his unique sense of the general comedy of living.
The memory of the Garden entails the knowledge of the Fall.

Geismar continues:

The life of his imagination would take on more complex, darker
hues of emotion; his own judgment of his social period and country become sharper and brilliantly prophetic; in the first decade of
the twentieth century he wrote one of his greatest books, *The*

157

Autobiography of Mark Twain—one of the great books of our literature. In the last half of his life, indeed, Sam Clemens produced some of his best writing—much of it newly released to the public eye—and the whole thesis of his being a childhood writer destroyed by the pressures of maturity falls to the ground. In terms of a broad cultural psychology, rather, he was a writer who carried his edenic vision of life to the very end; and it was precisely that vision, embedded in his deepest spirit, untouchable, uncorruptible, which created his whole remarkable description of our human pilgrimage undertaken amidst so much laughter and so many tears.

As Geismar interprets the crisis of Mark Twain's later life, it was the crucible in which he underwent testing and purification, the refining and strengthening of his vision and his mission. But not until 1897, according to Geismar, did Mark Twain manage to define for himself "the essential underlying conflict of all his work": the opposition "between primary nature and civilization." He accomplished this in what most Mark Twain critics consider to be an incidental and inferior book, *Following the Equator.*

In elevating this work to prominence in the Mark Twain canon, Geismar—as he does in elevating the *Autobiography* to a still higher place—relies on his conception that in his truest literary being Mark Twain "was not a novelist or a fiction writer at all." He "was a poet-prophet on the model of Walt Whitman even more than that of Melville." He was "the prophet and conscience of his country at the end of the Old Republic." Intensifying his conception of Mark Twain as a poet, Geismar declares that he was "a true folk bard" of the Old Republic. In this connection Geismar goes so far as to make the astounding declaration that—in contrast to the twentieth-century "expatriate" literature—genuine "American literature was as a whole until 1910 a folk art." But in making much of Mark Twain as a folk bard, Geismar hardly insists that he is a poet nearly anonymous. Like all modern poets, he is preeminently a self; but unlike most of them, he did not suffer from a locked-in ego. "It takes a bard, a large and various talent," Geismar explains, "to talk about himself and without tedium since he is in fact talking about the world with which he is inextricably and pantheistically joined at the very moment he is so separate and original as an individual voice." Another way to put this is to say that Mark Twain is the embodiment of "the cultural concept of the double soul." In him the "pagan-plenary and primitive man [is] conjoined with the moral-historical-social vision which is clearly the result of civilizational repression." His range of awareness, so to speak, comprehends existence before the fall and after the fall. And this awareness is the range of his art. Mark Twain agreed with Freud, Geismar comments, in his "harsh dictum that all civilization is developed at the price of human repression." But "art and the artist . . . as Otto Rank perceived, and as Sam Clemens intuitively knew, are based on the edenic pleasure principle always conjoined, always in conflict with man's 'statutes.' "

Placing such an emphasis on Mark Twain's intuition of the edenic principle reduces the complex motivation of the perplexed, confused, disturbed—the historical and actual—Mark Twain to a mystical and murky emotionalism. The knotty question of Mark Twain's attitude toward slavery and the Negro is referred to his "natural affinity with the black slave." The "real fascination of *Pudd'nhead Wilson,* its true meaning which was perhaps unknown to the artist who wrote it," is that "Sam Clemens was the first and only writer, among all the early [American] ones, to rush into the 'ambush' of blackness and dusky nature, to embrace it with all his soul, and hence to reenrich his whole life with it." Such an uncritical declaration represents a kind of forced literary integration which removes Mark Twain from an historical relation to the "peculiar institution." It amounts, to be sure, to an ahistorical strategy; for it eliminates, whether deliberately or not, the need to deal with the awkward problem of Mark Twain's connection with the South and slavery as a part of the story of the Old Republic.

In elaborating his notion of Mark Twain as a bardic artist and prophet, Geismar—although he does not seem to be fully aware of doing so—sets forth a vision of American history in which the old Republic is Eden. It expressed a wish to be free from history. History proving to be too powerful to allow the new Republic to become a state of pastoral permanence, the Garden was corrupted by the intrusion of civilization in the form of modern capitalism and industrialism; and the fall of man was repeated in the rise of the "American Empire." In his role in this representation of American history, Mark Twain did not, as the fallen critics say, succumb to the corruption of the second fall but was victor over it. He was victorious not only over the personal tragedies of his life but over the dispossession of the Old Republic by the Empire. In his spirit the Eden that had been America entered upon an inviolate existence. If Mark Twain is viewed as a prophet, he is logically the prophet of a second American regeneration.

Still, Geismar's interpretation of Mark Twain's victory over civilization is divided. He sees a process of suffering on Mark Twain's part: his personal experience of "all those civilizational discontents which he . . . felt so vividly and personally at the center of his being." Following the logic of this insight, he proposes that Mark Twain effected through his art a resolution or catharsis of his suffering. He is a tragic figure, closer to the Freudian than to the Rankian emphasis. But Geismar simultaneously maintains his dominant bent toward the Rankian analysis. The source of Mark Twain's victory is to be found in the "untouched spring of pagan, plenary, and edenic innocence" located in his innermost being. This is to say, in a pure relationship with nature. The divided interpretation suggests a considerable uncertainty in Geismar's mind about the ultimate significance of the triumph over civilization he so confidently claims for Mark Twain. If Mark Twain is looked upon as finally a tragic figure, he is not in any very convincing sense a figure of regeneration. If he is finally seen as a child of nature, he is placed outside any experience of regeneration. In the last part of *Mark Twain: An American Prophet*, Geismar attempts to reconcile the "catharsis" and "pagan-plenary" interpretations of Mark Twain's later career—to bring into harmony the idea that Mark Twain's later writings are a purgation of all his despair and the idea that they are a demonstration of the pleasure principle. The result is an interesting confusion, out of which more or less clearly emerges still another concept of the old Mark Twain. (It is one Geismar suggests early in the game, when he remarks: "For Clemens . . . in his best moments completely dissipated the whole psychological syndrome of 'guilt-anxiety-shame-and-self-punishment' which might apply to ordinary mortals.") Geismar finds, as anyone must, that Mark Twain has his best moments in his final works when he identifies himself with the transcendent figure of Satan, seeking a point of view far beyond that of ordinary mortals.

Of Adam and Eve, who also appear prominently in the latter-day writings, Geismar says that they constitute "a study in the primary narcissism which betokens the unconscious pleasure in the functioning of the animal organism, and as Mark Twain's true ancestors delight in their innocent fleshly grace" before "they receive unknowingly the first blow of civilization: clothes." But Mark Twain's primary identification is not with Adam and Eve, it is with Satan. Geismar works hard to relate the feeling Mark Twain has for Satan to the thesis of the repressed pagan-plenary soul. "Satan becomes not merely Twain's confidante in these later years," he says, "but in Jungian terms, say, the earlier-repressed but now reversed and dominant half of Twain's soul; and in Rankian terms, more accurately, the repressed primitive soul which took rightful power over the 'rational' social soul." Yet, we ask, is Mark Twain's fascination with Satan to be described like this? In Mark Twain's conception Satan is impeccably mannered and infinitely rational. He is, in fact, refined beyond all civilization, for he is possessed of the reason and imagination of the angels. He is at once completely innocent and completely knowing. The "crucial dark and mysterious Angel of human history," he has a total understanding of what the fall of man meant. It meant the introduction into the human being of the Moral Sense, the sense on which civilization is established. This obviously is not an understanding that wells up from the instinctual knowledge of the repressed primitive soul; and plainly Satan does not symbolize to Mark Twain the repressed primitive soul. Indeed—and it is a little startling to realize this—Mark Twain conceives the lost paradise of man not as an earthly and earthy state of existence in natural pleasure. It is an angelic state of being. Before Eve eats of the fruit of the tree of knowledge in "That Day in the Garden," Satan tells her:

> In your present estate you are in no possible way responsible for anything you do or say or think. It is impossible for you to do wrong, for you have no more notion of right or wrong than the other animals have. You and they can do only right; whatever you and they do is right and innocent. It is a divine estate, the loftiest and purest attainable in heaven and in earth. It is the angel gift. The angels are wholly pure and sinless, for they do not know right from wrong, and all the acts of such are blameless. No one can do wrong without knowing how to distinguish between right and wrong.

Geismar's assumption that this version of Eden is allied to the reassertion of the primal in Mark Twain and that it is simply a presentation of the "original, beneficent, natural harmony of animal existence" is more than doubtful. Satan is describing a "divine estate," one given as "an angel gift," the gift of an ineffable transcendence beyond nature and beyond civilization.

Mark Twain's enigmatic quest for transcendence receives its fullest expression in *The Mysterious Stranger*. Geismar devotes considerable space to this story, reading it as Mark Twain's great emotional catharsis. Mark Twain, who never attempted to deny the basic tragedy of life, discovers in *The Mysterious Stranger*, Geismar argues, the ultimate nature of tragedy in the cosmic indifference of the universe. But because of his "gay, pagan, pleasure-loving spirit," Mark Twain's "desperate nihilism" is transformed into "a comedy, a parody of evil." Belonging as much to man as to the Gods, laughter is catharsis and salvation. There is something to this argument; Geismar fails nonetheless to convince us that in *The Mysterious Stranger* Mark Twain truly resolves the pain of living in the capacity for laughter. We cannot fail to recognize that Mark Twain's relationship with the "Great Prankster," as Geismar calls Mark Twain's Satan, is in the interest of acquiring his angelic power. Geismar himself observes that if Satan can dispose of his fatal gifts at Marget's birthday party "with such equanimity," man could receive them "with equal and knowing equanimity." In doing so man can become liberated from his humanity—is this not the implication?

Geismar awkwardly avoids such a conclusion. To the end he persists in his efforts to yoke the disparate images he projects of Mark Twain, the bardic and the angelic. In summation, he comments:

But the plain fact is, as I hope the pages of this book illustrate, that Mark Twain not only survived and surmounted life's worst things, but in his later work far surpassed his earlier vision. It too is a celebration of life but with all its tragic depths; much more aware and complex than the rather simplistic innocence of Huck and Tom. The Fallen Angel in Mark Twain is still the supreme and satanic observer of the world; and all the better for his fall from that innocence he always cherished but never quite lost.

This evaluation, muted in contrast to some other summary evaluations Geismar has made along the way, is still fundamentally confused. It implies that Mark Twain underwent a "fortunate fall," though this is irreconcilable with his identity with the "satanic observer of the world." Geismar is moved always to try to interpret Mark Twain as essentially the regenerate American, one who preserved in his soul the essence of redemptive primal American innocence, the bard of the truth of his people. Even so, Geismar is drawn toward rendering the subject of his study as superior to moral categorizing. He sees what Mark Twain wanted to be, in other words, but he has to deny him his ambition. What Geismar hits on of first importance—in spite of his futile and tiresome attention to a consistent explanation of them—is the realization that in Mark Twain's later writings there is a sense of celebration. There is a kind of joy in them. It is, however, not the joy of life fulfilled but of the state of being transcended.

It may be a fundamental mistake to try to explain Mark Twain on the basis of his opposing a salvational primary nature to civilization. From the beginning of his writing career, he exhibits a skeptical attitude toward mankind's capacity for moral regeneration under any conditions. In spite of the poignant way he glimpses this possibility at times, he continually rejects any redeeming relation between man and nature. As Mark Twain sees him the human being's chief characteristic is his need to deceive himself about his own existence in general. Deception is the principle of existence; from the early

164

sketches about the good boy and the bad boy through *The Mysterious Stranger*, this is the theme. This is not suddenly to shift the ground of the present argument; it is to say that Mark Twain experienced fully the pathos of regeneration. He knew acutely the kind of suffering Americans go through because they believe that by virtue of being American they are regenerate, when at the same time they suspect that they are not reborn men and are, consciously or unconsciously, deceiving themselves. Not only this perhaps but suspect that they must as Americans deceive themselves about their doubt—that as Americans they are under a heavy obligation to believe that America is for the regeneracy of man. Mark Twain experienced the inner drama of American history as intensely as Melville. He felt the profound dubiety that lies at the very core of the experience of being an American: the Great Experiment may be the Great Deception (or the Great Confidence Game); Americans may have staked everything on a grand endeavor to deceive themselves as to the nature of man and history.

Whatever else it does, *The Mysterious Stranger* celebrates a liberation from the Great Deception. It is Mark Twain's ultimate response to the pathos of regeneration. Left in a fragmentary state by the author, it is not a complete response. But it indicates the logic of a decisive answer, which simply lies in realizing the nature of the motive of the deception. This is to be found in the rationalism of the Enlightenment. In his essay "The Angelic Imagination," Allen Tate speaks of the American Republic as "a society committed to the rationalism of Descartes and Locke by that eminent angel of the rationalistic Enlightenment, Thomas Jefferson." Accepting this drastic oversimplification of Jefferson with due caution, we can yet venture to establish a connection between Jefferson and Mark Twain's Satan. Jefferson was strongly attracted to the notion that man has the power in a new world to will his intellect to conceive his own regeneration in a new unity of spirit and nature. This Enlightenment conception of the American as a new man was a rationalistic defiance of all the limitations imposed on man by tradition and religion. America, as William Dean Howells said, is an idea; the American, he might have added, is a thought. After a lifetime of much doubt and vexation, Mark Twain, in *The Mysterious Stranger*, has, through the agency of Satan, a vision of the true logic of the American idea of man. He discovers the true and terrible freedom of the American Dream. Satan tells little Theodore: "It is true, that which I have revealed to you: there is no God, no universe, no human race, no earthly life, no heaven, no hell. It is all a Dream, a grotesque and foolish dream. Nothing exists but You. And You are but a *Thought*—a vagrant Thought, a useless Thought, a homeless Thought, wandering forlorn among the empty eternities!" In one of the several descriptive epithets he applies to Mark Twain, Geismar calls him "this demonic angel of an artist." This is more than an epithet; it is an insight. Save for Geismar's commitment to the pathos of regeneration, he might have made it central instead of incidental to his book. But the commitment carries its interest, and it is still ours, as it was still Mark Twain's even as he struggled to transcend it.

ᴇᔆ William Faulkner and the Fall of New World Man

THE SOURCE of William Faulkner's powerful vision of the American South, duly allowing for his innate genius, was fundamentally not the accident of birth which made him a Southerner but the accident of birth which made him a modern. Unlike Southerners of the last century and, unfortunately, many of this century, Faulkner knew that the history of American Southern culture is an integral part of the crisis of modern Western civilization. This crisis—which by now seems to have assumed total proportions—announced itself in one significant way in 1751, when Jean-Jacques Rousseau won a prize from the Academy of Dijon for his essay asserting that the arts and sciences have done more to corrupt than to aid human beings. Rousseau's attitude prophesied the aftermath of the Enlightenment, indicating that in the very midst of the century which coined the word "civilization" a profound discontent with civilization had begun to arise. From that time until the present the existence of this element of dissatisfaction has been a major characteristic of the literary and artistic expression of Western culture. Indeed Western literature may be said to have become modern only when this virulent discontent began to get into the central nervous systems of writers. "It seems to me," Lionel Trilling observes, "that the characteristic element of modern literature, or at least of the most highly developed modern literature, is the bitter line of hostility to civilization which runs through it."[1]

Why did a deep unhappiness with civilization become manifest at the moment when Voltaire thought that Europe, in spite of all its political and religious differences, had achieved intellectual unity; and when the French Encyclopedists believed that the advancement of human knowledge was going to create an almost perfect world? The least satisfactory answer is the oversimplified notion of "the rise of romanticism." Romanticism was only superficially a cause. Basically it was a symptom of a drastic historical displacement of the individual in relation to the world. This dislocation occurred, Hannah Arendt argues, when the ancient distinction between the "public realm" (the realm of the *polis* in Greece and of the *res publica* in Rome—the realm in which the individual person could be seen and heard and through his actions and words achieve a kind of permanence) and the "private realm" (the realm of the family—the undisclosed, impermanent area dominated by the sustenance of the physical life process) began to be reversed and finally more or less erased by developments anticipating the modern appearance of one great social realm. By the twentieth century, a utilitarian mass world dominated by abstract scientific and technological processes threatens to absorb the realms through which Western man has traditionally ordered his existence and maintained his world. "What makes mass society so difficult to bear," Professor Arendt points out, "is not the number of people involved, at least not primarily, but the fact that the world between them has lost its

1   Lionel Trilling, "On the Modern Element in Modern Literature," in William Phillips and Philip Rahv (eds.), *Partisan Review Anthology* (New York, 1962), 264.

power to gather them together, to relate and to separate them." [2]

As the traditional world was replaced by modern society, a typical response of the sensitive mind to the loss of order was "romantic individualism." This emphatic, introspective individualism found one motive in a longing to discover or to rediscover the primal, instinctual sources of life. If mankind could begin over again! The translation of this impulse into possibility was no more than a wishful hope in the congested European metropolis. But out on what Walter Prescott Webb calls "the great frontier," especially on that portion of it existing in what is now the continental United States, modern man could express his frustration with the civilized condition in an actual search for new ways of defining and ordering his existence to be developed out of a vitalizing new relationship between the individual and nature in a virgin wilderness.

Lewis Mumford has an interesting theory in this regard that, I think, can be adapted to the argument I am attempting to set forth here. According to this theory, Old World man began in the eighteenth century to try "to find a new way out from the repetitive impasses of 'civilization' by making a fresh start on a more primitive basis. This effort, imposed by the very need to survive in the raw American wilderness, brought modern man face to face with the ancient realities of paleolithic and neolithic culture, on which the life of the indigenous Indians was based: in the New World modern man turned to . . . pre-civilized existence . . . and lived on this older level with a new intensity, as a conscious *release* from civilization—though fortified both with many civilized skills and with infiltrations

---

[2] Hannah Arendt, *The Human Condition* (New York, 1959), 48. Cf. W. H. Auden, "The Poet & the City," *The Dyer's Hand and Other Essays* (New York, 1962), 80–81.

of . . . Christian morality."[3] But New World man had in a sense too many civilized skills, in particular his rapidly increasing mechanical ones. The opening of the New World, Mumford remarks, was accomplished with the help of many technological innovations—the navigation chart, the chronometer, the rifle, the railroad. In his desire to conquer the land, New World man destroyed the possibility of making a truly fresh beginning in mankind's social and moral history by allowing his mechanical side to take precedence over his romantic inclinations. He did not, in other words, effect a "synthesis of the romantic and utilitarian elements." He did not keep "alive the new values that he had experienced" in his contact with a virgin world. Instead "once he had conquered the wilderness he surrendered abjectly to the instruments that had made his conquest so swift—and his life so rootless. . . ." Mumford declares, "Properly interpreted . . . the rise and fall of New World man is a more significant drama than anyone has yet portrayed, though the pioneer himself was doubtless only partly aware of the significance of his actions and the implied goal of his efforts."[4]

I

One way to look at Faulkner's great saga about the South, it seems to me, is to examine the complex relation it bears to the drama of the abortive New World man.

In writing his stories Faulkner participated in this drama in the prophetic role which has characterized the literary artist during the final phase of the transition in Western civilization

---

3 Lewis Mumford, "The Golden Day Revisited," an introduction to the Beacon paperback edition of *The Golden Day: A Study in American Literature and Culture* (Boston, 1957), xx. *The Golden Day* was originally published in 1926.
4 *Ibid.*, xx–xxi.

from a traditional to a modern society. The setting of the Yoknapatawpha stories is the frontier South and this same South after the frontier passed away. Of all the frontiers that offered to Old World man the chance of a fresh start—the hope of a new relationship with nature—the territory of the American South was surely one of the most promising. It offered a beneficent climate, vast tracts of rich soil, an abundance of water, many forests, and a great variety of game. Here, if anywhere, the discontented Old World man might seek to bring the utilitarian and the romantic into a creative synthesis.

But this did not happen. The Southern frontier was early saddled with the anachronistic institution of chattel slavery. A chance to throw off this labor system at the end of the eighteenth century was lost when certain technological inventions made slavery indispensable to the rapid expansion of the South. First came the cotton gin, soon the steamboat, and then the railroad. Together slavery and technology began the task of destroying the vast wilderness world, and technology finished the job. Among many other things in his chronicles of Yoknapatawpha County, Faulkner tells us the story of this massive destruction and its consequences.

In telling the pre-Civil War portion of his saga, he emphasizes the damnation of slavery more than the damnation of technology. Still, more than once, both implicitly and explicitly he dramatizes the ironic relationship between the two. For example, we may consider a wonderfully suggestive scene in "Red Leaves," when Issetibbeha, the Indian chief, is discussing with his fellows what to do with a parcel of African slaves they have on their hands. Their discussion of "the Negro question" takes place while they are "squatting profoundly" beneath the gilded names above the doors of the staterooms of a steamboat. Long ago, Issetibbeha's father, the man called

Doom, had had his Negroes spend five months moving a deck house across the wilderness, after removing it from a steamboat which had run aground, so that he could make it his house. The Indians talk:

"We cannot eat them," one said.

"Why not?"

"There are too many of them."

Finally, they decide—as they meditate beside the relic of the white man's mercenary technological invasion of the woods—that they must do as the white men do. They must "raise more Negroes by clearing more land to make corn to feed them, then sell them. We will clear the land and plant it with food and raise Negroes and sell them to the white men for money." One asks:

"But what will we do with this money?"

They thought for a while.

"We will see."

The implications of this situation in "Red Leaves"—that is, the corruption of the paleolithic culture of the Indians—might be considered at some length. Let us here allow it to stand simply as a preface to a consideration of Faulkner's most profound treatment of the conquest of the wilderness by slavery and technology. This is to be found in the long version of "The Bear."

II

In this complicated and difficult story Isaac McCaslin comes closer than any of Faulkner's characters to realizing the idea of the development in the New World of a new version of man. Tutored by the old half Indian, half Negro, Sam Fathers, he enters into a relationship with the wilderness which clearly suggests Mumford's notion of modern man returning in the New World to a more primitive level of existence and living on this "older level with a new intensity, as a *conscious* release from civilization," although deriving support both from civilized skills and Christian morality.

Following his initiation into manhood when he kills his first deer and Sam Fathers ritualistically smears his face with the blood, Ike completes his induction into not only the skills but the mystique of the hunter when he first sees Old Ben, the great bear, who is a kind of primal god. To see the bear Ike has to divest himself, Sam Fathers tells him, of his gun—the gun being of course a prime symbol of civilized man's technological domination of the woods. "You will have to choose," Sam tells him. Ike makes his choice one morning before daylight and leaves the hunting camp without his gun and enters the forest. He takes with him nonetheless two major devices of modern civilization: a compass and a watch. After nine hours during which he goes far deeper into the wild country than he has ever gone before, he still has not seen Old Ben. And he thinks: "It was the watch and the compass. He was still tainted." "A child, alien and lost in the green and soaring gloom of the markless wilderness," Ike brings himself to relinquish "completely to it."

Having abandoned the watch and the compass and even a stick he has carried along for protection against the numerous snakes, the boy loses all sense of direction. But he does not panic. "He did . . . as Sam had coached and drilled him: made this next circle in the opposite direction and much larger, so that the pattern of the two of them would bisect his track somewhere. . . ." At the same moment he discovers the bush on which he had hung his compass and watch, he sees the fresh tracks of the bear. Then he sees the animal itself:

It did not emerge, appear: it was just there, immobile, fixed in the green and windless noon's hot dappling, not as big as he had dreamed it but as big as he had expected, bigger, dimensionless against the dappled obscurity, looking at him. Then it moved. It crossed the glade without haste, walking for an instant into the sun's full glare and out of it, and stopped again and looked back at him across one shoulder. Then it was gone. It didn't walk into the woods. It faded, sank back into the wilderness without motion as he had watched a fish, a huge old bass, sink back into the dark depths of its pool and vanish without even any movement of its fins.

Having thus "released" himself from civilization and having entered with proper respect and humility into a living relationship with the wilderness, Ike has achieved newness of life. He has won for himself the right to moral freedom. Now, we think, he can use his gun throughout a long career as a hunter in Yoknapatawpha County prudently and wisely. In his hands mechanical power will not destroy the great values of the human heart: "courage and honor and pride, and pity and love of justice and liberty." But is Ike the New World man truly redeemed from the impasses of civilization?

One distinguished student of modern literature, R. W. B. Lewis, attempts in an essay on "The Bear" to prove that Ike actually becomes something like a new man in a new world, that he is a figure of a modern salvation. In a long and arresting argument which I cannot reproduce in the limited space of this essay, Lewis contends that Ike is "the hero of the New World" and that in his "honorable long career" he "moves in a world of light—a light still meagre but definite; a new world in which values have been confirmed by being raised to a higher power; not the new world beyond the frontier—that is precisely what is transcended—but a world so perpetually new that Ike sometimes seems to be its only living inhabitant." Lewis carries the parallel between Jesus and McCaslin far enough to suggest that the Yoknapatawpha hunter is possibly a new incarnation, "a miracle of moral regeneration." [5]

This is hardly so. Although Ike voluntarily gives up his title to the property of his family because the land has been cursed by slavery, he is, I would agree with Robert D. Jacobs, in his total aspect "a pathetic figure, slightly comic, certainly ineffectual." He represents only the nostalgic possibility of modern man rising in the guise of New World man to a new and better moral condition. In reality New World man in his effort to follow Rousseauesque discontent into a new condition was creating another Fall of man and binding himself more securely by the fetters of society than ever before. In Faulkner's works Ike serves not, I believe, as a hero. He is a witness, the primary witness in Faulkner, to what Stephen Spender has described as the "Second Fall of Man." The English poet, commenting on theories of modern culture like Eliot's famous idea of a "dissociation of sensibility," says:

In all these theories there is perhaps concealed the idea of a Second Fall of Man in the industrial age. The operative cause of this Second Fall was the concept of individualism [in contrast, Spender apparently means, to the feudal concept of community], which led from the Renaissance onward, to the scientific era. Knowledge of science and industry here plays the role of eating of the tree of knowledge. The Second Fall is considered so much worse than the first one that Original Sin can be looked back on as the sign of man's comparative innocence, whilst it is precisely the loss of the sense of Original Sin which is the peculiar worse-than-damned condition of men in the period of exile which is the Second Fall. For the sense of Original Sin offers man the possibility of redemption whereas the loss of this sense condemns him to a life deprived of all moral significance. [6]

5   R. W. B. Lewis, "The Hero in the New World: William Faulkner's The Bear," in Charles Feidelson, Jr., and Paul Brodtkorb, Jr. (eds.), *Interpretations of American Literature* (New York, 1959), 348.

6   Stephen Spender, "What Modern Writers Forget," *Saturday Review*, XLV (January 20, 1962), 33.

175

When I say that Ike is Faulkner's chief witness to the Second Fall, I do not mean to suggest that he is a fully aware witness. I mean that through his perspective as a kind of moral philosopher he affords us an ironic and dramatic commentary on the Second Fall. About God's intention in revealing the New World to mankind Ike theorizes:

Dispossessed of Eden. Dispossessed of Canaan, and those who dispossessed him dispossessed him dispossessed, and the five hundred years of absentee landlords in the Roman bagnios, and the thousand years of wild men from the northern woods who dispossessed them and devoured their ravished substance ravished in turn again and then snarled in what you call the old world's worthless twilight over the world's gnawed bones, blasphemous in His name until He used a simple egg to discover to them a new world where a nation of people could be founded in humility and pity and sufferance and pride of one to another.

But the spiritual redemption of the New World was prevented by greed and pride. These sins inspired the effort to possess and to exploit the virgin land by means of chattel slavery, which is the subject of the fourth section of "The Bear," and by the ever-increasing use of the instruments invented by the technological-industrial revolution. More especially by the last. For—and I state what I think Faulkner implies—slavery was a curse, but a curse bears a moral significance rooted in man's original sinfulness. Technology masks greed and pride in the amorality of scientific and industrial "progress." It separates man from his sense of involvement both with his fellow man and with nature and dehumanizes him.

Do we not see this in the last section of "The Bear"? Did not Faulkner choose, among other reasons, to place the story of the eighteen-year-old Ike's return to the wilderness rather than that of the twenty-one-year-old Ike's meditation on slavery in the plantation commissary at the end of "The Bear" for the sake of emphasis? In any event in the final section—the time is

176

after the end of slavery—Ike sees with his own eyes the coming doom of the wilderness in the form of a new planing mill. He sees the mill already half completed, covering two or three acres of what had been untouched forest land. He sees "what looked like miles and miles of stacked steel rails red with the light bright rust of newness and of piled cross ties sharp with creosote, and wire corrals and feeding-troughs for two hundred mules at least and the tents for the men who drove them. . . ." This irrepressible attack on the wilderness had been preceded by the work of an insignificant little locomotive used for several years in a small logging operation:

> It had been harmless then. They would hear the passing log-train sometimes from the camp. . . . They would hear it going out, loaded . . . flinging its bitten laboring miniature puffing into the immemorial woodsface with frantic and bootless vainglory, empty and noisy and puerile, carrying to no destination or purpose sticks which left nowhere any scar or stump. . . . But it was different now. . . . It was as though the train (and not only the train but himself, not only his vision which had seen it and his memory which remembered it but his clothes too, as garments carry back into the clean edgeless blowing of air the lingering effluvium of a sick-room or of death) had brought with it into the doomed wilderness, even before the actual axe, the shadow and portent of the new mill not even finished yet and the rails and ties which were not even laid; and he knew now . . . why Major de Spain had not come back, and that after this time he himself, who had had to see it one time other, would return no more.

At the conclusion of "The Bear" Ike is walking through the woods when he comes upon a large rattlesnake. Not only does he see the snake, but with the acute sensory perception of the woodsman he smells him: "the thin sick smell of rotting cucumbers and something else which had no name, evocative of all knowledge and of pariahhood and of death." As the snake glides away, Ike addresses him in the primal tongue he had heard Sam Fathers use six years ago when they had confronted a large buck deer in the wilderness: "Chief," he said: "Grandfather." Shortly after this mystical moment with the snake, Ike hears "a sound as though someone were hammering a gun-barrel against a piece of railroad iron, a sound loud and heavy and not rapid yet with something frenzied about it, as the hammerer were not only a strong man and an earnest one but a little hysterical too." He comes upon a gum tree where he is to meet Boon Hogganbeck, the more or less irresponsible hunter who two years earlier had finally put an end to the legendary bear, Old Ben, and had thereby, as Robert D. Jacobs says, symbolized "the abrogation of the old relationship between man and nature." In the years before, Major de Spain and the others had hunted Old Ben each year as a ritual rather than as an act of depredation. Ike witnesses this scene:

At first glance the tree seemed to be alive with frantic squirrels. There appeared to be forty or fifty of them leaping and darting from branch to branch until the whole tree had become one green maelstrom of mad leaves, while from time to time, singly or in twos and threes, squirrels would dart down the trunk and then whirl without stopping and rush back up again as though sucked violently back by the vacuum of their fellows' frenzied vortex. Then he saw Boon, sitting, his back against the trunk, his head bent, hammering furiously at something on his lap. What he hammered with was the barrel of his dismembered gun, what he hammered at was the breech of it. The rest of the gun lay scattered about him in a half-dozen pieces while he bent over the piece on his lap his scarlet and streaming walnut-face, hammering the disjointed barrel against the gun breech with the frantic abandon of a madman. He didn't even look up to see who it was. Still hammering, he merely shouted back at the boy in a hoarse strangled voice: "Get out of here! Don't touch them! Don't touch a one of them! They're mine."

We remember the story of Eli Whitney, the inventor of the cotton gin: how he sent the rifles the Army had ordered from him—a box of barrels, a box of triggers, etc.—and thus announced the invention of interchangeable parts. Or we may remember this story. Whether or not Boon's confounding is linked specifically with the history of technology, it effectively symbolizes the combination of greed and mechanical power which destroyed the wilderness and its creatures. That the power has momentarily failed only makes Boon a more striking example of the Second Fall.

In "Delta Autumn," a tale about Ike in his old age, he is a witness to one of the ultimate results of the Second Fall, the creation of a wasteland out of the great Delta forests of Mississippi:

Now a man drove two hundred miles from Jefferson before he found wilderness to hunt in. Now the land lay open from the cradling hills on the east to the rampart of levee on the west, standing horseman-tall with cotton for the world's looms . . . — the land in which neon flashed past them from the little countless towns, and countless shining this-year's automobiles sped past them on the broad plumb-ruled highways, yet in which the only permanent mark of man's occupation seemed to be the tremendous gins, constructed in sections of sheet iron and in a week's time . . . —the land across which there came no scream of panther but instead the long hooting of locomotives: trains of incredible length and drawn by a single engine, since there was no gradient anywhere and no elevation save those raised by forgotten aboriginal hands as refuges from the yearly water and used by their Indian successors to sepulchre their fathers' bones, and all that remained of that old time were Indian names on the little towns.

Lying in his tent alone, old Ike conceives of the judgment upon the Second Fall of man:

This Delta. *This land which man has deswamped and denuded and deriverbed in two generations so that white men can own plantations and commute every night to Memphis and black men own plantations and ride in Jim Crow cars to Chicago to live in millionaire's mansions on Lake Shore Drive; where white men rent farms and live like niggers and niggers crop on shares and live like ani-*

mals. . . . No wonder the ruined woods I used to know don't cry
for retribution! . . . The people who have destroyed it will accomplish its revenge.

Ike's bitterness assumes that the Second Fall has not completely obliterated the element of Rousseauesque discontent
that drove modern man to seek to return to nature. It may be,
however, that Faulkner is one of the last writers to experience
fully the Rousseauesque tradition of discontent—that is to say,
a writer who really feels what it means for modern man to have
lost the chance to enter into a living, instead of a bulldozing,
relationship with nature. We may now be entering the age of
"post-modern man." A major characteristic of this age will
be the full acceptance of a mass-technological society as the
one and only way of existence. No doubt the people who live
in the post-modern world will accomplish the revenge of "the
ruined woods," but will they realize it? Punishment is meaningless when the punished have no moral norm to which they
can relate their punishment, and nature as a moral or ethical
norm has become almost meaningless.

III

Faulkner was always aware of this ironic dilemma. Not, I
would emphasize, as a dilemma or a problem as such. He was
aware of it in the complexity of his feeling for the drama of
modern Southerners who are modern human beings. His
awareness is strongly implied in that strange early work he
called *Sanctuary* and in that stranger later work, a play, he
called *Requiem for a Nun*. Published in 1951, *Requiem for a
Nun* is a sequel to the story of Temple Drake as it is related in
Sanctuary, a novel published twenty years before.

Sanctuary, the most notorious of Faulkner's novels, has been
reprinted more often than any of his other works. It has been
analyzed in many ways. In my opinion, it is surely one of the

most telling reflections on the fall of New World man (which is, more generally speaking, the Second Fall) in modern literature. The chief character, Temple Drake, is the daughter of an aristocratic Mississippi family. How "bad" she is at the beginning of the story is not clear; but the fact that her name is inscribed on the "foul, stained wall" of the men's room in the railway station at Oxford suggests that her reputation is not unblemished. When she agrees to slip off a train taking students to a baseball game at Starkville in order to take a trip in a risqué manner with Gowan Stevens, a spoiled youngster who cannot hold his liquor, she ends up in a bootlegger's nest. Here she is raped by a gangster named Popeye Vitelli, violated in a way that even the most sophisticated will agree is intriguing. Subsequently she is taken to a Memphis house of prostitution by Popeye, who, because he has no sexual capacity at all, supplies her with a lover named Alabama Red, another gangster, and enjoys himself watching them make love. This scandalizes even Miss Reba Rivers, the madam and high priestess of the house, but it goes on until Red is killed when he tries to slip into Temple's room without Popeye. Popeye is a jealous lover even though he has to make love by proxy. In the ins and outs of the story that follow, Red is buried after a grotesque funeral held in a road house. When the orchestra plays "Nearer, My God to Thee," a drunken woman in a red dress comes in yelling, "Whoopee . . . so long, Red. He'll be in hell before I could even reach Little Rock." Lee Goodwin, a bootlegger, is charged with the rape of Temple at the beginning of her adventure. Temple allows her false testimony to send Goodwin to his death at the hands of a lynch mob. The mob sets him on fire after drenching him with gasoline. Popeye is apprehended for a murder he did not commit and is hanged in Alabama.

Wherein does the peculiar power of this lurid tale lie? We do not have to follow the allegorical interpretation of George

Marion O'Donnell in which Popeye is said to represent literally "Amoral Modernism," but, I would insist, *Sanctuary* develops, perhaps to some extent in a concealed way, the controlling image of modern literature: the wasteland of modern industrial, mechanical society. Look at the scene, for instance, which Temple sees when she arrives in Memphis in Popeye's automobile:

> At the foot of the bluff below Main Street Popeye turned into a narrow street of smoke-grimed frame houses with tiers of wooden galleries set a little back in grassless plots, and now and then a forlorn and hardy tree of some shabby species—gaunt, lopbranched magnolias, a stunted elm or a locust in grayish, cadaverous bloom —interspersed by rear ends of garages; a scrap-heap in a vacant lot; a low doored cavern of an equivocal appearance where an oilcloth-covered counter and a row of backless stools, a metal coffee-urn and a fat man in a dirty apron with a toothpick in his mouth stood for an instant out of the gloom with an effect as of a sinister and meaningless photograph poorly made. From the bluff, beyond a line of office buildings terraced sharply against the sunfilled sky, came a sound of traffic—motor horns, trolleys—passing high overhead on the river breeze; at the end of the street a trolley materialised in the narrow gap with an effect as of magic and vanished with a stupendous clatter. On a second storey gallery a young negress in her underclothes smoked a cigarette sullenly, her arms on the balustrade.
>
> Popeye drew up before one of the dingy three-storey houses, the entrance of which was hidden by a dingy lattice cubicle leaning a little awry. In the grimy grassplot before it two of those small, woolly, white, worm-like dogs, one with a pink, the other a blue, ribbon about its neck, moved about with an air of sluggish and obscene paradox. In the sunlight their coats looked as though they had been cleaned with gasoline.

This is the world of Popeye Vitelli, who fears the sights and sounds of nature, wears a hat resembling a modernistic lampshade, has eyes like rubber knobs, and, in his black suit, seems to be stamped out of tin. Sexually impotent, he is further iso-

lated from sensory experience by his allergy to alcohol. None
of the terrible things he does can be blamed on drunkenness.
He is a sheer horror, representing a stage in the Second Fall of
man a good many degrees below that represented by poor old
Boon Hogganbeck. He is the complete reversal of the idea of
the New World man living in new connection with nature; he
is the entire perversion of the value of the instinctual life.

But Temple is the greater horror in *Sanctuary*. If the dream
of the rise of New World man developed in its purest form in
the mystique of American girlhood, we have in the story of
Temple Drake the record of the absolute defilement of this
mystique—a defilement all the more absolute because Temple
is a violation of the mystique of Southern American girlhood,
and, still more absolute, because she is a violation of Southern
American Mississippi girlhood. The full picture of Temple
does not emerge in *Sanctuary*. Her motivation is not made
explicit until she appears, eight years older, in *Requiem for a
Nun*. The reason for this may be that Faulkner was not fully
cognizant of her motives himself. But the careful reader may
find her motivation strongly implied. She wants Popeye to as-
sault her; she tells the sordid tale to Horace Benbow, the lawyer, "with actual pride." She could escape from the Memphis
house, but she doesn't because she loves life there. She could
save Goodwin's life. She does not because she has no com-
passion whatsoever. At the end of *Sanctuary* Temple and her
aristocratic father are in the Old World, in Paris, in the Luxembourg Gardens. It is what may well be reckoned one of the
key scenes in American literature:

It had been a gray day, a gray summer, a gray year. On the street
men wore overcoats and in the Luxembourg Gardens as Temple
and her father passed the women sat knitting in shawls and even
the men playing croquet played in coats and capes, and in the sad
gloom of the chestnut trees the dry click of the balls, the random

shouts of children, had that quality of autumn, gallant and evanescent and forlorn. From beyond the circle, with its spurious Greek balustrade, clotted with movement, filled with a gray light of the same color and texture as the water which the fountain played into the pool, came a steady crash of music. They went on, passed the pool where the children and an old man in a shabby brown overcoat sailed toy boats, and entered the trees again and found seats. Immediately an old woman came with decrepit promptitude and collected four sous.

In the pavilion a band in the horizon blue of the army played Massenet and Scriabine, and Berlioz like a thin coating of tortured Tschaikovsky on a slice of stale bread, while the twilight dissolved in wet gleams from the branches, onto the pavilion and the sombre toadstools of umbrellas. Rich and resonant the brasses crashed and died in the thick green twilight, rolling over them in rich sad waves. Temple yawned behind her hand, then she took out a compact and opened it upon a face in miniature sullen and discontented and sad. Beside her her father sat, his hands crossed on the head of his stick, the rigid bar of his moustache beaded with moisture like frosted silver. She closed the compact and from beneath her smart new hat she seemed to follow with her eyes the waves of music, to dissolve into the dying brasses, across the pool and the opposite semicircle of trees where at sombre intervals the dead tranquil queens in stained marble mused, and on into the sky lying prone and vanquished in the embrace of the season of rain and death.

We recall other American girls in our fiction who go to Europe. One is Henry James's Daisy Miller, the "little American flirt," who in her American innocence is victimized by corrupt European manners, yet who in dying wins a moral triumph over this corruption. We think, more especially, of Milly Theale. The highest reaches of James's mystique of American girlhood are glimpsed in this beautiful, frail girl, the sacrificial victim who in death spreads her wings of love over the Old World schemers who have destroyed her. Both Daisy and Milly are redeemers sent from the New World to save the

Old World; or, at least, to show it up for what it is. Seated in the Luxembourg Gardens—listening indifferently to the music of the last great romantics crashing about her, wholly sensate, wholly amoral, and completely isolated in the present, for she has no sense of the past—Temple symbolizes the utter end of the dream of the moral regeneration of mankind in the beautiful and fertile Garden of the New World. For her there is no salvation.

Twenty years after he left Temple in the Luxembourg Gardens, Faulkner came forth with his second work about her, *Requiem for a Nun*. Why did he write this drama? He said that he got interested in the question of what would happen if Gowan Stevens, the boy who was too drunk to help Temple when they were stranded in the bootlegger's lair, falsely sacrificed his vanity by marrying her. A more compelling reason Faulkner had in writing *Requiem for a Nun* may have been his compulsion, not to save Temple's soul, but to give her one that might be saved. He does this in a bizarre manner; yet the melodrama makes explicit the logic underlying it: namely, if man is to be saved from the Second Fall, he must once again be persuaded of the First Fall, or of the necessity of believing in Original Sin and in mankind's community in sin.

In the second story about Temple, duly and properly married, she lives in Jefferson with Gowan in a modern suburban bungalow. She and Gowan enjoy the pleasures of the local cocktail set, who like to entertain liberal social and political opinions while they sweat out their hangovers every Sunday morning in their church pews. The group Temple now belongs to believes that the enlightened opinions of her and her husband have led them to bring into their home as a nurse for their two children an ex-dope fiend and ex-prostitute Negro named Nancy Mannigoe. Actually Temple has employed Nancy because she can speak the language Temple still yearns to hear, the language she learned in Miss Reba's sporting house in Memphis. "You know," Temple tells the Governor in the confessional scene when she futilely seeks a pardon for Nancy, "the long afternoons, with the last electric button pressed on the last cooking or washing or sweeping gadget and the baby safely asleep for awhile, and the two sisters in sin swapping trade or anyway avocational secrets over Coca-Colas in the kitchen. Somebody to talk to. . . ." Nancy, however, does not cure Temple's boredom with the role of middle-class mother and wife. So, when Pete, a younger brother of her dead lover, Alabama Red, shows up to blackmail her with some obscene letters she had written years ago to Red, she tells him that she will pay his price if he will take her away with him. Seeing the situation, Nancy—in what one critic terms "the most insane solution to the problem of a broken home ever presented in fiction"—strangles Temple's baby in a last desperate effort to keep the family together. The basic motive of the solution is more fundamental. The lawyer Gavin Stevens puts it this way: Nancy murdered the baby because she believes that "little children, as long as they are little children, shall be intact, unanguished, untorn, unterrified." This is what Christ meant when he said, "Suffer the little children to come unto me." He would protect them as long as they were children from the universal and necessary sinning and suffering of all mankind. When Gavin asks Nancy, "The salvation of the world is in man's suffering. Is that it?" she replies, "Yes, sir." And when he asks, "You have got to sin, too?" she says, "You aint got to. You cant help it. . . . He dont tell you not to sin. He just asks you not to. And He dont tell you to suffer. But he gives you the chance. He gives you the best He can think of, that you are capable of doing. And He will save you." At the end of the play Temple, who has expressed doubts about whether or not there is a God, still appears to be in a labyrinth of doubt. She

186

has come to the point of saying in effect that if she has a soul and nobody wants it, then she is "sunk." And, "We all are. Doomed. Damned." Temple realizes what she is incapable of realizing at the end of *Sanctuary*. Man is a fallen creature who longs for salvation.

What may be called, albeit somewhat loosely, the Christian theme is prominent in the dialogue portions of the three acts into which *Requiem for a Nun* is divided. The dialogue, it is important to recognize, is only part of the play. Each act is preceded by a long prologue about the history of Yoknapa-tawpha County done in some of the most elusive rhetoric Faulkner achieved in a long career of writing slippery rhetoric.

The ironic theme of the prologues might be said to be "was" in relation to "progress." What they emphasize—Faulkner said he intended them to be contrapuntal to the dialogue sec-tions—is the overwhelming rapidity of the Second Fall of man. "There was no time." This is a major note in the prologues. It reaches a climax in the last one, which is devoted to the mean-ing of the jail in Jefferson, the oldest building in the town, somehow surviving, even though remodeled, and although inevitably doomed to be replaced:

And still—the old jail—endured, sitting in its rumorless cul-de-sac, its almost seasonless backwater in the middle of that rush and roar of civic progress and social alteration and change like a collar-less (and reasonably clean: merely dingy: with a day's stubble and no garters to his socks) old man sitting in his suspenders and stock-ing feet, on the back kitchen steps inside a walled courtyard; actu-ally not isolated by location so much as insulated by obsolescence: on the way out of course (to disappear from the surface of the earth along with the rest of the town on the day when all America, after cutting down all the trees and leveling the hills and moun-tains with bulldozers, would have to move underground to make room for, get out of the way of, the motor cars) but like the track-walker in the tunnel, the thunder of the express mounting behind him, who finds himself opposite a niche or a crack exactly his size in the wall's living and impregnable rock, and steps into it, inviolable and secure while destruction roars past and on and away, grooved ineluctably to the spidery rails of its destiny and destination; not even—the jail—worth selling to the United States for some matching allocation out of the federal treasury; not even (so fast, so far, was Progress) any more a real pawn, let alone knight or rook, on the county's political board, not even plum in true worth of the word: simply a modest sinecure for the husband of someone's cousin, who had failed not as a father but merely as a fourth-rate farmer or day-laborer.

The "new people" in Jefferson—"outlanders, living in new minute glass-walled houses set as neat and orderly and antiseptic as cribs in a nursery ward, in new subdivisions named Fairfield or Longwood or Halcyon Acres"—have no contact with the jail. Only the "intractable and obsolescent of the town who still insist on wood-burning ranges and cows and vegetable gardens and handymen who had to be taken out of hock on the mornings after Saturday nights and holidays" know the jail. That is, "until suddenly you, a stranger, an outlander, from say some suburbia in the East or the North or the Far West," happening to pass through Jefferson, go with one of the townspeople to see the jail. You are somewhat embarrassed because the jailer's wife is preparing a meal; but you go into the kitchen anyway to see one of the jail's best-known historical features: a name and a date scratched thinly on a window pane—"Cecilia Farmer April 16th 1861." Who was this name? She was, the old people of the community know, a "fragile and workless" girl, daughter of the jailer of nearly a century before. During a battle in and around Jefferson during the Civil War, she was standing, as usual, musing at the window on which with a diamond ring she had some time earlier etched her name. A Confederate soldier saw her for a moment. There was no communication between them. He did not speak to her; nor did he find out her identity. But after the war he came all the way back from Virginia to take this "maiden muse" for his bride—not, however, to some Eden in the Virgin West, unravaged by war, where they would be "engaged only with wilderness and shoeless savages and the tender hand of God." Their destiny is with a farm in Alabama, a land "rendered into a desert . . . by the iron and fire of civilization." What became of this girl of "invincible inviolable ineptitude"? You wonder. Did she have a "long peaceful connubial progress toward matriarchy in a rocking chair nobody else was allowed to sit in, then a headstone in a country churchyard"? This, you decide, was not enough for that face. "No symbol there of connubial matriarchy, but fatal instead with all insatiate and deathless sterility; spouseless, barren, and undescended; not even demanding more than that; simply requiring it, requiring all—Lilith's lost and insatiable face drawing the substance—the will and hope and dream and imagination—of all men (you too: yourself and the host too) into that one bright fragile net and snare; not even to be caught, over-flung, by one single unerring cast of it, but drawn to watch in patient and thronging turn the very weaving of the strangling golden strands. . . ." Was Cecilia Farmer actually Lilith, in Hebraic lore the first wife of Adam, who became a demon, the enemy of children, and merciless seducer and murderer of men? Or was she a "demon-nun and angel-witch," or a siren? You feel compelled staring at the scratching on the window pane, which seems "to have entered into another sense than vision," to decide who this "girl in the window" was—"not *might* have been, nor even could have been, but *was*: so vast, so limitless in capacity is man's imagination to disperse and burn away the rubble-dross of fact and probability, leaving only truth and dream. . . ." Then you are gone "to unfumble among the road signs and filling stations to get back onto a highway you know, back into the United States; not that it matters, since you know again now that there is no time: no space: no distance. . . ." You have heard a voice "across the vast instantaneous intervention, from the long long time ago: 'Listen, stranger; this was myself: this was I.' "

The human imagination, Faulkner appears to be saying, although it may be diverted from contemplating the nature of man in the time of the Second Fall, when even "little lonely lost farmhouses" glitter and gleam with "automatic stoves and washing machines and television antennae," can still "burn away the rubble-dross of fact and probability" to discover "truth and dream." This is what happens to you, the out-lander, when you leave the booming, industrial-technological United States and go into the obsolescent jail, where Cecilia musing at the window marked her identity upon it so that you could see it nearly a century later and wonder what she was like. So that you could decide that she might have been a primal demon. Not just idly wonder but be compelled to wonder, because, as the description of Cecilia keeps emphasizing, she was, or is, a muse, a source of wisdom. We are not divorced from her by our illusory absorption in the present, for the human brain carries in it all time.

What happens if we seek a more specific interpretation of the meaning of Cecilia by connecting her with Temple? I am not sure at all. Yet Faulkner apparently intended to suggest at least the possibility of an implied comparison between the two. Cecilia, a Mississippi girl, may have been in some sense the demon Lilith, killer of children and devourer of men. (Compare a comment on Eula Varner in *The Town*: "that damned incredible woman, that Frenchman Bend's Helen, Semiramis—no: not Helen nor Semiramis: Lilith: the one before Eve herself whom earth's Creator had perforce in desperate and amazed alarm in person to efface, remove, obliterate, that Adam might create a progeny to populate it. . . .") In *Requiem for a Nun* Temple says it was she, not Nancy, who killed her baby. She committed the murder eight years earlier when she kept her illicit tryst with Gowan. Gavin Stevens observes to the Governor that Red, Pete, and Gowan were all drawn to Temple "enough to accept, risk, almost incredible conditions." Does there survive in Temple the ancient destructive power of the insatiable, sterile Lilith? Through Cecilia Farmer, a blonde muse whose presence is still felt in the jail, is Temple brought into the realm of the myth of the White Goddess, who according to Robert Graves in his book about her is the ultimate source of Truth? Surely no firm answer can be given. Yet it may well be that Faulkner with his inclination to multi-dimensional complexity and his vision of single human lives projected against the background of all human history intended in the concluding act of *Requiem for a Nun* to juxtapose the myth of the White Goddess and the myth of the usurping male God of Christianity. If man is to find his way out of the modern wasteland, if he is to find salvation for the Second Fall and to achieve a life of moral significance, he must understand how his nature comprehends both the destructive lust of Lilith and the merciful love of God represented by the Christ embodied in Nancy.

⮑ O'Donnell's Wall

WHEN THE late George Marion O'Donnell taught at Louisiana State University for two years after the end of the Second World War, the wall above his desk in his Allen Hall office was decorated with three objects. In the center, suspended horizontally, was the sword of an officer, CSA; to the right of the sword hung a vintage photograph of his maternal grandfather in the uniform of a major in his Mississippi regiment; to the left of the sword hung a photograph of the death mask of Marcel Proust. During the twenty years and more since I first saw it, I have often gone back in retrospect to this woeful yet somehow awesome emblazonment and puzzled over its significance. Lately after reading Walter Sullivan's brilliant essay on the "death by melancholy" of modern Southern writers, I found myself again returning to O'Donnell's wall. I was led to think of O'Donnell again not so much by Sullivan's specific argument as by the stern religious moralism it shows and by two evocative phrases in it, which I quote bare of context: "As the whole world empties, its metaphysical concepts draining away. . . ."[1]

1   Walter Sullivan's "Southern Writers in the Modern World: Death by Melancholy" should be read in connection with two related essays by him: "In the Time of the Breaking of Nations: The Decline of Southern Fiction" and "The New Faustus: The Southern Renascence and the Joycean Aesthetic," *Death by Melancholy* (Baton Rouge, 1972).

The display O'Donnell stuck on his wall was an affectation of course—more than a little ostentatious and snobbish, I suppose, and altogether somewhat absurd. (It was comparable to the theatrical, decayed pomp of a dinner party given by O'Donnell, at which, having made adequate spiritual preparation around a bottle of Dixie Belle gin, the guests dined ceremoniously by the light of a treasured family silver candelabra on mustard greens and corn bread.) And yet did not O'Donnell's somber wall signify more than an eccentric social and literary vanity? In the wake of a long period of fairly diligent reading in the Southern writers, up to and including Walter Sullivan, William Styron, and others, I seem now to conclude that it was a significant attempt to represent that twentieth-century apocalypse of the Southern literary imagination we have come to call with historical certitude "the Southern literary renascence." In the early 1930s, O'Donnell had gone from his native Mississippi (he was born in 1914 on Silver Home plantation and grew up on Blue Ruin plantation, both places near a small town named Midnight) [2] to mould his early literary promise at Vanderbilt University, the leading center of what was coming by this time to be recognized even by non-Southern literati as a singular literary flowering in the South. Becoming a disciple of the Agrarian school (and of the school of Southern New Critics then in process of formation), O'Donnell contributed to the Agrarian-Distributist Symposium *Who Owns America?* (1935) and by the late thirties and early forties had founded a literary reputation on the basis of a small but distinguished body of poetry, fiction, and criticism, some of it published in *The Southern Review*; when he came to LSU in 1947, he seemed likely to become a figure in modern Southern letters, taking his place in the movement of the re-

2   The names are real. Midnight is located about halfway between the towns of Hard Cash and Louise.

nascence in close succession to Ransom, Tate, Davidson, Warren, Brooks, and not least, Faulkner—whose central role in the renascence began to be grasped by the Southern critics only when O'Donnell pointed it out in an essay in the *Kenyon Review* entitled "Faulkner's Mythology" (1939).[3] Indeed O'Donnell, in spite of his Agrarian allegiance and selfconscious Southernism, tended to be more of the renascence as a whole than his mentors. His discipleship to the renascent spirit included Faulkner in his isolation at Oxford, Mississippi, as well as the Agrarians and New Critics in their academic camaraderie in Nashville and Baton Rouge; in fact, the sign he placed upon his office wall witnessed to the latitudinarian complexity the renascence assumed as it developed. To O'Donnell the strange and bold conjunction of historical and literary pieties—the combined expression of fealty to the gentleman soldier of the South, to the War for Southern Independence, and to Proust—symbolized a modern community of literary aspiration, and not less of faith, to which he had been admitted by birth, talent, and education. It signified what may be called, assuming a certain license in terminology, a metaphysical doctrine: an established faith in the power of the imagination of a writer like himself to make real the presence of the Southern past in the present. A belief, in other words, that poetry, stories, and criticism could effect, in the stricter sense of the term, a renascence of the Southern past, giving the past virtually an ontological status. This doctrine (probably most explicitly expressed by Allen Tate and William Faulkner) is what O'Don-

---

3 When he was in high school, O'Donnell had formed an avid acquaintance with Faulkner's writings. Emily Whitehurst Stone records an interesting meeting between Faulkner and a number of high school students in 1930; O'Donnell served as the spokesman for the students. See Mrs. Stone's "Some Arts of Self-Defense" in James A. Webb and A. Wigfall Green (eds.), *William Faulkner of Oxford* (Baton Rouge, 1965), 95–100

nell had dedicated himself to; and to fulfill his dedication he intended to write a trilogy about the South, to be called "No More, My Ladies," that would be comparable, however imprecisely, to *A la recherche du temps perdu*. This intention is what he specifically declared on his wall. He declared as much because he thought he could do it.

But he never did. Possibly his ambition exceeded his talent. Still, I would conjecture that the sad incompleteness of O'Donnell's career bears a relation to something other than his capacities as an individual—to a tangled, if not contradictory, metaphysical situation in the modern Southern literary mind that O'Donnell, not without an awareness of it, also symbolized on his wall. When we try to analyze this situation, we may, I think (borrowing a term from R. P. Blackmur), reduce it to something like the following description: an "irregular metaphysics" of remembrance taking on the incomplete form of an "irregular metaphysics" of restoration.

The Southern literary mind began to operate on the basis of a metaphysics of remembrance when the decision of the Civil War placed it under a maximum obligation to memory. Remembrance was the cultural imperative of a people defeated in an effort to attain national identity in the historical age of integral nationalism—a beaten people who must return to the fold of a larger nation which was, as C. Vann Woodward has said, living a unique legend of victory and success.

I have in my possession—an incidental acquisition in the passing of things in a Southern family—one of those crude Civil War mementoes constructed of bits and pieces of battlefield debris. It features grapeshot, a Minié ball, some fragments of shrapnel, and a small chunk of wood (apparently from a breastworks). Looking at the underside of the base of this garish little sculpture, peering intently at it under the glare of a fluorescent lamp, one can make out faint words and figures inscribed in pencil: a date in the 1880s, not quite legible, and then clearly one word, *Remember*. . . . What follows may be the name of a battle, or possibly the place of a veterans' reunion. But the hand that wrote the plea was simply repeating an appeal that by the 1880s was inscribed everywhere in the South; it expressed a compulsive need that had passed from need into a revealed faith: in defeat the Confederacy had lost a cause but preserved the truth of a civilization. We can see this development in the Southern memory in many writings of the later nineteenth-century South, an outstanding example being Thomas Nelson Page's address, "The Old South." Moreover, we can see a certain mood of expectancy rising in the Southern literary mind: those faithful to memory have intimations of revelations yet to come. There was a good deal of foolishness in this veneration of memory; but essentially the Southern renascence originated in a prophetic revelation of memory, more complex than any preceding one, but nonetheless a fulfillment of the promise of memory. This revelation occurred in the Southern literary mind when, following the First World War, it came directly and vividly into contact with the general apocalyptic mood of the modern Western literary renascence. The literature of this spectacular resurgence of the Western literary spirit, which begins at least as far back as the 1880s and 1890s in Yeats, Mann, Proust, and others, envisions the active destruction of the classical-Christian past by all that is sanctioned under the name of Progress: industrialism, technology, the economy of consumption, communism, naturalism, behaviorism, in short by everything that constitutes modern materialism. It expresses at once a profound nostalgia for the past of Western civilization and a moral determination to conserve the past as the true dimension of existence. This determination had exceedingly rich and various results. Broadly speaking, it led to Proust and his

196

struggle to achieve an intensely personal vision of the presence of the past as a liberation from "all contingency," an "extra-temporal essence"; and to T. S. Eliot and his struggle to achieve an impersonal vision of the presence of the past as the prescriptive ground of religious and moral order. These struggles, and the whole effort to make the past present that we find in modern literature, became the enlarged context of the Southern literary sensibility. In this context the Agrarians expanded and intensified the meaning of the Southern past. They discovered (whether literally or metaphorically or somehow in both ways) the true meaning of the defeat of the South in the Civil War: it was a defeat of the traditional humanistic-Christian community of the West, a part of the general defeat of this community in modern history. This was an exciting discovery; it made the Southern past seem immensely important, and it moved the Agrarians toward transforming the metaphysics of remembrance into a metaphysical basis for restoring order—the movement that is documented in the Agrarian manifesto, *I'll Take My Stand*. At the same time the Agrarians, sophisticated and attuned to the ironic temper of modern times, could not fail to recognize, though trying not to do so, that the inner and spiritual history of the South is rooted not only in conflict between the South and the outside world but also in the contention between Southern traditionalism and an innovating materialism within the South itself. The South, Old and New, belongs to modernity. This truth, inescapable as feeling if not as fact, made it difficult for the Southern writer to believe faithfully in a restoration of tradition.[4]

4 It is instructive to contrast O'Donnell's discipleship to the Agrarians with that of the late Richard M. Weaver. Such a comparison has been facilitated by the publication of Weaver's LSU doctoral dissertation in English under the title, *The Southern Tradition at Bay*, edited by M. E. Bradford and George Core and with a Foreword by Donald Davidson. (New Rochelle, N.Y., 1968). M. E. Bradford's *Rumors of Mor-*

Out of his striving with this difficulty comes the pathos we find in the career O'Donnell started and left unfinished. I cannot recall for sure whether or not he had on his wall, in a less conspicuous spot and removed from his central symbols, a picture of Eliot, as he did of Joyce and Yeats. He was, I know, devoted to Eliot and listened with religious solemnity and delight to Eliot's recorded readings of "Gerontion" and other poems on an archaic, hand-winding Victrola. And, it is obvious, he imitated Eliot in his own practice of poetry and criticism; it is less obvious how thoroughly he was given to Eliot's feeling that the modern poet has a moral responsibility to oppose tradition to "pseudotradition." In "A Note on Poetry," which prefaces his section of poems in *Five Young American Poets* (1940), O'Donnell says that as a Southerner he belongs "naturally to a particular cultural tradition" and that he is tempted "to regard the tradition in my poetry as though it were operative." But "the very existence of the tradition is precarious" and his "own piety in it defective." Although "tempted to impose personal judgments disguised as traditional evaluations," he tries always, he states, not "to yield to my temptation." The rigor of O'Donnell's subtle battle against yielding is written in his work, and perhaps more eloquently in what he did not write. With his faith in the vision of the presence of the past fading, and any hope he took in the mission of the Southern writer to restore community draining away, O'Donnell was increasingly drawn to the Proustian vision of the past as revealed through the introverted, solipsistic consciousness. This is why he responded acutely to the complexities of Faulkner when other Agrarian critics had not yet paid Faulkner much attention. He saw Faulkner as the tradi-

tality: An Introduction to Allen Tate (Dallas, 1969) is a valuable study of the impulse to moral restoration in Agrarianism, especially with respect to Tate's poetry.

tional moralist in an antitraditional world. Out of this tension, O'Donnell recognized, Faulkner had created a unified series of works that assume the shape of "a great myth." But for all his achievement there is, O'Donnell observes, a large failure in Faulkner's stories: "Mr. Faulkner is unable to sustain his traditionalism at all, and the forces of antitraditionalism become the protagonists." O'Donnell makes a graphic equation between Faulkner himself and one of his chief characters, the doomed Quentin Compson: "In a way Quentin's struggle is Mr. Faulkner's struggle as an artist." For Quentin the past is an overwhelming presence; it is the presence of the purest reality, death, and he fulfills his futile struggle with time by drowning himself.

Penetrating though it is, O'Donnell's view of Faulkner is too narrow, for Faulkner's genius comprehends and commands all of his characters and all the forces at work in his stories. One feels in "Faulkner's Mythology" that the critic must have himself in view more than his subject and that it may be more accurate to say that Quentin's struggle is O'Donnell's instead of Faulkner's. One wonders if O'Donnell did not secretly identify himself with Quentin; one wonders if the metaphysics of remembrance did not become a complete trap for O'Donnell and if finally he was not locked into the dimension of the past as tightly as Quentin, whose very body (O'Donnell quotes the line in his essay) "is an empty hall echoing with sonorous defeated names." In 1947, when the Southern renascence still seemed to be an onward going movement, O'Donnell published (in *A Southern Vanguard*, edited by Allen Tate) a remarkable poem entitled "Time's Well." In this poem the poet describes how, dressed in a ponderous modern diving suit and helmet, he is lowered by friends into the well of time on a mission "to find what did not die." He gets caught in the well; his friends try to extricate him, but they cannot pull him upward beyond a certain level, while at another level below he must heed a sign, "Stop! Do not descend!" He is dragged up and down, and the well "Became a heaven for me,/And an earth too, and hell." He is

> by ceaseless motion
> Perpetually transformed,
> Cold as the depths of the ocean
> And yet by friction warmed,
>
> Until I forgot my name,
> Forgot the friends above
> And in time's dark well became
> The piston plunge of love.

It seems somehow an appropriate coincidence that when he died in 1962 O'Donnell had left the South and was living in New England, where about fifty years earlier Quentin Compson, not long before he died, had breathed in the hard, alien darkness and said that he did not hate the South. Appropriate in an indirect and indistinct poetic way, even though O'Donnell died in New Haven, not Cambridge, and his death was quietly natural. According to a newspaper report, he got out of a chair to walk across a room and fell dead. The same report said that he had been for some years engaged on a work he called "No More, My Ladies."

⸎ The Southern Novelist
and Southern Nationalism

THE CIVIL WAR, Richard M. Weaver says in his essay entitled "The South and the American Union," confirmed in the South "the feeling that it was in spirit and needs a separate nation." Weaver continues: "It [the South] might be viewed as an American Ireland, Poland, or Armenia, not indeed unified by a different religious allegiance from its invader, but different in its way of life, different in the values it ascribed to things by reason of its world outlook. . . . The South has in a way made a religion of its history, or its suffering, and any sign of waning faith or laxness of spirit may be met with a reminder of how this leader endured and that one died, in the manner of saints and saviors. . . . Being a Southerner is definitely a spiritual condition, like being a Catholic or a Jew; and members of the group can recognize one another by signs which are eloquent to them, though too small to be noticed by an outsider."[1]

Weaver is speaking of the Southerner in a general way; but if we assume he speaks primarily out of his own experience of affiliation with an intensely self-conscious intellectual and literary community of Southerners, we may recognize in his comment an unusually frank confession of a modern Southern writer's sense of identity. His statement may strike one famil-

1 Louis D. Rubin, Jr., and James Jackson Kilpatrick (eds.), *The Lasting South* (Chicago, 1957), 63–64.

iar with the history of the literary vocation in the South as the revelation of a hidden motive; for he associates his role as a writer not in the conventional way with the concept of a Southern regionalism but more nearly with the concept of the South as a spiritual nation. He implies, or almost does, that the South is a special redemptive community fulfilling a divinely appointed role in the drama of history. In so doing, Weaver, I think, recognizes that the true form of Southern nationalism (I mean basically literary or cultural nationalism but I also mean political nationalism) is not to be found in an image of the South as a region, or even as a section. The image of the South that lies at the heart of the modern Southern writer's imagination of the South is more integral. Even though it may be an image that so repels him in its blatant self-consciousness—in its aspect of Southern chauvinism—that he denies it, it is nonetheless fundamental to his imagination of himself as a writer and to his relation to his subject, the condition of human existence in the South. The Southern writer has tended to be a kind of priest and prophet of a metaphysical nation, compelled in his literary construction of human existence in the South—whether he is historian, philosopher, critic, poet, or novelist—toward representing it as a quest for a revelation of man's moral community in history. The revelation may be ironic, tragic, humorous; it may be all three at once, but it is salvational. The quest for it is an underlying motive in the major imaginative works of the brilliant Renaissance in Southern letters during the past forty years, a flowering that can hardly be said to have ended yet. And it is notably present as a motive in the most prolific and extensive accomplishment of the Renaissance, the large body of remarkable fiction it has generated.

I am going to set down some notes and make some comments on the image of the South as a spiritual nation in Southern literature with particular reference to the bearing this subject has on Southern fiction. My remarks, perhaps more impressionistic than analytical, will fall into two general divisions: the emergence of the idea of the South as a spiritual nation; selected aspects of the development of this idea in the one hundred years or so from the 1820s down to the 1920s and 1930s, when it reached fulfillment as a controlling image in modern Southern fiction.

I

It is probably impossible to determine when a Southern literary imagination began to develop or when it began to move toward the idea of the South as a redemptive community, but I doubt that we can precisely place either phenomenon earlier than the age of the American Revolution. By this time, it is important to note, the image of New England as a spiritual nation had reached an advanced stage of development. Since the effort to define the connection between the South as a spiritual nation and Southern fiction may be considerably illuminated by looking at the relationship between New England as a spiritual nation and New England fiction, let us for a moment consider the situation in New England, particularly in the case of Nathaniel Hawthorne.

The rise of New England as a spiritual nation was integral to the origins of New England, which was established as the result of an exodus of a chosen people from an Old England, a world in which they had become spiritual aliens. To purify and to fulfill their personal and corporate relationship to God, they set out on an "errand into the wilderness," explicitly identifying their errand with that of the Israelites. In the primitive wilderness, according to one of the metaphors they used to describe their achievement, they set up a city on a hill. According to another metaphor, they made a garden and enclosed it in a wall. This garden became their place, and New Englanders developed a deep sense of locality. Scarcely had the New England garden been made before it was threatened by evil forces. Among these the most powerful and insidious were not from outside but from inside the garden. Some of these evils—including the love of money—were ancient ones, but they assumed their immediate meaning in the little New England community as a part of the massive secularization of the mind that had begun to occur in Western civilization by the seventeenth century. The New Englanders could not wall out this process in their own minds. By the time of the second generation of the Puritans, the unity of their errand had been broken. Declamations against apostasy and nostalgic laments for an irrecoverable time of wholeness and purpose became common. "But O! Alas! Our great and dangerous declensions!" Thomas Prince cries in 1730, longing for that first generation of his people who, in contrast to the present one, "made a heaven upon earth." In other words, history soon began to happen to the people of New England; they ceased to be a people transcendent over history. What happens to a chosen people when history begins to complicate their vision of redemptive community? When they begin to realize that their vision exists in the context of the disorder of history and that this disorder has invaded, often brutally, often subtly, the very sanctuary of their vision, and that the vision so invaded resists purification? They look for another revelation which must surely come. In a way the American Revolution provided this second revelation for New England, and from this time on New England identified its older sense of being a redeeming community with the rise of the Union as a redemptive nation. There were members of the New England community in the first years of the Republic who became separatists— those arch Federalists who began the seccessionist movement that finally came to a dead end in the compromising of the secessionist issue in the Hartford Convention of 1814. The Hartford secessionists like Timothy Pickering told their fellow Yankees "again and again that they were the earth's chosen people, that the Constitution was weighted against them, and that the annexation of Louisiana absolved them from all obligation to remain in the Union."[2] But the New England effort to embody in political form the surviving pure spirit of the New England mission was not accomplished. By this time the mission of New England had become identified with the idea of the destiny of the new Republic in such a way that New England would from now on represent the ethos and mystique of the Union. In this mystique the United States was identified with the providential growth of modern scientific and capitalistic materialism, that is to say, with the eschatology of Progress.

And yet the distinctive New England of the mind and spirit scarcely lost its being. In the New England literary imagination it became a ripened myth. As New England became more cosmopolitan in its literary education, it was the old intense sense of New Englandness that provided for the self-conscious community of writers I have elsewhere called the New England "clerisy"—and for the very substance of the New England Renaissance.[3] "I see New Englandly," Emily Dickinson said. So did Emerson, Thoreau, and most especially Hawthorne. Hawthorne, speaking of the first Hawthorne to come to New

2   Samuel Eliot Morison and Henry Steele Commager, *The Growth of the American Republic* (New York, 1942), I, 427. An important recent book for the student of New England nationalism is A. W. Plumstead (ed.), *The Wall and the Garden: Selected Massachusetts Election Sermons, 1670–1775* (Minneapolis, 1968). See pp. 183–220 for Thomas Prince's "The People of New England," from which I have quoted a sentence.

3   See "Joseph Stevens Buckminster: The Rise of the New England Clerisy" in this volume.

England in 1630, said that he gave him "a sort of home feeling with the past." The myth of New England came to possess the imaginations of its poets and storytellers. They were conscious not only of the New England past but of their own part in the drama Emerson refers to as the "interior and spiritual history of New England." [4] The myth lived in them. Out of this sensibility some of them lived what they conceived to be a fulfilling version of the myth in action in their times. This we can see in the history of the Abolitionist movement.

But Hawthorne began to live with the myth of New England in an ever deepening meditation on the history of the human spirit of New England. This became the center of his literary achievement. In his mind the myth of New England as a spiritual nation reached the stage of consciousness in which it lived at once both in the past and in the present, both in piety and irony. It was alive, if we may compare greater to lesser things, in somewhat the same way the myth of the Middle Ages was alive in the consciousness of Dante. Out of Hawthorne's meditation came a series of stories, climaxed by *The Scarlet Letter*, which is not only one of the indisputably great romances in nineteenth-century literature, but also a synthesis of the inner life of New England.

There were various reasons why Hawthorne chose to introduce *The Scarlet Letter* with a long essay called "The Custom House." One undoubtedly was to get back at some people he thoroughly disliked in Salem, who had, he believed, caused him to be fired from his political job as the surveyor in the Salem Custom House, But there is, I think, a deeper reason. Hawthorne understood that his story is a realization of the whole myth of New England as a redemptive community. He felt the need to make this clear, although it meant fabricating

4 Stephen E. Whicher (ed.), *Selections from Ralph Waldo Emerson* (Boston, 1960), 3.

a tale—in a playful way with no intention of literally fooling anyone—about finding documentary evidence for the story of Hester and Dimmesdale in the ancient custom house. This was a way of bringing the past into the present and showing, to use the notable words William Faulkner gives to Gavin Stevens in *Requiem for a Nun*: "The past is never dead. It's not even past." Into the midst of his concern about his job and about the fate of the artist in the materialistic society he mocks and condemns in "The Custom House" (this place of business being a symbol of the death of the spirit from "the daily materiality of life"), Hawthorne introduces the discovery of old Surveyor Pue's papers and "a certain affair of fine red cloth, much worn and faded." Hawthorne centers his story on the fall of the hero of the New England myth, a charismatic minister, the Reverend Mr. Dimmesdale. Further, he centers the last great scene of the story on Election Day, an annual occasion in each New England colony (and later in each New England state) of a sermon before the legislature and the public. Election Day was a day when the minister, the chief figure in the redemptive community of New England, gave what amounted to an official revaluation of the state of the chosen people. His sermon, prepared with the utmost care and art, was usually in part a record of apostasies from the original sense of the errand into the wilderness, to some degree an expression of nostalgia for an irrecoverable past, and a forecast of the future. Immediately before Dimmesdale reveals to the chosen people his own awful corruption of their mission, he has spoken to them, with an eloquence and authority such as they have never heard before, on the subject of "the relation between the Deity and the communities of mankind, with a special reference to the New England which they were planting in the wilderness." It has been suggested that in his final sermon Dimmesdale makes the greatest of all conversions: he converts himself. When he does so he is led inevitably to reveal on the scaffold the sin he has committed and the emblem of it upon his breast, "his own red stigmata . . . the type of what has seared his inmost heart." "As one who, in the crisis of acutest pain, had won a victory," the hero of the chosen people, who has been worshipped to the point of apotheosis, sinks down upon the scaffold and dies his "death of triumphant ignominy before the people" of New England.[5] With consummate irony and piety Hawthorne tells the inner and spiritual history of New England, making the scarlet letter the symbol of a chosen people—the redemptive community of New England, in all of its complex, tortuous, ironic historical dimensions.

These dimensions, we must observe, were those of a relatively latitudinarian world. After the second generation of Puritans, New England had become, not an open, but at least a half-way open society. (This began to happen by the time of the "half-way covenant" in 1662.) Both heresy and reaction were logical and coherent, the attack on and the defense of a well-developed metaphysic. The New England mind was at no time given to excesses of nostalgia for the past. Past and present were a continuum, both for the conservatives and liberals. This was true down through the age of Emily Dickinson, even down through the time of Henry Adams. And we can see the lines of coherence extending into the careers of Robert Frost and, yet a little later, of Robert Lowell. Still, by the time Henry Adams knelt before the Virgin in the Cathedral of Chartres at the end of the last century, all the coherence was

5 Passages from Hawthorne's novel are quoted from the edition in the New World Writers Series edited with an Introduction and Notes by Terence Martin (Cleveland, 1967). Martin makes the suggestion concerning Dimmesdale's self-conversion (236–37n).

in effect lost. The image of New England as a redemptive community was shattered.

But at this time the image of the South as a spiritual nation had only begun to reach the stage of coherence in the Southern literary imagination.

II

Although, like the myth of New England, it has been basically an assertion against the materialistic way of life, the myth of the South as a spiritual nation is considerably more complicated than the myth of New England. I mention several of the leading reasons for this.

To put it in a negative way, the Southern myth is more complex because it did not originate in a systematic and intricate Protestant theology expounded by a class of learned clerics. Although the religious motives in the establishment of the colonies in the South were strong, the migration to these colonies in the seventeenth century did not have the unity of an inspired biblical exodus from the Old World. The revelation that they were a special people came to Southerners only after the Republic had been launched, and then it did not come with any clear illumination. A large general reason for its lack of focus and intensity is that by the time of the founding of the United States the secularization of the Western mind—at the level of the intellectual class—had been consolidated in the American Enlightenment. We can say, in other words, that at the literary and intellectual level the Southern myth originated primarily in eighteenth-century rationalism and humanism—in the concepts of nature, human nature, and the new concept of history. The Southern literary imagination, no matter how much the mass of nonliterary Southerners subscribed to a Protestantism motivated by the Christian sensibility of a millenial apocalypse, was not compelled by a vision of the South fulfilling a millenial destiny. The Southern literary imagination was not to be heavily influenced by Christian historical determinism until later.

I think we can approach an understanding of the origins of the myth of the South as a spiritual nation by referring to Thomas Jefferson's *Notes on the State of Virginia*, a work Jefferson intended for limited distribution when it first came out in 1787 but which soon became widely and, among his enemies, notoriously known. The most famous passage in it is Jefferson's description of Virginia as an agrarian (or, more precisely as will be argued, a pastoral) civilization made up of self-subsistent yeoman farmers. It comes in Query XIX, one dealing with the question of manufacturing.

Those who labour in the earth are the chosen people of God, if ever he had a chosen people, whose breasts he has made his peculiar deposit for substantial and genuine virtue. It is the focus in which he keeps alive that sacred fire, which otherwise might escape from the face of the earth. Corruption of morals in the mass of cultivators is a phaenomenon of which no age nor nation has furnished an example. It is the mark set on those, who not looking up to heaven, to their own soil and industry, as does the husbandman, for their subsistance [sic], depend for it on the casualties and caprice of customers. . . . While we have land to labour then, let us never wish to see our citizens occupied at a work-bench or twirling a distaff . . . let our work-shops remain in Europe. It is better to carry provisions and materials to workmen there. . . . The loss by the transportation of commodities across the Atlantic will be made up in happiness and permanence of government.[6]

6 Thomas Jefferson, *Notes on the State of Virginia*, ed. William Peden (Chapel Hill, 1955), 164–65. I am indebted in some of my remarks to the brilliant interpretation of Query XIX by Leo Marx in *The Machine and the Garden: Technology and the Pastoral Ideal in America* (New York, 1964), 116–44. As will be apparent, I am generally indebted to William R. Taylor, *Cavalier and Yankee: The Old Society and American National Character* (New York, 1961).

Although Jefferson ostensibly is making an economic argument in this celebration of a self-subsistent, yeoman farming world, he is in truth projecting a vision; he is setting forth a revelation of Virginia as the pastoral repudiation of the Old World dominated by cities, factories, customers, mobs, and wars. Virginia is to be the purification of civilization—the reassertion of man's timeless relation to the mothering earth, which is the source of all virtue. Both Hebraic and classical in inspiration, this passage primarily represents the pastoral (and essentially non-Christian) humanism which was first fully articulated by Virgil and which has been a constant shaping force on the Western literary imagination in its search to transcend the confines of history and society.

We usually think of Jefferson's revelation of the redemptive economy of pastoral—the community of yeoman farmers—as having reference to Virginia generalized as America and the new nation. And it no doubt is. At the time Virginia was, we recall, the largest and the most populous of the states formed out of the old colonies. Jefferson envisions a free, Anglo-Saxon moral American community—the moral result of natural liberty regained in the Revolution—a community freed from avarice and power, existing in peace and permanence of government. Essentially in Query XIX Jefferson envisions a people not chosen to fulfill history but a people freed from history, living in a mortal but indeterminate dimension of time we might call "Arcadian time," a dimension of pastoral permanence.

But we seem always to overlook the fact that the context of this beautiful poem, born of the pure spirit of Hebraic and pastoral humanism, is a vexed treatment of the problem of slavery—the distinctive and peculiar problem of the plantation world of Virginia and the South, in which Jefferson, the master of that perfection of plantations, Monticello, lived and died

211

as the owner of around ten thousand acres and two hundred chattels. Indeed it is against the background of the plantation world of masters and slaves, and in startling contrast to it, that Jefferson projects his vision of the redemptive yeoman community. I refer to the discussion immediately preceding the one celebrating the yeoman, Query XVIII. I also refer to Query XVII (on religion). At the end of Query XVII, Jefferson gives a gloomy forecast about what will happen as the Revolution ends. His prediction is based on a dark view of human nature, which is, to be sure, a part of the eighteenth-century rational view of humanity. After the Revolution, Jefferson says, money making will take over again and the shackles on freedom left unbroken by the Revolution will never be struck. Paradoxically no shackles were more binding on the American sons of liberty, Jefferson understood, than the shackles on the African slaves they owned. He moves from Query XVII into the most thorough denunciation of slavery he ever penned. In Query XVIII he seems to find the problem of slavery so monstrous that it may be beyond the scope of rational solution. It may be solved by an apocalyptic intervention.

There must doubtless be an unhappy influence on the manners of our people produced by the existence of slavery among us. The whole commerce between master and slave is a perpetual exercise of the most boisterous passions, the most unremitting depotism on the one part, and degrading submissions on the other. Our children see this, and learn to imitate it. . . . The parent storms, the child looks on, catches the lineaments of wrath, puts on the same airs in the circle of smaller slaves, gives a loose to his worst of passions, and thus nursed, educated, and daily exercised in tyranny, cannot but be stamped by it with odious peculiarities. The man must be a prodigy who can retain his manners and morals undepraved by such circumstances. . . . With the morals of the people, their industry also is destroyed. For in a warm climate, no man will labour for himself who can make another labour for him.

Jefferson's revelation of the full horror of slavery comes to a climax: "And can the liberties of a nation be thought secure when we have removed their only firm basis, a conviction in the minds of the people that these liberties are the gift of God? That they are not to be violated but with his wrath? Indeed I tremble for my country when I reflect that God is just: that his justice cannot sleep forever: that considering numbers, nature and natural means only, a revolution of the wheel of fortune, an exchange of situation, is among possible events: that it may become probable by supernatural interference!" Query XVIII concludes with the hope that a "total emancipation" of the slaves may come about before the "extirpation" of the masters.[7]

The language of this inquiry into manners is no more sociological than that of Query XIX is economic. Query XVIII is a heightened, dramatic projection of feelings originating, it may be, no less in Jefferson's intimate experience of slavery than in his Enlightenment conviction of the universal nature of man in freedom. The conception of slavery in Query XVIII must be read, however, in the context of notions about slavery Jefferson expresses elsewhere, including some in an earlier part of the *Notes on the State of Virginia*, in which he makes a case for the inferiority of the Negro by reason of color and faculty. In the Great Chain of Being the Negro race belongs in a place below the white race. Jefferson remained convinced of this as an absolute principle of natural history. Taken out of the context of this conviction, Query XIX seems more socially revolutionary than it is. When Jefferson speaks of emancipation, he means only emancipation by foreign colonization of the freed slaves. In Roman times, he points out, slaves, who

7 Jefferson, *Notes on the State of Virginia*, 161, 162–63. On Jefferson and slavery see in particular Winthrop D. Jordan, *White Over Black: American Attitudes toward the Negro, 1550–1812* (Baltimore, 1969), 429–81; William Cohen, "Thomas Jefferson and the Problem of Slavery," *Journal of American History*, LVI (December, 1969), 503–26.

were whites, might be freed to live in the society in which they had been enslaved. Natural history and social history did not come into conflict. But in America an unprecedented situation existed. Jefferson describes it: "Among the Romans emancipation required but one effort. The slave, when made free, might mix with, without staining the blood of his master. But with us a second is necessary, unknown to history. When freed, he is to be removed beyond the reach of mixture." [8]

Emancipation by colonization—Jefferson knew that such an unprecedented action in the history of slavery was probably beyond historical possibility. It might well be beyond the grasp of the imagination of the majority of the master class— he knew this also. Query XVIII in *Notes on the State of Virginia*, although it ends with a glimpse of hope for the South, is close to being an apocalyptic vision of the doom of history to be visited on it. Against the background of this vision, the vision that follows of the redemptive community of yeomen laboring in the earth represents a kind of counter apocalypse. It is a golden revelation of freedom in a society emancipated from the historical necessity of being what it is, an uneasy and insecure society dominated by the relationship of white masters and black chattels.

Looking at Jefferson's hymn to the chosen people against the background of his fearful contrary vision of the fate of the slaveholding world, we conclude that in Query XIX Jefferson is struggling to awaken from the nightmare of the history in which he was intimately involved as a Virginian and a slave master. History, we may say, had happened to Thomas Jefferson; or, we may say, history had chosen his fate, and his image of a yeoman people chosen of God is an effort to resign from it. At any rate, in the *Notes on the State of Virginia* we are

8   Jefferson, *Notes on the State of Virginia*, 143.

in the realm of a distinctly Southern sensibility. We are within the realm of the sensibility of what John Alden has called "the First South." By the age of the Revolution the South had indeed been chosen to have a special role in the spiritual and moral history of America, but the terms of the choice were not clear. In fact they were ambiguous. It was not clear whether the South had been chosen for salvation or damnation, whether it was to be a redemptive agrarian civilization or a doomed slavocracy.

In the years before the Missouri question came up, there is some indication that if slavery could have been allowed to lie passive in the mind, the Southern imagination might have created a coherent vision of a nonmercenary, redemptive South. I mean that the antimaterialistic ideal of Southern agrarianism might have achieved a clearer focus. We glimpse such a vision here and there in Jefferson's writings, still more in the works of John Taylor of Caroline. Taking his stand against the "paper aristocracy" of the North, Taylor became a strongly self-conscious Southerner. Convinced that America must choose between agrarianism and capitalism, he at times generated a vision of the South that suggests an agrarian metaphysic with a Christian coloration.[9]

But significantly about this time there began to appear in the Southern imagination an image of the South as a dispossessed world. Consider the mind of John Randolph of Roanoke. Thoroughly versed in the imaginative literature of the classical ages and the eighteenth century, a neurotic genius, the poet as orator, Randolph foreshadows a resistance of the Southern literary mind to the formulation of any image of

9 See especially Number 59 of Taylor's *Arator* essays. This is reprinted in *Literature of the Early American Republic,* ed. Edwin H. Cady (New York, 1950), 262–65.

the South's role in history save a fatalistic one. Randolph was the first "last gentleman" of the South. According to his aristocratic code, the values of the gentleman are "*truth*, courtesy, bravery, generosity, and learning, which last, although not *essential* to it, yet does very much to adorn and illustrate the character of the true gentleman. . . ." These values came increasingly to Randolph to have an antique cast. Although he regarded Jefferson as a leveler and called him "St. Thomas of Cantingbury," Randolph had no real capacity for opposing democracy. He indicates how the feeling of a historical impasse was building up in the Southern mind and how this early turned the Southerner of poetic or dramatic temperament toward substituting nostalgic retrospection for any struggle to achieve a vision of a stable present and future. "The old gentry have disappeared," he declared with finality. Their world was gone. "I made a late visit to my birthplace," Randolph says in a letter in 1814. "At the end of a journey through a wilderness, I found desolation & stillness as if of death—the fires of hospitality long since quenched—the hearth cold—& the parish church tumbling to pieces, not more from natural decay than sacrilegious violence. This is a faithful picture of this state from the falls of the great river to the sea-board." [10]

Meanwhile, the self-consciousness of the South increased. If we follow Jefferson on the Missouri question, we begin to feel how remorseless the operation of history began to seem to a philosophe who had once believed that man might direct history—how caught up in historical necessity the Southern dream of freedom and permanence in an ahistorical, non-materialistic agrarian civilization became.

In 1821, Jefferson wrote to John Adams:

10 The passages from John Randolph are quoted in Jay B. Hubbell, *The South in American Literature, 1607–1900* (Durham, N. C., 1954), 223–29.

Our anxieties in this quarter are all concentrated in the question, what does the Holy Alliance in and out of Congress mean to do with us on the Missouri question? And this, by-the-bye, is but the name of the case, it is only the John Doe or Richard Roe of the ejectment. The real question, as seen in the States afflicted with this unfortunate population [slaves], is, are our slaves to be presented with freedom and a dagger? For if Congress has the power to regulate the conditions of the inhabitants of the States, within the States, it will be but another exercise of that power, to declare that all shall be free. Are we then to see again Athenian and Lacedemonian confederacies? To wage another Peloponnesian war to settle the ascendency between them? Or is this the tocsin of merely a servile war? That remains to be seen; but not, I hope, by you or me. Surely, they will parley awhile, and give us time to get out of the way. What a Bedlamite is man! [11]

III

It was under pressure of the knowledge of the fatal separation of the Union by slavery that the South's full awareness of its existence as a historical entity developed; and it was under this pressure that the South began to seek a redeeming identity as a people. The South obviously represented more to Southerners than the dissolution of the Union. Did not the South represent the truth of the American Republic? This question is an implied theme in the crisis of self-consciousness that rose in—indeed that *created*—"the mind of the South." I refer to the mind of the pre-Civil War, or Old South, and in a sense to all the minds of all of the Souths envisioned by Southerners down to the present day. One way, and not the only way but one way, to describe the history of Southern fiction, the Southern novel in particular, as it begins to develop from the 1820s on is in terms of the effort of Southern storytellers to focus the idea of the South as the truth of the Republic in a coherent

[11] Andrew S. Lipscomb and others (eds.), *The Writings of Thomas Jefferson* (Washington, D.C., 1905), XV, 308–309.

image. In doing this they altered—shall we say "fictionalized"?
—the "interior and spiritual history" of the South as this had
been developing in the historical First South; and thus helped
to create that illusory South which would, after the Civil War,
become known as the Old South.

Let us regard for a moment the situation in antebellum
Southern fiction.

Antebellum Southern novelists were given the drama which
emerges from the *Notes on the State of Virginia* and, generally, from the letters and papers of Jefferson and other Southern intellectuals from the 1780s on. The implied plot of this
drama concerns the permanence of liberty in opposition to
historical necessity. The leading figures in it are the philosophe
(the eighteenth-century rationalist), the master of the plantation, the yeoman farmer, and the African slave. (In the
Notes on the State of Virginia we can see that the first three
are all guises of Jefferson.) The last figure, although he is interpreted as a distinctly inferior human being, is yet an alien
and threatening presence. He is a threat to the rational man
who in his rationality regards the slave as a lesser human form
in the Great Chain of Being and the potential destroyer of its
beautiful harmony; he is a threat to the yeoman whose self-
subsistent relation to nature will be destroyed if he acquires
slaves; he is a threat to the master whose soul he corrupts by
fascinating him with the love of power and of money and by
alienating him from the restoring source of virtue, labor in the
earth. Whether the Garden of the South is thought of as a
farm or a plantation, the slave is an evil in it.

Obviously if Southern novelists could have realized the
potential of the drama of the inner history of the South as this
may be seen in Jefferson and Randolph, a Faulkner might have
been Hawthorne's contemporary. From the First South the
Southern novelists inherited a divided vision: the South as a

218

world of sturdy and independent yeomen and the South as a possibly doomed plantation society of masters and slaves. The conflict in a society trying to subscribe to such antithetical images of itself would seem to be rich matter for the literary imagination. How much so, as a matter of fact, is suggested to a degree in such a novel as George Tucker's *The Valley of Shenandoah*. In this story something of the struggle between the Southern yeomanry and an insecure plantation aristocracy that is aware of the evil of buying and selling slaves is suggested; as of course it is suggested in a number of antebellum Southern novels. But after Tucker's novel, published in the mid-1820s, whatever may be made of the yeoman world in Southern fiction, it is dominated by the image of the plantation. The informing rationale of the antebellum Southern novel was dictated by the need—accentuated after 1830 by the nullification controversy and antislavery agitation—to establish the image of the South as a redemptive plantation order. Logically, the Southern novel, under the compulsion to defend slavery, must seek to define the Southern plantation as the static image of a community of chosen people existing in a pastoral dispensation which it is America's destiny to fulfill. The logic of definition further demanded that the planter be made into a pastoral patriarch (not, it must emphasized, a feudal lord) and that somehow the slave be conceived as a pastoral figure. The Southern plantation would then emerge as a version of pastoral unique in literary history but continuous with the tradition of Western pastoral as a celebration of the nonmaterialistic realm of existence.

Some such version of the plantation South as the pastoral redemption of America was created by the antebellum Southern novelists. All of them were influenced by the literary strategy John Pendleton Kennedy employs fully in the prototypical plantation romance, *Swallow Barn*. This resembles the strategy of Arcadian time Jefferson used in Query XIX of *Notes on the State of Virginia*. Kennedy aims to foster the illusion that in contrast to the disorder of the present (to innovating materialism justified by a spurious faith in Progress) Swallow Barn plantation represents a life of pastoral permanence. But to idealize the plantation in the pastoral mode, opposing the image of the plantation to the historical present, was difficult. Indeed it proved to be impossible. One notes from the beginning of the literary plantation that it exists not in an indeterminate or ideal time but in an indeterminate past time, in nostalgic time, in the dimension, as Swallow Barn plantation, of "old-fashioned" time; and it is filled with old-fashioned persons, notably the two figures whose relationship comes to be central and critical in the plantation novel, the old-fashioned planter-master and the old-fashioned slave.

They had to be creatures of nostalgia because the literary imagination could not reconcile the distance between their historical existence and the sense of pastoral time. To do so would be to conceive of them in a natural relationship transcending slavery; when their actual relationship to the source of all virtue, the earth, was a bondage that confounded them both.

If virtue is rural, if it stems from labor in the earth, then the slave should be as virtuous as the master—acting in some sense as the peasant was imagined to act in the capacity of an intermediary between the virtue conferred by direct contact with the soil and the lord's supervision of his labor and his life. But the slave was a chattel, in brutal economic terms, a thing. As Allen Tate has pointed out, he did not even belong to the land as the peasant did; he was a barrier between the master and his affiliation with the earth, connecting the master logically with the marketplace, where the product of the slave's labor was sold and where he himself might be sold. The slave, moreover, was as much a cog in the industrial machine as he was a laborer in the earth, the product of his labor being the raw material of the mills of New England and Europe. Also, it might be observed, if as a kind of lame afterthought, the European pastoral tradition did not include Africans among the herdsmen and swains who sing in the pastoral gardens of literary imagining, even though a slave might be named Theocritus or Virgil.

In sum, the image of the South as a redemptive community in the ideal of the plantation portrayed in the antebellum novels was not convincing. Southern storytellers were not able to dramatize a vital mythic opposition between a redemptive plantation life and the materialistic drive in society. And there was no way out of the dilemma they were placed in by historical necessity. They were compelled by the ideology of slavery, centering in an absolutist defense of the peculiar institution as an agrarian institution (when in fact the context of slavery was the industrial revolution, not an agrarian restoration), to make the plantation the central image of the South.

Nonetheless, the Southern novel, seeking to reveal a moral and spiritual South in the community symbolized by the literary plantation, amounts to a good deal more than a mere rationalization of the slavery system. From George Tucker's *The Valley of Shenandoah* through the works of William A. Carruthers and John Esten Cooke, Southern novels are a part of a yearning, and of a struggle, in the Southern literary imagination to discover in the life of the plantation South an image of the South transcending historical existence.

Such an image would emerge after the evolving myth of the South was liberated from the static world view demanded by the defense of slavery, and the South as a spiritual nation became subject both to the nostalgic and apocalyptic modes of perception in the literary mind. I mean after the Southern literary imagination experienced the most intense form of historical consciousness known in the modern age—an age when nationalism has been the chief form of existence in history. This is the consciousness of the spiritual condition of the invaded, defeated, and occupied nation.

IV

I cannot explore this consciousness in any detail here. Let me merely suggest that after the Civil War—the war the South called the War for Southern Independence—the defeated Confederate States of America, began to emerge out of the older image of the South in the form of a sacramental nation. Purified by the war, the South in defeat more than ever symbolized to its citizens the truth of the Republic, to which it had, in the Republic's corrupted state, been forcibly returned. To its citizens the South would continue in an America reunited and yet divided to represent this truth. What the South now stood for, as a matter of fact, was more expansive and transcendent than before the war. The cause of political and economic Southern nationhood was lost but not the cause of Southern civilization: redemption from the ever increasing power of modern materialism. In his highly influential history of the Civil War from the Southern point of view (1866) Edwin A. Pollard, editor of the Richmond *Examiner* during the war years, warns against the South's concentrating upon "recovering the mere *material* prosperity" and admonishes Southerners to assert their well-known superiority in civilization. If the South has lost its political autonomy, it has not lost its "peculiar civilization" nor its "schools of literarture and scholarship" nor its "forms of . . . thoughts" nor its "style of . . . manners." Moved by this conviction the Southern imagination began to establish a mystique of Southern identity based on a poetic attitude toward victory-in-defeat. "But once the War was over," Robert Penn Warren has observed, "the Confederacy became a City of the Soul, beyond the haggling of constitutional lawyers, the ambition of politicians, and the jealousy of localisms." Warren continues, "We may say that only at the moment when Lee handed Grant his sword was the Confederacy born; or to state matters another way, in the moment of death the Confederacy entered upon its immortality."[12]

But the impulse to divinize Southern civilization did not proceed alone from military defeat; it proceeded more powerfully from the reaction to the massive effort of the conquering power to impose "reconstruction" upon the aborted nation. The martyrdom of the South became more nearly Reconstruction than military catastrophe, and the metaphor of the destiny of Southern civilization became the Christian Resurrection. Thomas Nelson Page in his once famous address "The Old South" proclaimed in the late 1880s:

> Two-and-twenty years ago there fell upon the South a blow for which there is no metaphor among the casualties which may befall a man. It was not simply paralysis; it was death. It was destruction under the euphemism of reconstruction. She was crucified; bound hand and foot; wrapped in the cerements of the grave; laid away in the sepulchre of the departed; the mouth of the sepulchre was stopped, was sealed with the seal of government, and a watch was set. The South was dead, and buried, and yet she rose again. The voice of God called her forth; she came clad in her grave-clothes, but living, and with her face uplifted to the heavens from which had sounded the call of her resurrection.[13]

In such an imagining of the Southern destiny, the image of

12 Edwin A. Pollard, *The Lost Cause: A New Southern History of the War of the Confederation* (New York, 1866), 751; Robert Penn Warren, *The Legacy of the Civil War: Meditations on the Centennial* (New York, 1964), 14–15.

13 Thomas Nelson Page, *The Old South: Essays Social and Political* (New York, 1892), 4.

the redemptive South is obviously transformed from the Arcadian image into one primarily derived from Christian eschatology. The South represents a truth of man and society that God will not allow to remain dead but summons back to fulfill its divine mission in history.

Page creates the impression that the whole of the Civil War and Reconstruction constitutes an apostasy not only from the true principles of the Union but from the true principles of Christian civilization. Both sets of principles are based on the conservation of moral qualities as opposed to materialistic desires; the South stood, Page says, on the overall principle of "the reduction of everything to principles." And Page offers the hope that the South can yet save the American Union "from the materialistic tendencies" which still threaten its existence. At the same time in his address, "The Old South," Page is drawn toward creating the impression that the Old South represented a unique, doomed, and irrecoverable civilization, for which the present can only have the greatest nostalgia. But more significant than the tension between apostasy and nostalgia Page sets up is the reason he gives for the South's defeat in the War. It was lost because the Old South did not create a literature. And the Old South did not do so, paradoxically, because of her lack of interest in material wealth. Page has the idea that the South failed to set up a publishing industry and a literary market place because Southerners did not want to become materialistic about letters. Southern writing consequently did not become a profession, and when the crisis came the South did not have the literary resources to solicit "the outside support" she needed. The North got this help. Page says: "Only study the course of the contest against the South and you cannot fail to see how she was conquered by the pen rather than by the sword; and how unavailing against the resources of the world, which the North had commanded through the sympathy it had enlisted, was the valiance of that heroic army, which, if courage could have availed, had withstood the universe."[14]

But now the story of Southern civilization must be told: "The heroic story of the Old South . . . must be sung through the ages." Not out of any simple motive of nostalgia. Southern writers, in Page's terms, become in effect the priests of a literary resurrection which will be the resurrection of the South.

I dwell on Thomas Nelson Page because it seems to me that he is the continuator of the literary plantation who is the direct prophet of the literary apocalypse that is modern Southern storytelling. In setting up an image of the South as a redemptive nation, he was motivated both by the conviction of an apostasy from the Southern moral order and by nostalgia for the Old South. In Page apostasy and nostalgia fuse to provide a mythic perspective for the Southern storyteller. Most importantly, the South becomes a coherent revelation that occurs within the storyteller's imagination; and not only this, the revealing of the revelation becomes the imperative of his identity. In a hyperbolic paradox Page links the Southern writer to the doom of the South. It was a literary failure—the absence of the writer, the failure of his presence, which was in itself a result of the South's nonmaterialistic civilization—that caused the South to lose the War for Southern Independence. Now at last the writer is himself to become a redemptive figure in the fulfillment of the South as a redemptive community. Page discovers that the Southern literary imagination is the medium through which the revelation of the meaning of the interior and spiritual history of the South is to be completed. This was potentially a momentous discovery.[15]

14 Ibid., 150.
15 For lack of space I am isolating this discovery in Page. Other writers, notably Joel Chandler Harris and George Washington Cable,

But Page was more a prophetic Southern apologist than a storyteller. His novels and short stories are notably lacking in the dimension of the imagination that would bring about the full participation of the Southern storyteller in the ripening myth of the South. Page had, you might say, an excess of piety and a deficiency of irony. He lacked the sense of irony required if a Southern writer is to control the myth of his people as a Hawthorne does.

V

It would take another generation and another great war, the First World War, before Southern writers would experience the revelation of the plantation South as a redemptive community with something approaching full artistic comprehension. The writers of the Southern Renaissance—John Crowe Ransom, Allen Tate, Donald Davidson, Robert Penn Warren, William Faulkner, Eudora Welty, and a number of others— experienced this, as I have tried to show elsewhere, when they became conscious of the coalescence of their sensibility as modern American writers and as modern Southern writers.[16] When they became sufficiently aware that the South is a part of the apocalypse of modern civilization: the revelation of the horror of a scientific-industrial-technological machine which operates completely on the principle of endless consumption, and is in fact consuming the world.

Of the Southern writers the one who most adequately realizes the apocalypse is William Faulkner. Like Hawthorne he became a lonely and withdrawn man and after making two

---

should be considered in relation to it, as indeed should Mark Twain, who, however, is a special case. But the sensibility of Page, now mostly unread, is central in the history of the Southern literary imagination.

16 See "The Southern Writer and the Great Literary Secession" in this volume.

or three more or less false starts in his writing, he had a revelation of the history of that little postage stamp of a world which was his own world, and that became Yoknapatawpha County —and not less than the whole South and, for that matter, not less than the whole world. But Yoknapatawpha County remains the South, as Hawthorne's New England, for all its universalism, remains New England—a special place inhabited by a people who have perceived an image of themselves as a chosen and redeeming community. The storytellers, the poets, of such a community are both shaped in this image and help to fashion it. Eventually in a late stage of this community the mind of one of the storytellers, who is gifted with great literary genius, possesses—in piety and irony—the whole struggle of his people, in all their differences, to know their meaning. And the revelation is given culminating form. He writes down the inner truth of his people.

He writes it down, as Faulkner said, in agony and sweat; for the modern prophetic writer, Faulkner knew, as Hawthorne knew (and some modern writers have failed to see) is not an incarnation of God. I think of "The Bear" and one of the greatest scenes in Faulkner, that night in the McCaslin plantation commissary—the commissary as a symbol of Old South materialism may be one way to take the setting—when Isaac McCaslin tries to reveal to McCaslin Edmonds a revelation that he (Ike) has had in his heart: slavery has cursed the very earth of the South, and the only way he can attone for the curse is to dispossess himself of all title to the McCaslin land. Ike does not in any literal way suggest Dimmesdale to us. He does not tear off his shirt and reveal a slave brand burning his flesh. But in a way he does preach an eloquent sermon. Ike talks about the revelation that has come to him in the light of biblical revelation. Cass reminds him what the Old Testament says about the sons of Ham. If the sons of Ham were not

227

meant to be slaves, then the storytellers in the Bible are liars. Ike says, "Yes. Because they were human men. They were trying to write down the truth out of the heart's driving complexity, for all the complex and troubled hearts that would beat after them." [17] Ike is talking about the revelation of the community of human kind that comes from the complex and troubled heart of the biblical storyteller, who was seer and prophet, who meditated deeply on the story of a chosen community's constant and doomed involvement in the struggle between freedom and necessity. The storyteller told his people their story out of his own heart and out of his own art as God gave him the power to tell it.

It was this role that Faulkner himself assumed, once he found out it was the role that had been given to him. This is not to confuse Faulkner with Ike, still less to say that he was a scribe of God, but it is to say that he was a scribe—both pious and ironic—of a people seeking a revelation of themselves as a redeeming community. Faulkner was a poet of the complex and troubled heart—of the interior and spiritual history—of the South. Focusing this history in the plantation legend, he embraced finally the wholeness of the diversity of Southern history, to become the writer who has made the most complete synthesis of the spiritual condition that was and is now the American South. Faulkner's achievement is the measure of the revelation of the South that is the substance of modern Southern fiction.

17 The quotations are from "The Bear" as it appears in Malcolm Cowley (ed.), *The Portable Faulkner* (New York, 1964), 294–95.

✌§ The Southern Writer
   and the Great Literary Secession

RECEIVING THE National Medal for Literature from the National Book Committee in 1967, W. H. Auden—a United States citizen since 1946—accepted it not in the name of his fellow American writers but "in the name of all my fellow-citizens in the Republic of Letters, that holy society which knows no national frontiers, possesses no military hardware, and where the only political duty on all of us at all times is to love the Word and defend it against its enemies." And yet I wonder if Auden paradoxically has been anywhere more the American writer than he is in this cosmopolitan declaration. His profession of faith in the catholic, sacramental community of letters invokes the power of an imagination of literary order which—in spite of the effort of nationalistically minded critics and historians to put the label "made in America" on all our writing—has been a dominant motive in the twentieth-century American vocation to letters.

We find this motive at work not only in our literary wanderers, exiles, and expatriates—James, Pound, Eliot, Hemingway—but in some of our writers who have been associated with the species of American nationalism known as regionalism. We will of course think of the South and of William Faulkner. I am thinking now especially of the motive of the American Southerners of the 1920s and 1930s known as the Fugitives and Agrarians—of Andrew Lytle, Robert Penn Warren, and all of them, but particularly of the three central figures of the famous Agrarian group: John Crowe Ransom, Donald Davidson, and Allen Tate. They are suspected, today as yesterday, of being inspired by a paranoiac Southern nationalism—of being unreconstructed neo-Confederate fascists plotting the reconstruction of the South, perhaps of the whole nation, as an agrarian totalitarianism. But when they are considered in the light of their *essential* historical motivation as men of letters, their inspiration, I would argue, did not derive from what we ordinarily consider to be politics. It came from their struggle to imagine the authoritative role of the modern Southern writer in the attempted restoration of a politics of the Word or polity of letters. How this is so emerges when we study the Agrarians in the context of the history of the imagination of literary order in modern Western letters. In this context they illuminate the role of the writer generally in modern times and particularly the role of the Southern writer.

I

At the time the poets to become known as the Fugitives, and later as the chief figures in the Agrarian group, gathered in Nashville, Tennessee, we see a great upsurge of literary and artistic activity in Western civilization. A response to the catastrophe of the First World War, this took the form of an apocalyptic creativity, echoing Paul Valéry's famous loud tolling of the bell for Western civilization in his 1919 essay, "The Crisis of the Mind": "We later civilizations . . . we too know that we are mortal. . . . And now we see that the abyss of history is deep enough to hold us all. We are aware that a Civilization has the same fragility as a life. The circumstances that could send the works of Keats and Baudelaire to join the works of Menander are no longer inconceivable; they are in the newspapers."

Here is the anxious, fascinated realization of cultural mortality that haunts—and yet animates—the profound and comprehensive literary imaginations we associate with the group of writers now called "the traditionalist moderns."

It is, notably, a fascination with the mortality of words, and it implies a recognition of the manner in which Western civilization is preeminently a verbal one, founded on the power of the conscious, educated use of words or letters, that is, on literary discipline. This is a great power but mortally subject to the fragility of words and the precariousness of the use of letters. Edward Gibbon makes a classical statement of this recognition in *The Decline and Fall of the Roman Empire*: "The Germans, in the age of Tacitus, were unacquainted with the use of letters; and the use of letters is the principal circumstance that distinguishes a civilized people from a herd of savages incapable of knowledge or reflection."

Aware of complexities and subtleties in the use of language Gibbon did not dream of—and nevertheless inescapably the inheritors of his vision of the artifice of words—twentieth-century poets, novelists, and critics became preoccupied with the twin themes of language and the renewal of language. Moreover, without fully divining the basic inspiration of their effort, twentieth-century men of letters became preoccupied with the "Republic of Letters." In the years following the First World War they reaffirmed the notion of representing the literary existence as one of the orders of Western society—to support, that is to say, the faith that the "spirit of letters" represents a separate realm of being and the belief that this realm offers the possibility of walling us against the abyss and of bringing order out of chaos. To grasp this, however—to under-

231

stand what Auden is talking about in his speech—is not easy. We must study the struggle to symbolize the life of the mind under the aspect of letters over a long period of time, for the past two thousand years and over. We must involve ourselves in a study that calls for us—especially those of us who are in some sense consciously literary people—to examine the structure of a commonplace notion about our existence that we may assume without knowing we assume it.

How was the "holy society" Auden proclaims his allegiance to created? To start at some point less remote than the age of stone tablets, we can find the symbolic discrimination of the literary realm developing in Alexandrian and in Athenian times, but we do not find the basis of a literary universalism rising until the Roman world, through the appropriation of Greek letters and art, brings cosmopolitanism into being. Thus we come to the ideal cosmopolis of the Stoics (the cosmopolis to which men belong because they participate in the Logos); and we come to Arcadia (which represents, Bruno Snell says in *The Discovery of the Mind*, Virgil's vision in his *Eclogues* of the pastoral mode as an independent world of literary art). The unfolding distinction of the realm of letters as a realm of being is enhanced—ultimately if not appreciably for several centuries—by the Christian ecumenicalism of the Word. By later medieval times the City of God or the Republic of Christ distinctly nurtured the literary cosmopolitanism of later Roman times. In the preservation of the ancient writers and in the development of the concept of the university, the medieval clerks provided for a distinction of the realm of letters from the Church and the State that had not been known before.

How "historically concrete" did the polity of letters become? It became visibly expressed, we can see, in the humanists and philosophes—in the lives of Erasmus, Voltaire, Franklin, Jefferson—and in the universities, the academies, and eventually in the clubs, salons, coffee-houses, and the correspondence of men of letters. In the Renaissance the term "Republic of Letters" became a commonplace, and in its commonplaceness asserted the realm of letters as a realm of moral being—all the more so as the Reformation destroyed the unity of Christendom. The assumption of the reality—the substance and power —of the literary republic reached a climax in the full tide of the eighteenth-century Enlightenment; when, divided though they were by many animosities, men of letters were at the same time united—in their hostilities as well as their friendships. In the middle of the eighteenth century Voltaire declared that the Republic of Letters had been consolidated in Europe—"a great fellowship of intellect, spread everywhere and everywhere independent." From St. Petersburg in the Russia of Catherine the Great to Philadelphia, Williamsburg, and Boston, the fraternity and authority of men of letters (philosophes and Augustans) was the bond of a common citizenship.

In the heyday of the Enlightenment a kind of precarious balance of power among Church, State, and Letters was effected. This was achieved as the Enlightenment appropriated and synthesized in the context of reason the symbols of literary order inherited both from ancient times and medieval times and from Renaissance humanism. (The Jeffersonian doctrine of the separation of Church and State implies the separation of Church, State, and Letters. The autonomy of the "third realm" is the necessary source of the intellectual discrimination between the first two.) And yet, even in its greatest age, the success of the Republic of Letters was threatened by novel historical forces: integral nationalism, equalitarian democracy, scientific specialization of knowledge, industrial and technological specialization of function, and the dynamics of a capitalistic market economy. The complex operation of these forces would accelerate what Hannah Arendt in *The Human*

Condition terms "the rise of society." Making a gloss on the margins of her distinguished book, we might say that we see in the rise of the social the absorption of the orders of being into society—that mingling of all private and public life which, she says, "always demands that its members act as though they were members of one enormous family which has only one opinion and one interest." Deeply implicit in the rise of society—in the confusion of Church, State, and Letters—is the remarkable self-consciousness that has marked the vocation of the man of letters for almost two centuries: characterizing, let us say for the sake of immediacy, a Norman Mailer or a Robert Lowell. Both are end results of the historical loss of literary order or autonomy; of the user of words and letters having to locate the sense of transcendent literary autonomy within himself.

Toward the beginning of the nineteenth century the literary realm entered into a prolonged state of crisis, which we are more than ever in today, and of which Valéry's mood in "The Crisis of Mind" or Auden's mood in his National Medal award speech may be taken simply as latter-day manifestations. The literary history of the past century and a half—pointedly the history of the vocation to literature—centers in the participation of writers in this crisis. By this I mean the struggle of the man of letters to represent the imperatives of the Word—in spite of the pressing medley of demands upon him exerted by the politics of nationalism and the politics of democracy, by specialization and money, and by the whole intricate apparatus of the technological materialism in which and by which the modern age uniquely lives in history. This spirit of representation is, I assume, integral to the careers of two of the writers mentioned in the passage I have quoted from Valéry: Keats and Baudelaire. Baudelaire speaks out of it when he says, "The man of letters is the world's enemy." This declaration is the slogan or the text of the great modern movement in literature. Marked by the defection of the most original literary minds from society, this may be called the Great Literary Secession. This defection governs the concept of the literary vocation which gives us the modern image of the man of letters as a prophet-priest-artist. At once a man of solitude and a member of a community, or an order, of literary alienation, he is a figure often absurd yet often heroic.

II

Two outstanding features of the national American literary history are: one, it falls almost entirely within the period of the crisis of the literary order; two, under the comparatively naked cultural circumstances of American life, it represents a more definitive expression of this crisis than does modern European literary history. These facts ought to be taken into account in any theory of American literature, and of the American writer, and I have attempted in some places elsewhere to do so. But I have never more than suggested what keeps forcibly reoccurring to me in studying nineteenth-century Southern writing and writers: a cardinal aspect of American literary history is that in the South the crisis of the literary order took a singularly acute form. It acted effectively to prevent Southern writers from participating in the primary literary power of their time—that is, the creative power generated by the Great Literary Secession. It cut them off from experiencing the self-consciousness which is the major literary resource of modern times; it denied them the resources of alienation.

How productive these resources could be in America is shown to varying degrees in the careers of Emerson, Thoreau, Hawthorne, Melville, and (I think with some reservations) Whitman. And of course I must add Poe—most of all, the

Southerner Poe, one may say, the paragon of alienation. Baudelaire deified him and prayed to him. But Poe's enigmatic career is, I trust, the exception that demonstrates my thesis. Poe's career had a strong relation to his life outside the South; however we may explain it, we cannot do so basically in terms of his integral Southernism.

Let us settle for a minute on Henry David Thoreau, who in *Walden* created one of the outstanding documents of the Great Literary Secession. The book is written from the point of view of the first person. "I . . . require of every writer, first or last," he says in the beginning, "a simple and sincere account of his own life, and not merely what he has heard of other men's lives, some such account as he would send from a distant land; for if he has lived simply, it would be a distant land to me." The pages that follow are anything but simple. In this complex, long-meditated, carefully structured, exquisitely written, and desperate work, we have possibly the most complete and satisfying portrait of the American writer as a figure of alienation in our literature. The authorial "I" emerges in perfect moral purity as the prophet-priest-artist struggling against the democratic-technological materialism of his age. He emerges, furthermore, in the guise of an Arcadian or pastoral prophet-priest-artist. How significant this is may be estimated if one studies Leo Marx's noted book, *The Machine in the Garden: Technology and the Pastoral Ideal in America*. Adapting Marx's argument somewhat here (Marx does not deal with the Agrarian group), I would observe that Thoreau in *Walden* brings to a logical climax the American—let us say the Jeffersonian—affinity for the pastoral, as opposed to the urban image of literary order and the literary vocation. Descending into the American Enlightenment from Virgil's imagining of an independent realm of literary art, the pastoral mode of literary order dominated the American imagination of literary order on into the time, as I shall shortly indicate, of the Southern Agrarians. As Americans conceived of the Republic of the United States as a pastoral republic, American writers were drawn toward a concept of the Republic of Letters as constituting a pastoral order. In the crisis of the literary order Thoreau makes the right response: he sets up a controlling image of the literary vocation. Walden Woods becomes one of the redemptive homelands of the modern literary spirit.

Well, why did not Henry David Thoreau have a contemporary in the South? Why not a literary renaissance in the South? If in the American appropriation of the symbols of literary order and vocation, the pastoral symbol had been favored over the urban symbol, the nineteenth-century South should have been the place for it to flower. Indeed the pastoral image of literary order was beautifully and fully embodied in Thomas Jefferson's Monticello; on his little mountain three miles from the small town of Charlottesville, Virginia, the American Republic of Letters found a leading center. The New Englanders were aware of this. Before young George Ticknor—Federalist that he was, a Bostonian's Bostonian, and thus supposedly a true-blue despiser of Jefferson—began his famous literary sojourn in Europe in 1815, he traveled with considerable difficulty all the way to Monticello. He wanted to get letters of introduction from Jefferson to men of letters in Europe, but he also wanted to get his blessing. The winding road up Jefferson's mountain, Ticknor understood, led to the heart of the Republic of Letters. Figuratively speaking, Thoreau also made the journey to Monticello, and his was more significant than Ticknor's. The distance from the hut in Walden Woods to Monticello was not so far as from Beacon Hill to Monticello. Thoreau drew more literary power from Jefferson than did the conservative Ticknor. This may be measured by the beginning sentences of Thoreau's greatest plea for the

independent order of the literary artist, "Civil Disobedience."
Thoreau approves heartily of Jefferson's dictum "that government is best which governs least" but goes the logical step
further to say "that government is best which governs not at
all." Thoreau, nonetheless, does not suggest that this "best"
government is for everyman. At the end of his essay he makes
it clear that it is for "a few." And although he does not describe them, does he not mean men of letters like himself and
Jefferson, the members of the literary patriciate? The conclusion of "Civil Disobedience" is a vision, rarefied though it is,
not of anarchy, but of the transcendent, autonomous literary
order.

But no such relationship as that between Jefferson and
Thoreau developed in the mind of any of Thoreau's Southern
contemporaries. The literary fruits of estrangement from the
scientific-industrial-technological revolution did not ripen in
the Southern sun; there were in fact no plants to bear them.
This was not, I conjecture, because the midnineteenth-century
South did not have the right potential conditions for fruitful
literary alienation. Potentially it had better conditions than
the North. By the 1830s the inheritance of the Jeffersonian
pastoral sense of literary order in the South came up against
the leading force of American history—an evolving technological materialism—in a most dramatic way. By this time the
Southern area of the Great American Garden—of all the areas
the richest by far: temperate in climate, abundant in water,
fertile in soil, lush in forests and vegetation, teeming with
birds, fish, and animals—had not only been invaded by machines, but had yoked the age of machinery to its anachronistic
"peculiar institution" of chattel slavery. Machines—the cotton
gin, the steamboat, the railroad—made the Southern Garden,
including a good deal of it which was virgin frontier, into the
Cotton Kingdom. The Cotton Kingdom was no isolated

agrarian world; it was a vital part of the raw-materials supply system of the developing industrial-technological complex of Western society.

In this situation, it seems logical to suppose, the South might have had two or three Thoreaus, who, discovering a condition so contrary to pastoral virtue, might have taken to cabins in the piney woods to meditate upon the ironies of the invasion of the Southern Garden by the machine. But there was no pastoral detachment of the literary self in the South. The only Southern writers (after the early 1830s when the last debates in the South about slavery occurred) forcefully to attack the industrial materialism of their day did so in the name of slavery. Everyone who studies Southern literature reads David J. Grayson's "The Hireling and the Slave," a long poem in classic couplets which presents the degraded condition of the industrial hireling of the Northern factory in contrast to the secure, happy condition of the slave in the little cabin on the plantation:

> The cabin home, not comfortless, though rude,
> Light daily labor, and abundant food,
> The sturdy health that temperate habits yield,
> The cheerful song that rings in every field,
> The long, loud laugh, that free men seldom share.

Literary cabins in the South were built for occupancy by contented but illiterate slaves. None were constructed by alienated intellectuals. In the Old South, literary pastoralism became devoted wholly to the defense of slavery instead of the defense of poetry.

The reason Southern writers so completely lost their capacity for ironic disaffection, or simply for ironic detachment, is that in the South the crisis of the literary order did not express itself, and this because in the South the literary realm virtually disappeared. With the realm of the Church it was

239

assimilated into the realm of the State, which came finally to allow only the politics of Southern nationalism; and this was only the politics of slavery. Or, possibly it is more accurate to say that in the Old South, Church, State, and Letters were all three absorbed by the rise of a Society dominated by a class convinced that its existence depended on fostering a social order centered in "only one opinion and one interest." This class, the planter class of the antebellum South and those associated with its interests, advanced the notion that for both racial and economic reasons chattel slavery was an absolute necessity. Although the majority of Southerners did not own slaves, they agreed to this proposition. Whether or not this agreement was absolute (as the consensus thesis of Southern history holds) or relative to an appreciable amount of dissent from Southern abolitionists and Unionists, it was pervasive enough to qualify the image both of the ecclesiastical order and the literary order and to circumscribe the role both of the man of God and the man of letters. In this situation the literati of the Old South tended—in spite of the South's cultural and social pluralism and its stubborn personalism—to become an ideological community on the issue of slavery. The only heroic guises they could project for the man of letters in the South were those of the gentleman planter and the chivalric hero. These were more disguises than guises, especially for a gifted man of letters like William Gilmore Simms—who is, if we make Poe a special case, the central figure in antebellum Southern letters. In his attempt to fulfill the literary vocation, Simms, who began his career aspiring to citizenship in the cosmopolitan literary world descended from Jefferson, committed himself in the 1840s to the defense of slavery; and he ended up as the self-appointed, parochial laureate of South Carolina— the only flower, he said, of modern civilization. (Which is a heavy burden even for South Carolina to bear.) In view of his great talent, if not genius, Simms's history, filled with as much suffering as Poe's, is in a way a literary horror story more depressing than Poe's. Poe eventually emerged a saint of the alienated. But poor Simms! Allen Tate in "The Profession of Letters in the South" holds him up as a horrid example of the literary failure of the antebellum South. Simms alone seems to be a sufficient explanation of why a literary renaissance did not occur in the South of the 1840s and 1850s.

III

"With the war of 1914–1918, the South," Allen Tate has observed, "re-entered the modern world—but gave a backward glance as it stepped over the border; that backward glance gave us the Southern renascence, a literature conscious of the past in the present." This interpretation of the origin of the great period of writing in the twentieth-century South has almost become classic. It is, I think, subject to some revision. The South, I have suggested (and I believe we must grant), has historically been inseparably a part of the modern world since the founding of the nation, an event coinciding with the invention of the cotton gin. We can say, I think, that after the First World War the South entered the modern world in a special sense: Southern writers joined the Great Literary Secession. So doing of course they reentered an old world—that is, the literary realm of Western High Culture, the world of Voltaire, Gibbon, and Jefferson, which had been carried on in its strongest expression by the literary secessionist movement of the nineteenth century, continuing, reinvigorated, in the twentieth.

At this point we may well pause to ask: Why did not the post–Civil War Southern writers join in the literary secessionist movement? This is a good and difficult question, but it is one that I cannot in the limitations of space deal with here except in gross generalities. If we make a special case of Mark Twain as a Southern writer (and I think that along with the instance of Poe, we must do so) we do not find Southern writers in the half century before the First World War expressing a vivid discontent with the burgeoning scientific-industrial-technological order.* Sidney Lanier had strong intimations of such discontent, but he did not set up an opposing construct of literary order (like Thoreau's *Walden*), nor did he consciously seek to make of himself an image of the alienated writer. What seems to have happened is that the Southern literary mind by and large continued to operate in the political realm—dominated by a politics that, whether it expressed a defense of the Old South or a vision of the New South, was essentially a politics of apology or justification. The South—and this is something we do not at times understand, allowing ourselves to be misled by terms like regionalism and sectionalism—was a defeated national polity. It was a nation, the Confederate States of America, that had been defeated in history, and by history, and had to justify the continuing historical existence of its people under the conditions of this defeat. For half a century Southern writers, attempting to explore and to define these conditions, were still emotionally assimilated by the political realm. The imagination of literary order and/or the role of the writer was subordinate to the politics of apology—the latter-day self-conscious justification of an aborted national will.

When this defense took the form of a nostalgic postbellum apology for slavery, it still often implied a criticism or distrust of industrialism. But in Thomas Nelson Page and others who supported the Lost Cause through the plantation legend, there

---

* The most important discussion of Mark Twain as a Southern writer is found in Louis D. Rubin, Jr., *The Writer in the South: Studies in a Literary Community* (Athens, Ga., 1972), 34–81.

is no edge to this distrust. And it is scarcely present in the popular type of romantic plot which features the reconciliation of North and South through the love of a pure Southern lass and a Yankee lad of irreproachable morals. In fact, save for Robert L. Dabney and a few other hardcore, dedicated throwbacks to John Taylor of Caroline, Southern literati managed to weep for a lost past and either tacitly accept or glorify New South industrialism at the same time. Indeed as Southern nationalism assumed the mien of the New South, an association between the potential greatness of the South industrialized and a potential renaissance in Southern letters developed. This is how we get people like Edwin Mims and Henry L. Snyder, in the first two decades of the twentieth century, envisioning the voice of the machine and of the poet in the South speaking together.

A half century or more after the secession of the South and the establishment of the nation of the Confederacy, Southern writers still had not found a convincing image of their existence as *modern* writers.

IV

The public and formal announcement of the Southern literary secession was made in 1930 with the issuance of the famous Agrarian manifesto, *I'll Take My Stand*, in which the key issue of modern culture is seen as *Agrarian vs. Industrial*. Issued by the most intense and coherent literary group in America since the Transcendentalists, this document implies at once the Southern discovery of the crisis of the literary order, the image of the modern writer as the estranged heroic prophet-priest-artist, and the necessity of restoring the Third Realm—the literary order—as a redemptive force in Western civilization. These implications were not clear to the makers of the manifesto, not even to the leaders, Ransom, Tate, and Davidson.

243

But during the decade when they were Fugitives, they had a growing vision of the crisis of the literary order and of the vocation to letters. Its unfolding was slow, but it had something of the force of a revelation. As a matter of fact, when we study the Fugitives with reference to a developing vision of literary order, they appear to have followed the pattern of withdrawal and return common in the psychology of visions.

The time of the meetings of the Fugitive poets and of the publication of *The Fugitive* in the early 1920s was one of the dissociation of the Southern literary mind from the South, of release from the politics of apology. This detachment was obviously fostered in part by the South's general acceptance of the First World War as an expression of the reunited nation's messianic role in history, now proclaimed to be to "save the world for democracy." The Lost Cause in its purest form passed into the trust of the surviving members of the United Confederate Veterans, and Southern youth, volunteers and willing draftees, embarked for adventures at Belleau Wood and St.-Mihiel. The Southern literary mind underwent a kind of liberation from its pietistic obligation always to celebrate in some way what might have been. It became possible to see the disaster of 1861–1865 for what it was, a historical episode. But the withdrawal of the Fugitives from the politics of apology is not to be explained simply by the First World War. The war helped to confirm a sophistication of outlook that had begun to develop in the mind of John Crowe Ransom several years earlier. Skeptical, subtle, urbane, Ransom brought to the Nashville world of the early 1920s an antisentimental, aesthetic aloofness, which charmed, puzzled, and at times, irritated the younger poets who sat in the Fugitive circle. One of them recognized Ransom for what he was: "The first modern among us." How he got this way is not easy to explain; personal genius as well as a cosmopolitan education must be considered. In any event, in his pursuit of an aesthetic sensibility that would counter the abstractionist tendency of the modern mind, Ransom discovered the split between reason and feeling that is the crux of modern poetry. He had the awareness of the modern complexity that we see in T. S. Eliot, and he had it as soon as Eliot did. Ransom brought to Nashville in the Fugitive days an awareness of the crisis of the literary order. This awareness informs the affirmation of the literary realm we see in the Fugitive documents. Louise Cowan in *The Fugitive Group* quotes Donald Davidson writing to Laura Gottschalk in 1924: "Literature is a serious business with us. We are for no compromise in the arts . . . we wish to reach, and are reaching, the intelligent few everywhere in whom lies the real hope of American literature." Mrs. Cowan also quotes Allen Tate to Marjorie Swett a year before. Tate strikes the note of conscious, deliberate detachment from the South for the sake of literature: "But we fear very much to have the slightest stress laid upon Southern traditions in literature; we who are Southerners know the fatality of such an attitude—the old atavism and sentimentality are always imminent." By 1927 Tate could write an essay like "The Revolt Against Literature," in which he identifies the scientific order as the enemy of the literary order, and argues for the concept of the "organic community" (saying "a great poetry cannot be written without the background of a perfectly ordered world which men have assimilated to their attitudes and convictions"). By this time Tate had become fully aware of the crisis of the literary order and of its defense by the traditionalist moderns. Moreover, since he makes no mention of the South, it would seem that Tate had made a full withdrawal from self-conscious Southernism.

But this omission is deceptive. By 1927 the Fugitives were showing a marked tendency to make a re-identification with the South. Not, however, according to the patterns of the old

245

loyalty, though this is a motive they never really lost, but in terms of the traditionalist moderns' allegiance to the literary order as a redemptive community opposed to the wasteland of modern industrialism. Their quest for literary meaning led them to become not simply modern contemporaries of Yeats, Eliot, and Pound but to become modern Southern American contemporaries of such figures. In so doing they transformed their consciousness of the South into the image of a redemptive cultural community and a homeland of the alienated literary spirit.

Precisely how this happened I cannot pretend to say (though of course I am pretending to say it in an imprecise way). I think we find a major clue to an answer in the displaced New Englander, born Middlewesterner, T. S. Eliot, whose work as a critic of modern civilization became a central and a controlling influence on his age. His metaphysics of literary order in "Tradition and the Individual Talent" (1919) took on a scriptural authority, resting in the dogma that may be defined as tradition by historical labor. Eliot says: "Tradition . . . cannot be inherited, and if you want it, you must obtain it by great labor. It involves . . . the historical sense; and the historical sense involves a perception, not only of the pastness of the past, but of its presence." In "The Function of Criticism" (1923) Eliot elaborates on the meaning of literary order: "I think . . . of the literature of the world, of the literature of Europe, of the literature of a single country, not as a collection of the writings of individuals, but as 'organic wholes,' as systems in relation to which, and only in relation to which, individual works of literary art, and the works of individual artists, have their significance. . . . Between the true artists of any time there is, I believe, an unconscious community. And, as our instincts of tidiness imperatively command us not to leave to the haphazard of unconsciousness what we can attempt to

246

do consciously, we are forced to conclude that what happens unconsciously we could bring about, and form into a purpose, if we made a conscious attempt."

To bring about and form into a purpose through conscious criticism the unconsciously assumed community of the literary mind—this is the challenge Eliot discovered as he pondered the structure of (using his own revealing phrase) "the polity of literature and of criticism." Even if we do not grant Eliot's primary influence on them (which is well documented) we can see that the Agrarians responded to a like challenge.

The response was virtually built into the Southern writer of the 1920s who had gone far enough with his education in modernity. From the 1820s on, the Southern mind had been self-consciously constructing images of polity. Calhoun's "Greek Democracy," the "Cavalier South," "The Lost Cause," the "Old South," the "New South"—these were constructs of self-justification but they were also poetic constructs of order in which the Southern mind had sought to assert the identity of the South in history. Save for the last one—so deliberately contrary to the others—all of these constructs were intended to invest the South with the authority and fraternity of the traditional community. In the making of them, there may be detected something like the kind of labor Eliot speaks of when he says that it is work to inherit a tradition. The Southern mind has always had to do this kind of work; for—and this perhaps may still seem heresy to some—tradition in the South has never simply been given. Tradition has never simply been given at any time anywhere in the United States, a nation invented in the full light of history—at the moment when history took over from tradition as the guiding force in culture. More pressed by this circumstance than other American writers, Southern writers have worked hard and self-consciously to receive what in a traditionalist culture would have been handed to them in the form of cultural assumptions. From the time of early proslavery writings until William Styron's *Nat Turner,* they have in their own way been at the task of inheriting their cultural inheritance.

The Agrarians, liberated from the politics of apology, brought to the task more sophistication and refinement than their predecessors. This is why they more or less successfully convey the impression that their inheritance is something solidly given; although the trouble they take to give this impression reveals how much of the inheritance is artifice, how little merely "passed on." If I read them at all correctly, I would say that no American writers ever worked harder at inheriting their inheritance than the Agrarians. If ever they give the appearance of being securely possessed of it, the appearance, as Henry James might say, is their little secret. This secret was their will to believe that their primary literary inheritance was not agonizingly self-conscious and ideological but traditional, that the Old South constituted a traditionalist order. In 1925 Tate in his state of detachment from the South thought that the advantage the Southern writer had over the New Englander lay in the Southerner's cosmopolitanism. "The modern Southerner does not inherit, nor is he likely to have, a native culture compounded of the strength and subtlety of his New England contemporary's," Tate wrote in the *Nation.* "But he may be capable, through an empiricism which is his only alternative to intellectual suicide, of a cosmopolitan culture to which his contemporary in the East is emotionally barred." About twenty years later he looked back on the period in which he wrote these words to find that the Fugitives benefited from being "an intensive and historical group as opposed to the eclectic and cosmopolitan groups that fluorished in the East." In between these statements Tate had done a great deal of hard work at inheriting his inheritance. The result was his uncovering of the relation of Southern writers to a "common historical myth," a tradition.

By the time he wrote his celebrated "Ode to the Confederate Dead" in the mid-1920s, Allen Tate clearly was laboring on the formulation of this tradition. The poem is about the experience of the agonizing consciousness (the "solipsism," "Narcissism," the "locked-in ego," the "squirrel-cage sensibility," to employ phrases from Tate's noted essay, "Narcissus as Narcissus") of the modern intellectual. It is an implied portrait of the literary artist, who finds, not in Eliot's version of the Middle Ages, but in the South of the Confederacy the grace which could save his machine-age soul, if the grace were available to him. This is the grace of the spiritual unity of a traditional community as opposed to the evil of a specialized, mechanized society, with its demand that each individual be at best some fragment of a man. The "Confederate Dead" poem gives us the inner history of a protagonist who is something akin to J. Alfred Prufrock—an American, or a Tennessee cousin. The Southerner who stops on an autumn afternoon at the gate of a Confederate cemetery is not Tate; he may be, I suppose, a kind of dramatization of Tate (see "Narcissus as Narcissus"). Moved by an extravagant "active faith," Tate's Confederate soldiers are depicted as men who died without having had to make an agonizing personal decision about whether or not they wanted to die in battle. The soldiers were unaware of their state of blessedness in being slaughtered; but Prufrock's cousin, in his traumatic alienation from the modern world, realizes how blessed they were. In his psychic displacement, he glimpses a vision of their homeland, the Old South. And he makes us aware that "we who have knowledge carried to the heart"—we the poets who are captive aliens in modernity—have a spiritual homeland in the Old South. The Old South becomes a metaphor of spiritual and artistic community. This metaphorical community, furthermore, although not explicitly made so by the poem, is by association a pastoral world.

The Old South as a homeland of the estranged literary spirit is suggested more directly in Ransom's essay, "Reconstructed but Unregenerate," in *I'll Take My Stand*. Here Ransom describes the antebellum Southern aristocracy as "mostly homemade and countrified" (a "squirearchy") and contrasts the principle of peace represented by the Old South and "the boundless aggression against nature" represented by industrialism. This aggression created the New South which has threatened the leisure that permits "the activity of intelligence." In spite of New South knavery, "unregenerate" Southerners have kept the agrarian establishment going and have brought it into the twentieth century, although in a depreciated state. And they have kept going the life of the mind. In patched blue jeans they sit "on ancestral fences, shotguns across their laps and hound-dogs at their feet, surveying their unkept acres while they comment shrewdly on the ways of God." The fault is, Ransom says, "that their aestheticism is based on insufficient labor." But their indolence is fully justified. Indeed they are "heroic" figures in "their extreme attachment to a certain theory of life." For "they have kept up a faith which was on the point of perishing from this continent." They have kept the faith in the Southern establishment, "the most substantial exhibit on this continent of a society of the European and historic order."

Ransom has found, sitting on the Southern fences, heroes who are more useful, in a way, to the cause of literary power than Tate's Confederate soldiers. For they are none other than the rustic poet-shepherds of Arcadia, symbols of the free life of the mind and spirit in the pastoral convention. Thus Ransom brings the past into the present as a restoration of a pastoral South which has the authority of a literary establishment and the appeal of an alienated community of artists.

The association between the modern man of letters and the Southern writer is made more explicitly and dramatically in another essay in *I'll Take My Stand*, Davidson's "A Mirror for Artists." Like Ransom, Davidson emphasizes the descent of the South from an homogeneous community (that "eighteenth-century European America that is elsewhere forgotten") and offers the Southern agrarian community as the possible Arcadian homeland of the artist. But Davidson's essay is notable in its aggressive definition of the situation of the writer in the twentieth century. Davidson sees clearly the alienation of the modern writer: "He is *against* or *away* from society, and the disturbed relationship becomes his essential theme, always underlying his work, no matter whether he evades or accepts the treatment of the theme itself." Davidson, moreover, poses a solution to alienation: he calls for the literary artist to subordinate, even surrender, his vocation to engage in the reconstruction of an order in which the writer can once again live.

This [Davidson cautions] is no doubt a desperate counsel. . . . [But] harmony between the artist and society must be regained; the dissociation must be broken down. That can only be done . . . by first putting society itself in order. In this connection we must realize that discussions of what is good or bad art, no matter how devoted or learned, cannot avail to reëstablish the arts in their old places. Criticism, for which Arnold and others have hoped so much, is futile for the emergency if it remains wholly aloof from the central problem, which is the remaking of life itself. . . . As in the crisis of war, when men drop their private occupations for one supreme task, the artist must step into the ranks and bear the brunt

251

of the battle against the common foe. He must share in the general concern as to the conditions of life. He must learn to understand and must try to restore and preserve a social economy that is in danger of being replaced altogether by an industrial economy hostile to his interests.

To fight industrialism the artist, Davidson declares, "must enter the common arena and become a citizen," and, he goes on to say, "whether he chooses . . . to be a farmer or to run for Congress is a matter of individual choice; but in that general direction his duty lies." To reverse history—this is a desperate undertaking. To sacrifice the identity of the artist in order to do so—this is even more desperate. Going to such lengths, Davidson indicates how strongly by 1930 a Southern man of letters could assert the hostility between the writer and society. Considering Davidson in relation to the Agrarian sensibility, it is not too much to say that he indicates how fully Southern men of letters had begun to participate in the crisis of the literary order at the stage it had reached by the post–World War I period of the twentieth century. They could identify with the modern literary artist-priest-hero—even conceive of the Southern writer sacrificing himself for literature in an ultimate way: giving it up to be a congressman. The spiritual themes and psychic resources of what Stephen Spender calls "the struggle of the modern" became available to the South. The vocation to the cosmopolitan realm of letters became a possibility in the South, as it had not been since the days of Jefferson.

V

One major result of the Agrarian sense of the literary vocation was the New Criticism. As I would read it, the doctrine of literary autonomy so stringently advocated by the New Criticism is a symbolic expression of the autonomy of the literary realm. In its most fruitful expressions the New Criticism attempted to uncover the nature of literature as a form of knowledge superior to science (the creator of industrialism and technology), reaching one of its climaxes in Tate's essay, "Literature as Knowledge," in which he argues for poetry as "an experienced order" against the positivistic sciences as "an abstract order." He concludes that "however we may see the completeness of poetry, it is a problem less to be solved, in its full import, than to be preserved." The meaning is to preserve the poem whole in the culture (the discipline) of language and thus in a small way (I offer an underlying meaning) to preserve the realm of letters as an order of society. To the extent that, say, Brooks and Warren in *Understanding Poetry* conveyed this meaning, this noted text belongs as a primary document in the modern attempt to restore the literary order. It exemplifies the imperative Allen Tate states for the man of letters: "The state is the mere operation of society, but culture is the way society lives, the material medium through which men receive the one lost truth which must be perpetually recovered: the truth of . . . the 'supra-temporal destiny' of man. It is the duty of the man of letters to supervise the culture of language to which the rest of culture is subordinate, and to warn us when our language is ceasing to forward the ends proper to man. The end of social man is communion in time through love, which is beyond time."

By the time Tate said this in "The Man of Letters in the Modern World," an address made in 1952 to an international congress of men of letters in Paris, he had become conversant with Roman Catholic theology and had begun to see the literary order and the literary vocation rather explicitly in terms of religious order. But this was a change in degree of emphasis, not of substance. The vision of the Agrarians always had a strong religious and metaphysical quality. This indeed is the quality of the whole modern effort toward the renewal of letters, which ultimately is an expression of an increasing alienation of modern man from the mystery of the Word.

Tate's address in 1952 may possibly mark not only the terminal date of the New Criticism but of the whole modern movement toward the renewal of the literary order in America. In fact, the crisis of the literary order may have disappeared. Not because of a politicization of the realm of letters as in the Old South, but because of the displacement of the humanistic concept of the verbal center of civilization. In science and technology communication has ceased to an important degree to depend on words. In our society in general the "discipline" of letters is largely outmoded, and literary expression itself is becoming a marginal competitor for attention among the innovative modes of expression produced by technology. In the great technological fabrication which surrounds us—in the intricate artifice, the physical and biological process, no longer simply mechanistic, no longer simply industrial, in which we live—we have less and less use for an education in the assimilating function of words and letters. The "man of letters" has become obsolete. The Old South had plenty of use for men of letters and for words and letters in the service of society. Although Old South writers under their historical circumstances did not represent the humanistic polity of literature, the possibility of the renewal of this polity was present when and if the sense of the literary order should be restored to the South. But American society today does not conceive literacy to be a central need in the maintenance of civilizational order. The motive of literary alienation—the keeping alive of "the spirit of the letter"—is draining away. This is not to say that poets, storytellers, and critics are disappearing, only that writing no longer centers in literature. The dominion of literature is effectively gone. You cannot restore what is not needed: and this may be the significance of the story of the Agrarians and of the whole history of modern Southern letters.